PRAISE FOR PIERCE O'DONNELL AND HIS PREVIOUS BOOKS

"After reading *Last Pick* and relishing Pierce's sweet remembrances of his boyhood, I wish I had been there with him during his upbringing. It would have been wonderful (and fun!) to behold the making of this amazing, thoughtful, exciting, and hugely important legal icon. I am fortunate to be able to be both a client and friend of this outstanding individual."

—Lew Wolff, Chairman Emeritus, Oakland A's Major League Baseball Team

"The small-town kid who became one of the West Coast's hottest trial lawyers... describes his younger self as a nerdy 'fatso' who loved baseball with all his heart but had no talent for it."

—*Law360*

"One of the most influential lawyers in America."

—*National Law Journal*

"Pierce O'Donnell is the new Perry Mason in Hollywood."

—*Forbes Magazine*

"The $7 billion collected for his clients—including sale of the Los Angeles Clippers for $2 billion—makes him 'The Billion Dollar Litigator.'"

—*Variety*

"You watch [Pierce] walk into a courtroom, and he just fills up the room. You just think: Who is that? He looks pretty serious. We better settle."

—James J. Brosnahan, past president, Bar Association of San Francisco

"[*In Time of War: Hitler's Terrorist Attack on America* is] riveting—a blazing red flag of caution to any government hell-bent on tampering with constitutional rights in a time of crisis."

—John Grisham

"A masterful account of how the government and those we rely on to preserve our liberties can fail in moments of crisis. [*In Time of War*] is history that speaks to us today."

—Arthur R. Miller, professor, New York University

"[*In Time of War*] reads like a novel, only it's all true."

—David Cole (author of *Enemy Alien*, 2004 American Book Award winner)

"Pierce O'Donnell is the most creative trial lawyer I have ever faced. A true legal genius, he is also a gifted actor in the courtroom. His strategy for selling the Los Angeles Clippers for $2 billion was truly inspired."

—Bert Fields (author of *Summing Up: A Professional Memoir*)

"Pierce O'Donnell was a brilliant, fearless, and resourceful lawyer, much like his mentor Edward Bennett Williams. A graduate of Georgetown University Law School in 1972 and a clerk for Supreme Court justice Byron White,…O'Donnell was always willing to fight the good fight for a case and a client he truly believed in. He knew it would be a long, messy, uphill struggle [against Paramount Pictures for using Buchwald's story as the basis for the Eddie Murphy hit *Coming To America*], but O'Donnell was ready. The partnership of Buchwald and O'Donnell was off and running."

—Michael Hill, *Funny Business: The Legendary Life and Political Satire of Art Buchwald*

"*Fatal Subtraction* is a true and fascinating read."

—Winston Groom (author of *Forrest Gump*)

"Super lawyer Pierce O'Donnell and Dennis McDougal have written a step-by-step account of the now historic trial, and you won't put it down."

—Larry King

"'Legal whiz'" Pierce O'Donnell and his humorist client Art Buchwald nailed Paramount Pictures for using Buchwald's story to create *Coming To America* as recounted in this 'spellbinding' legal drama *Fatal Subtraction*.

—*Kirkus*

"Written in a free-flowing style told solely through O'Donnell's perspective. He's been called a tiger in the courtroom, but the book shows that he has an eagle's eye for detail."

—*Pasadena Star-News*

"Provocative." —*USA Today*

"[T]here's as much drama here as in a whole season of *L.A. Law*."

—*San Francisco Chronicle*

"This book is a landmark in that it was the first time that a…David won anything from a Hollywood Goliath…Hollywood is changed forever. A grand read."

—*The Martha's Vineyard Times*

"[*Fatal Subtraction*] is also filled with the kinds of gritty details the tabloids could never concoct—or *The Player* could even hint at."

—*Los Angeles Magazine*

"One absorbing book…provocative…skillfully written…a first-rate and candid depiction of the litigation process."

—*Los Angeles Daily Journal*

"*Fatal Subtraction* is the guidebook to Hollywood dealmaking…Authors Pierce O'Donnell and Dennis McDougal cut through the tangle of contract doublespeak and studio hot air to explain the real financial issues in movie making. Better yet, they do it with style and wit!"

—*Playboy*

"O'Donnell…clearly has a point. 'Net profits' are a scam—the fatal subtraction."

—*Washington Post*

"*Buchwald v. Paramount* is one of the most controversial cases of Hollywood going to court. *Fatal Subtraction* is one of the most revealing accounts of how studios make movies and lawyers make lawsuits. And as the title hints, this book is fun to read."

—Paul Weiler, Henry J. Friendly Professor of Law, Harvard Law School

LAST PICK

ALSO BY PIERCE O'DONNELL

Books

In Time of War: Hitler's Terrorist Attack on America

Dawn's Early Light

Fatal Subtraction: The Inside Story of Buchwald v. Paramount
(with Dennis McDougal)

Toward A Just and Effective Sentencing System: Agenda for Legislative Reform
(with Michael J. Churgin and Dennis E. Curtis)

Films

Home Team
(with Jeff Lewis)

America Betrayed
(Executive Producer)

LAST PICK

*A Whimsical Warmhearted Autobiography
of a Twelve-Year-Old Who Became a Great Trial Lawyer*

PIERCE O'DONNELL

RARE BIRD
LOS ANGELES, CALIF.

This is a Genuine Rare Bird Book

Rare Bird Books
6044 North Figueroa Street
Los Angeles, CA 90042
rarebirdbooks.com

Copyright © 2022 by Pierce O'Donnell

HARDCOVER EDIITON

All rights reserved, including the right to reproduce this book or portions thereof in any form whatsoever, including but not limited to print, audio, and electronic.

For more information, address:
Rare Bird Books Subsidiary Rights Department
6044 North Figueroa Street
Los Angeles, CA 90042

Set in Minion
Printed in the United States

10 9 8 7 6 5 4 3 2 1

Publisher's Cataloging-in-Publication Data available upon request.

To Carmen,
my beloved wife and champion

*"When you are old and grey and full of sleep
And nodding by the fire, take down this book
And slowly read, and dream of the soft look
Your eyes had once, and of their shadows deep"*

William Butler Yeats,
"When You Are Old"

"I never could catch very well, but even as a grade-schooler I could hit...[I]t's a good thing to be able to hit. You hardly ever get picked last...Despite my weak glove, I made the team. And I wasn't last picked."

Nancy Powers in Mike Schacht,
*Mudville Diaries: A Book of
Baseball Memories*

"The greatest thing in the world is to know how to belong to oneself."

Michel de Montaigne

"Everything that happens to you is your teacher. The secret is to sit at the feet of your life and be taught by it."

Mahatma Gandhi

CONTENTS

15 Author's Note
17 Preface
19 Prologue

WINTER
25 Chapter 1: Hometown Boy
36 Chapter 2: Nora the Ghost
42 Chapter 3: "All Aboard!"
51 Chapter 4: "Bless Me, Father"
58 Chapter 5: Muskrat
63 Chapter 6: Peter Pan

SPRING
79 Chapter 7: Spring Training
88 Chapter 8: Incense
96 Chapter 9: "Look It Up"
108 Chapter 10: Highballs

SUMMER
117 Chapter 11: Mr. Dibble
124 Chapter 12: Sister Act
131 Chapter 13: The Cousins
137 Chapter 14: Last Pick
149 Chapter 15: The Methodists

FALL
155 Chapter 16: "Yes, Miss Gehle"
162 Chapter 17: Happy Thanksgiving
169 Chapter 18: "What Did Your Mother Say?"
181 Chapter 19: Eating My Way Across Troy
191 Chapter 20: Chin-Ups

203 Epilogue
211 Acknowledgments

AUTHOR'S NOTE

In 1998, at the age of fifty-one, I started writing down some recollections of my childhood. These musings grew until I had the inspiration to write a memoir of my life growing up in rural upstate New York in the fifties and early sixties. I wrote this book primarily for myself. When I finished a year later, I shared the manuscript with my mother and three sisters—all of whom gave me some "corrections."

I made some changes based on their comments and my additional recollections about growing up together in a post–World War II nuclear family that played, prayed, and paraded together down Main Street on Fourth of July. Then I put the manuscript in a filing cabinet where it seasoned for over twenty years. When my wife Carmen and I moved in 2018, my only copy of the draft was lost, and I had no digital backup. I was crestfallen, feeling that a part of me had died.

My mother was fond of saying that "things happen for a reason." Miraculously, while we were again moving in mid-2019, Carmen found the draft at the bottom of a box. Manuscript in hand, I sat down and relived my childhood in vivid Technicolor, grinning from ear to ear and boisterously laughing out loud as I pored over the text.

I don't know how it happened, but I misplaced it again—and foolishly had not made a copy. As I tore my office and house apart, I cursed my stupidity. Despair and anger competed for center stage of my emotions.

Then, lightning in a bottle struck again: Carmen was cleaning out our garage. Amazingly, she discovered the twice-vanished velobound pages buried in the battered black trunk that my mother had used to go to college during the Depression, and which I took to Georgetown University three decades later. I vowed not to make the same mistake again, converted the PDF to Word, and started editing. But a funny thing happened on the way. Other than some stylistic and grammatical repairs, I barely changed anything.

What follows is the book that I wrote over twenty years ago when the events of my youth a half century earlier may have been fresher in my mind. But maybe not. As I scanned the text, I could close my eyes and conjure up the scene, whether it was fighting frostbite while shoveling snow, fishing at sunrise, meeting Mickey Mantle, or watching "The Boys of Summer" at a doubleheader at Ebbets Field in Brooklyn. The innocence of youth and the wonder of fresh discoveries filled many days of my boyhood. In Marcel Proust's words, I was reliving joys of "a long distant past" thanks to "the immense edifice of memory."

So, here it is. I hope that you enjoy reading the stories as much as I have recounting them. And see if you don't agree with NFL football star Jerry Smith: "Childhood is the most beautiful of all life's seasons."

PREFACE

I TURNED FIFTY-ONE THIS year (1998). One of those Baby Boomers born in the wake of World War II, I have four children—Meghan (fifteen), Brendan (thirteen), Courtney (three), and Pierce Dublin (eight months)—and a vivacious wife, Dawn. I've coached my oldest son's Little League teams for five years (three championships and two second place finishes). As a soccer dad, I have attended scores of my older children's soccer games.

One spring day, while accompanying Meghan's class on a hike in the Angeles National Forest in Pasadena, California, I walked by myself down the three-mile trail to the parking lot. The air was crisp, the woods still, and my breath audible. A rare but welcome serenity dispelled obtrusive thoughts of courtrooms and boardrooms.

Suddenly, as a red-tailed hawk glided against the azure sky, a flood of childhood memories overwhelmed me: fishing on the Old Mill Pond, standing on the sidelines as the other kids played sandlot baseball without me, praying the rosary with my mother and sisters kneeling around my parents' bed, Boy Scout camping trips in subzero weather, my Aunt Hunnah sorting mail at the post office, watching *The Ed Sullivan Show* with my family on Sunday nights, hanging out at my dad's liquor store, and dozens of other fragmentary images. I recalled the smell of nauseous incense at a funeral, the taste of my mother's creamed codfish on boiled potatoes, and the sound of crickets through my bedroom window on a hot August evening.

When I got home, I furiously filled a legal pad with scores of recollections of my childhood. Something later impelled me to organize those thoughts and feelings more systematically. Thus, this book—the autobiography of a twelve-year-old—was conceived.

After the draft was completed about a year later (thanks to time afforded by a lot of business travel on planes, trains, and ships, and nights alone in distant hotels), I tested my memory with family members. I peppered my three sisters (Mary Eileen, Helen Kay, and Maureen) about their recollections of our childhood. To my surprise, I learned that this is not the same boy, family, events, or town that my siblings remember. Their memories on some points are different or long gone, reminding me of these lines from Edward Hirsch's "Siblings":

> "The story of siblings is the story of childhood
> Experienced separately and together, one tree
> Twisting in different directions, roots and branches,
> One piece of land divided up into parcels,
> Acres and half-acres, parts of a subdivision,
> Memories carved into official and unofficial versions."

For better or worse, this is how I remember my boyhood.

PROLOGUE

I GREW UP RURAL.

In Upstate New York, about ten miles east of Troy in a sleepy village surrounded by lakes, streams, farmland, forests, and rolling hills.

I grew up in paranoid times.

At the height of the Cold War when the Soviet Union and China were determined to destroy the United States, and many families had an air raid shelter.

And I grew up cold.

In a tiny town strategically located at the crossroads of twenty-below-zero Arctic wind blasts and snowstorms blowing off Lake Erie and Lake Ontario.

It has been over thirty years since I left Averill Park, New York, to attend college in 1965. I returned frequently over the next decade, and then less regularly thereafter as I began my own family and moved to Los Angeles. Yet the passage of time has done little to dim my memory of childhood in that special place.

When I was growing up, there was a popular song "Turn! Turn! Turn!" recorded by Pete Seeger and later by The Byrds, based on a memorable passage from *Book of Ecclesiastes*:

> There is a time for everything,
> and a season for every activity
> under the heavens:
> a time to be born and a time to die,
> a time to plant and a time to uproot…
> a time to tear down and a time to build,
> a time to weep and a time to laugh

My season was 1959.

An insightful book by Fred Kaplan is titled *1959: The Year Everything Changed*. History will remember 1959 as the year of the Soviet-American race to space. General Charles de Gaulle became Premier of France, and Fidel Castro rose to power in Cuba. Pope John XXIII was elected. The other John was gearing up to run for President of the United States. And the Los Angeles Dodgers beat the Chicago White Sox in six games to capture the World Series.

In 1959, an Oldsmobile cost $3,000. You could fly from New York to Houston for $66.65. Harvard tuition was only $1,250 a year. A pair of blue jeans retailed for $3.95. A Coke was five cents.

That year, the United States had nearly eighty-five million television sets, one for every two Americans, and Alaska and Hawaii became states. Hula-Hoops were the rage.

America's love affair with the automobile resulted in a dubious historic first: total historical car accident fatalities of more than 1.25 million exceeded the death toll of all American wars.

British novelist Ian Fleming wrote *Goldfinger*, and memorable works were published by Saul Bellow, James Thurber, Ionesco, Gunter Grass, William Faulkner, Muriel Spark, Brendan Behan, Graham Greene, and John Updike. Jesuit Pierre Teilhard de Chardin revolutionized philosophical discourse with *The Phenomenon of Man*. Ending a thirty-year ban, a federal appellate court ruled that D. H. Lawrence's *Lady Chatterly's Lover* was not obscene. "Mack the Knife" was one of the year's most popular songs, *Ben Hur* won the Oscar for Best Picture, and Cecil B. DeMille and Billie Holiday died.

But I remember much more—events and people in my life—about the year I turned twelve…1959.

Nothing terribly noteworthy happened that year. My grades in school were average, I hadn't reached puberty, and once again, for the fifth year in a row, I didn't win a free bike in the Fireman's Field Day raffle.

By all objective standards, 1959 was just another year for me. Yet, for some reason, I have been drawn back to that time. Maybe because it was my *Age of Innocence*—that time of awkward transition just before a young boy starts to look, feel, and think like a young man. Or maybe it was merely because it was such a fun-filled, joyful chapter in my life. A time when an adolescent boy in soiled blue jeans could lie down in a field of dandelions, chew a piece of straw slowly, and daydream all afternoon long about how the heavens were made or why lilacs bloomed only in May.

I was making my passage, but I didn't realize it at that time. I started to think about and feel things that I had never thought about or felt before. But I never said anything to anyone back then because it was a weird, new sensation. You see, I wasn't sure if this was how you were supposed to think and feel when you turned twelve. I'd never been twelve before.

I don't remember any specific dates or anything like that. I was never particularly good about birthdays or anniversaries. I recall things by the time of the year, the season when something happened. Where I lived, there was no mistaking fall and winter or spring and summer. Winter melted into spring, and fall ushered in winter. Summer seemed to last only five weeks.

I was a boy for all seasons. Hockey and snow shoveling in the winter, baseball and selling pansies in the spring, Boy Scout camp and fishing in the summer, touch football and mink trapping in the fall. Somehow, I managed to squeeze in school, getting through sixth and seventh grade with As and Bs, except for a D in penmanship.

For whatever reason, I remember 1959 vividly, as if it were still happening. In fact, if I close my eyes in a tranquil place, I can still see a chubby, eager-to-please, blond-haired, Irish American kid: his black horn-rimmed eyeglasses sliding down his nose, a baseball mitt dangling from his Raleigh bike handlebars, and a fishing pole in one hand, pedaling down the dirt roads of his boyhood.

We'll start in the winter of 1958-59. Heavy snowfall and freezing temperatures. Man, was it cold outside, even for my hometown! But that's okay because in a few months, I'll be twelve. That's a really big deal. Twelve year olds can do a lot more things than eleven year olds. Like get a paper route and earn money so that when you become a teenager in just one more year, you can buy strawberry fizzes and vanilla Cokes at the Park Pharmacy and hang out with the older guys.

Come on, let's go.

WINTER

"People ask me what I do in winter when there's no baseball. I'll tell you what I do. I stare out the window and wait for spring."
—Rogers Hornsby

1.
HOMETOWN BOY

I WAS LIKE MOST other kids growing up. I lived with my mom and dad, three younger sisters, my mom's younger sister, Aunt Hunnah, who never got married, and stray cats that my sisters brought home. I used to sneeze a lot. Especially when I played with the cats and the roses were in bloom. My dad had the same problem when he was cutting the lawn. When I got older, he gave me some medicine that stopped the sneezing, but it made me sleepy. I've never been fond of cats or roses or lawn mowing.

We lived in a large white house with reddish brown gingerbread trim. It was built in 1850 by a country doctor, and my mom's family had lived in the Victorian-style house since 1875. The house had a cold, damp basement where the furnace burned coal for our heat. There were two stories for living—five bedrooms, a kitchen, dining room, two bathrooms, a front and back parlor, a front and back porch, the apartment that we rented out, and an attic with two levels that was cluttered with old furniture, paintings, and long-abandoned chests of clothes. There was a red brick chimney on the outside of the house, but the fireplace had been covered over before I was born.

There also was a ghost, but I don't want to talk about Norma just yet.

In the back of the house, off the kitchen on the ground floor, was my "bedroom." When I was about ten, my parents decided that my sisters and I should have separate rooms. There were only two bedrooms for the four kids, so my sisters divided up the bedrooms upstairs, and I got the former coal bin converted into a bedroom. Small but cozy, it featured a single bed, dresser, desk, tiny closet, and a linoleum floor. The radiator never worked.

In the winter, I slept under a lot of blankets and a thick comforter. It wasn't all bad though because my dad would wake up before me, turn on the kitchen oven, and leave the oven door open so that the heat would drift into my bedroom.

That was very thoughtful of him, but I dreaded putting my bare feet on the freezing linoleum on a winter morning.

I was raised in the sleepy village of Averill Park, in the town of Sand Lake, in Rensselaer County, in Upstate New York. Generously dotted with glacial lakes and man-made ponds and creeks, this rural area of farmers, dairymen, and sheepherders is located about ten miles east of Troy. It was a big deal when they installed a blinking traffic light where Route 66 and Route 43 converge on the map. You could literally hold your breath biking from one end of the village to the other—from the Mobil to Sunoco gas stations.

Averill Park had a third-class post office, two grocery stores, an A&P, a hardware store, two beauty salons, a pharmacy with a soda fountain, a news and candy store, a barbershop, an appliance store, a typewriter store, a seamstress, two funeral parlors, a doctor (Reid) and dentist (Dunn) who shared the same building, one phone booth, a lumberyard, a laundromat, a diner, and the Lakeview Hotel with a bar, restaurant, and bowling alleys. I wasn't sure why they called it a "hotel" because no one ever stayed there overnight. No one except the men who fell asleep in their cars in the parking lot after drinking too much beer.

One of my first jobs was a "pin boy" two nights a week at the bowling alley. We had semiautomatic pin setters which had to be fed with the bowling pins after each bowler had his two tries. I sat up on an elevated bench in the back of the pit, holding up my legs while the ball traveled down the lane and hit the pins. I would then jump down, send the ball back, pick up the felled pins—two to a hand—and place them in the pin setter. After the second roll, I would again send the ball back, put the rest of the pins in the rack, and pull a string so that the machine would lower and deposit the ten pins in their assigned spot.

We would handle two adjacent lanes at a time, jumping over a low barrier from one to another as balls and pins flew in the air. The job, which paid fifty cents per game, could be dangerous. I swore that the real "sport" for the beer-bellied bowlers was hitting the pin boy on the shins with a pin. Bruises were an occupational hazard. And if you didn't get bruised, you weren't moving fast enough.

Several days a week, milk was delivered to our front door by a white-coated deliveryman. The coal truck came once a month. Tommy Taiconia's fruit and vegetable truck stopped at our house three times a week.

"Mary," stoop-shouldered Tommy would always begin. "The watermelon is juicy sweet, the tomatoes are ripe, and the bananas are turning yellow."

My buddy Bob Campano liked to come to our house on Sundays because my dad made a fresh fruit salad that Bob inhaled. I think that he liked it because Dad spiked the fruit salad with some liqueur. We also had a lot of churches for the few people in our town. Besides St. Henry's Roman Catholic Church where my family attended, there were at least five Protestant churches, including the Methodist Church right next to our house. While a few Jewish families were scattered around town, they had no synagogue.

My hometown also had a liquor store—O'Donnell's Wine & Liquor Store on Main Street. It was my dad's place in the heart of the hamlet. The building (called a "salt box") had been built in the late 1700s as a rest stop for stagecoaches and mailmen on horses who were traveling between Albany and Boston. After he came home from World War II, my dad opened the store in this dilapidated building owned by my mom and Hunnah. In fact, he started business three weeks before I was born on March 5, 1947.

Our home was on Burden Lake Road, three houses and one Methodist Church down from Dad's store. Out our back door was Tin Can Alley and the Old Mill Pond. Not far away was Johnny Cake Lane. I figured out that Burden Lake Road got its name from the fact that it went from the village to the three Burden Lakes, separated by man-made dikes, a few miles away where people from Troy and Albany would come on weekends and some for the whole summer. But I could never get a decent explanation about why the narrow dirt road along the Old Mill Pond was called Tin Can Alley or how Johnny Cake Lane got its name.

Our area had been settled back in the seventeenth century by Dutch and German farmers. They couldn't grow many crops (except corn) in our climate, but they found that it was a neat place to raise cows for milking and soon the cows outnumbered people four to one. The hills were alive with the sound of mooing. I milked a few cows in my day, but I never could quite get the hang of it. I didn't like getting squirted in the face by the milk or hit on the back of the head by the cow's tail any more than I did shoveling manure. I milked, fed, and cleaned up after enough cows to earn the Dairy Farming merit badge as a Boy Scout, but I knew that I was not cut out to be a dairy farmer.

My mom's family on her father's side were the Kanes. They had left Ireland during the Potato Famine in 1848 when everybody was dying from starvation. My mom said the English were very cruel and let people starve on purpose. I never could understand why anybody would do something so horrible. My family was Irish to the core. Besides O'Donnell and Kane, my mother's mother was a Gleason whose parents, Mariah and Simon Gleason, emigrated from Ireland in the second half of the nineteenth century. My father's mother, Mary Katherine, was a Cussen who was born in 1883 in New Jersey shortly after her mother arrived in New York City from Ireland. His father Henry Joseph O'Donnell, a Protestant from Northern Ireland, emigrated to America in 1885. Another Irish relative on the Kane side (Jonathan Slauson) fought for the Union Army, was captured by the Confederates, and was imprisoned at the infamous Andersonville.

The Kane family eventually resettled in Troy, New York, on the east bank of the Hudson River a few miles north of Albany. Within twenty years, it was a fairly prominent family. In 1886, Nicholas Kane, who was born in County Waterford, Ireland and fought in the Civil War, was elected to Congress, but he died within six months of taking office. Another member of the family got involved in knitting woolen clothes and supplied uniforms to the Union Army during the Civil War. They started a knitting mill in our village and moved the family six miles east. I was named after my grandfather, Pierce Daniel Kane, who had various jobs (including being a railroad detective) but whose great passion was serving as a volunteer fireman.

I almost grew up in Kanesville.

When they were naming our hamlet back in 1880, people suggested that it be called Kanesville in honor of our family. But one of my great, great uncles refused the honor. He thought the place should be named after another local leading family Averill, one of the earliest settlers in the area. So that's how I grew up in Averill Park and not Kanesville.

Now, you have to understand something about Averill Park.

Nothing exciting had ever happened there for over two hundred years. The only thing that my mom ever told me about was the Anti-Rent Wars back in the mid-eighteenth century around the time of the Revolutionary War. She gave me a book called *Tin Horns and Calico* about the local farmers in the Hudson River Valley who refused to pay exorbitant rent to their Dutch landlords. Over the years, there were some battles, and people got killed.

Now that I think about it, there may have been one other important event in our village. When my mom was a young woman in her teens, Eleanor Roosevelt, wife of the then governor and future president Franklin Delano Roosevelt, visited our house and had tea with my mom's mother and a bunch of ladies from the neighborhood. She sat in the comfortable chair by the window in the front parlor. They talked for a few hours about the Depression, poor people, and Hitler.

I wasn't born until two years after Mrs. Roosevelt was no longer First Lady, but whenever I sat in that chair, I felt a little funny.

The only other famous person who came to Averill Park was the comic actor Jerry Lewis. In 1942, he lived with an aunt and uncle in a house across the street. While attending Averill Park High School, Lewis worked as a soda fountain "jerk" at the Park Pharmacy. When he became famous, the owner, Ben Silberg, put his name on a six-scoop sundae with three bananas, hot fudge, marshmallow sauce, strawberries, whipped cream, nuts, and cherries. I enjoyed a few "Jerry Lewis Specials" in my day.

My mom and her sister Hunnah were born in the Samaritan Hospital in Troy, the same place all the O'Donnell kids were born. It was an old brick building near Rensselaer Polytechnic Institute. I had my tonsils and appendix taken out there, too. The only thing that I liked about the hospital was the nice candy stripers who brought treats to kids.

When I was six and recuperating from my tonsillectomy, I left my room to explore the hospital. I found an area on another floor, and ever curious, I opened the swinging doors. I wasn't prepared for what I discovered. The people in there seemed all wacked out. Some were making funny noises while others were talking to themselves. I'd never seen anything like this before.

I don't know why, but I walked into the ward. After I took a few steps, someone started shouting at me. I looked to my left, and there in a hospital bed was an old lady with stringy, gray hair and no teeth. Her glassy eyes bugging out, she was pointing at me and screaming, "He's my son! He's my son!" I was so freaked out that I ran all the way back to my room and never told anybody about what I saw.

Dad was born in New York City and grew up in a slum neighborhood known as "Hell's Kitchen" on the lower west side of Manhattan. This was a tough community of mostly poor and working class Irish Americans dating back to the refugees from the Great Famine. "The walk to and from school could be a ten-round fight," Dad would say. "Maybe that's why I became a Golden Gloves boxer."

My dad had it rough as a kid. Like me, he had three sisters. But that's where the similarities end. His mother Mary was blinded in an industrial accident after he was born, and when he was eight, she died of uterine cancer in a Catholic pauper's hospital in Greenwich Village. My dad's father had what they called a "nervous breakdown" and was confined in a mental institution before his wife died. Dad and his three sisters—Marie, Bernadette, and Louise—were put in two

Catholic orphanages in Brooklyn—one for boys and one for girls. My dad adored his sisters, and whenever he could, he'd walk the two miles to visit them.

Dad was a good student, excelling in math. But he had to quit school in tenth grade so that he could get a job to support his sisters and himself who were taken in by his mother's sister, Katie O'Shea, and her husband. That story always made me sad because I couldn't imagine what it would be like to be cheated out of growing up with your mom and dad. Or not having a real childhood.

My parents met in the late 1930s when Mom played Mary Magdalene and Dad played a Roman centurion in an Easter Passion play at a Roman Catholic Church. My father was a stock trader on the New York Stock Exchange, and Mom taught high school English and Latin on Long Island. They were a beautiful couple. My sisters and I used to love to look at old photos of our parents when they were first dating. Dad was tall (6'3"), muscular, and really handsome with the waviest blond hair and the biggest blue eyes that you ever saw. Mom was a super pretty, intelligent-looking blonde with a gentle smile and enviable patience. No matter which photo we saw, my parents always looked happy together.

When I was a little boy, my dad told me how the Japanese bombed Pearl Harbor on a Sunday in December 1941, and he volunteered for the Army the next day.

"Why did you go to war, Dad?" I asked him one day.

"Simple," he responded without hesitation. "Our country's survival was at stake."

Dad wanted to defend his country against the Japanese and Germans who were trying to take over the whole world.

I wondered if I would ever be called upon to risk my life for my country.

Dad was really enthusiastic about being a soldier, but he had two big problems: his feet. He had size fifteen shoes, and the Army didn't make that size when he enlisted. Dad spent most of boot camp training at Fort Dix, New Jersey, wearing his street shoes. But he must have been a pretty good soldier because he made Sergeant by the time his Twenty-Ninth Division invaded Normandy in June 1944. And by then he had his own pair of size fifteen Army boots.

My sisters and I were studying German or French at school. We laughed every time he dusted off his command of foreign languages. "Achtung, Messerschmitt!" Dad would say, repeating the few German words learned by GIs before the Invasion of Normandy. They were also taught a smattering of French.

"Bon jour. Je suis Américain—votre ami."

Mom and Dad were married in March 1942. It was a small ceremony at a Roman Catholic Church on Long Island. Just a few friends and relatives attended. There is no wedding photo album. They didn't have time for a honeymoon, but they did spend their first married night together at the Hotel Pennsylvania in Manhattan.

Within a few months, Dad was shipped off to England and didn't return until late 1945. I asked my mom what it was like not to see her husband for over three years. She told me that it was difficult, she missed him, and she worried about him all the time because so many American men were being killed and badly wounded. The one thing that helped, she said, were the love letters that they regularly wrote to each other. My sisters found the hundreds of Dad's love letters that Mom had saved. We shouldn't have read them, but I'm glad we did. They really loved each other. "Mary," one typical letter began.

> We are still training. I cannot mention where, but we are doing everything we can to be ready. I cannot tell you how much I miss you. Your letters cheer me up and always remind me how much I love you. God willing, I will be home someday, hopefully soon. You mean the world to me and I pray for you and my sisters every day. Love, Harry.
>
> P.S. If I don't make it home, I owe my sister Louise $200. Please pay her back.

My sisters and I talked about how hard it must have been for Mom while Dad was away, risking his life for his country. The longing, the fear, and the dread of that knock on the door by a Western Union courier delivering a telegram from the US Army that begin "We regret to inform you…"

"I don't know how she handled it so well," Helen Kay commented as we read their letters one day. "She's always upbeat and encouraging in those letters."

"Well, she was able to take her mind off of it a little," Mary Eileen noted. "She taught high school English and Latin during the War."

"Yeah, but still," Bubsy said, "I can't imagine that the anxiety ever goes away."

My dad was a really good soldier. He got all kinds of medals and ribbons that I loved to pin on my shirt. For a young boy to have a father who was a war hero is really special. Dad used to let me wear his Army hats—both the thin cap and the fancier dress uniform hat with the shiny brow and Army insignia on the front.

I don't know how many times I asked him to tell me the story, but I will never forget Dad's description of the Invasion of Normandy on June 6, 1944. Training in England for two years, the soldiers had practiced boarding troop ships and assaulting a beach from amphibious landing craft. My dad realized that training was over when they gave all the soldiers ice cream on June 5 while they each read a letter from the Supreme Allied Commander, General Dwight David Eisenhower. The letter to the Soldiers, Sailors, and Airmen of the Allied Expeditionary Force read in part:

> You are about to embark upon the Great Crusade....The eyes of the world are upon you. The hopes and prayers of liberty-loving people everywhere march with you. In company with our brave Allies and brothers-in-arms on other Fronts, you will bring about the destruction of the German war machine, the elimination of Nazi tyranny over the oppressed peoples of Europe, and security for ourselves in a free world...I have full confidence in your courage, devotion to duty and skill in battle. We will accept nothing less than full victory!

As a boy, I held that letter in my hand, imagining my dad with an eighty-pound pack on his back and a rifle held over his head, as he waded ashore that historic morning that will forever be known as D-Day.

My dad told me that he was alive today because his unit in the Twenty-Ninth Division was in the second wave at Omaha Beach. Almost all the men in the first wave, some of them his buddies, were killed or badly wounded by the Germans' heavy machine gun and artillery fire from the bluffs above the beach. The sea was unusually choppy, and a lot of the men kept throwing up as their landing craft approached the beach. My dad told me that he was scared sitting in the boat, waiting for its big door to drop. When they "hit" the beach, they were in water up to their armpits with dead American GIs floating around them. Dad would choke up whenever he got to this part of the story.

For one year, my dad and the Twenty-Ninth Division fought from the beaches of France to the Rhine River in Germany. They fought under the leadership of General George "Blood and Guts" Patton in the Battle of the Bulge. ("His guts and our blood," my dad would always note.) As a boy, I asked him lots of questions about the war. We would take out a map of Europe, and Dad would show me the route that they fought and how to identify American, British, and German aircraft.

Dad didn't talk about it, but I learned from Mom that he was injured with shrapnel in the shin during the Battle of the Bulge in the winter of 1944–45. Luckily, he was brave, recovered quickly, and rushed back into battle where the temperature was twenty degrees.

I remember one story about his unit capturing some German soldiers.

"I don't know who was more relieved, us or them," my dad would sigh. "No one wanted to be killing each other. We were all just ordinary people who wanted to be home with our families."

Approaching one surrendering German soldier, a dirty-faced, emaciated boy, cowering in fear, only a few years older than me, Dad reached into a pocket.

"Nein! Nein! Nein!" the youngster pleaded.

The boy thought Dad was going to shoot him. Hitler had brainwashed the remnants of his tattered, conscripted army to believe that the Americans were vicious murderers who took no prisoners and gave no mercy to captives. In truth, Dad was reaching for a chocolate bar to feed the starving youth.

In September 1945, on a troop ship embarking from Le Havre, France, the soldiers had nothing to do. They had won the war and were coming home in victory. So they gambled all day and night. My father had some money from his last few months of combat pay (about fifty dollars per month). When he landed in Boston, however, he was broke. Fortunately, he had sent most of his pay to Mom.

My dad was a Sergeant throughout the war. There was a certain know-it-all First Lieutenant who really didn't know very much, and he liked giving my dad a hard time. One day they were playing cards on the ship as they sailed home, and Dad caught the officer cheating. Now, my dad was a pretty levelheaded guy, but this time he lost his cool and popped the officer in the nose. They busted my dad from Sergeant to Private.

When Dad returned from the war, he and his bride of three years settled in her hometown of Averill Park and took up residence in her family's home with her sister Helen Theresa Kane. I had unintentionally nicknamed her "Hunnah" when, as a toddler, I couldn't pronounce her first name. My mangled pronunciation stuck.

My dad never minded that he was living in Mom's home, and Mom never seemed to mind having her sister in the house. It was actually a good deal for the Kane sisters because my father cooked breakfast every morning, maintained the yard and home, and did all the grocery shopping. (Mom cooked dinner, and

Hunnah was a great baker.) And my dad really loved Hunnah and cared for her whenever she got sick.

Before the war, Dad was a successful stock trader on the floor of the bustling New York Stock Exchange. When he returned and moved to Averill Park, Hunnah gave him a job as a rural mailman. After a year of delivering mail to farmers, widows, and hermits, Dad scraped together enough savings and borrowed money to make a "donation" to a Democratic Party official in Amsterdam so that he could get a scarce state liquor store license. Years later, my father would recount the harrowing ride in his old Ford on bumpy roads from Averill Park to the rusting city of Amsterdam on the Mohawk River (famous for rug making) and his secret meeting with a stranger in a hotel dining room, where Dad said "Big Bill sent me" and handed over the envelope. And like that, he was in business.

The grand opening of O'Donnell's Wine and Liquor Store—three weeks before I was born—went largely unnoticed. After fixing up the rundown place, Dad had only enough money for a tiny inventory of a few bottles of whiskey, scotch, rye, gin, vodka, and cheap wine, all displayed in a space smaller than a bank vault. To add insult to injury, the first month was one of the coldest, snowiest, and iciest winters on record. My dad grossed less than one hundred dollars.

Fortunately, locals started to stop by this curiosity on Main Street and meet the friendly, talkative Irish American with the warm welcome and witty conversation. Over the years, standing behind the counter with his handsome looks and sleek physique, I saw him countless times put a smile on a customer's face with a funny joke and nonsensical sayings like: "The boy stood on the burning deck, eating peanuts by the peck."

When the store phone rang, Dad cheerfully answered: "O'Donnell's Wine & Spirits, Spirits speaking."

When my sisters and I were pushing back about doing some chore, Dad would say, "What did we do? Lose the war?"

My father's humor was not totally silly. More than once, I heard him say, "Many a true word is said in jest."

Then there was me. Pierce Henry Joseph O'Donnell. As a kid, I was an awkward work in process. Things just happened to me. Like the time that I got a bean stuck up my nose (really!) and had to get the local doctor to remove it. Or the time that one of my sisters closed a bedroom door and mangled my left index finger and then the right one was mangled in my dad's car door by my well-intentioned sisters who took me to the car for the trip to the hospital. And I will never forget my extreme embarrassment (unfortunately, more than once) when I climbed a tree and couldn't get down without a ladder.

So, that's my family and hometown. My father, the liquor store merchant. My mother, the local school librarian. My aunt Hunnah, the postmaster. Three sisters. Several stray cats. A hundred year old house.

And Nora the ghost.

2.
NORA THE GHOST

I DON'T BELIEVE IN ghosts.

I've never seen a ghost or a picture of one. As far as I'm concerned, they exist only in books and movies and people's imaginations. All you have to do is watch *Casper the Friendly Ghost* cartoons to figure out that there are no such things as ghosts.

When someone dies, they're dead. I was taught that their body decays in the ground, but their soul goes to heaven if they lived a good life, to Purgatory if they lived a so-so life, and to hell if they had too good a time on Earth. That's it. There's nothing left behind.

Now, I have to admit that what I'm about to tell you is loony tunes. Off the wall. Nutso. I'm almost embarrassed to mention it. But my family knows about it, and if I don't talk about it, they'll say that I didn't tell the whole truth about growing up in Averill Park.

You see, the rest of my family believes in ghosts. To be more accurate, they believed in Nora. She was our resident ghost, they claimed.

It's not just that they believed our house was haunted by a woman ghost. You see, they claim that they actually saw Nora. Four different people.

I once heard my mom talking to my dad about someone having skeletons in the closet. I wasn't sure what they meant. But I figured that they thought we had a ghost in the apartment.

Before I say anything more, I want you to know that I'm not making all this up. This kind of stuff is too serious to joke about. Little kids grow up weird if you lie to them about things like ghosts.

The first person to tell me about Nora was my father. One day, as the family ate Sunday dinner, Dad told us about his encounter with our resident ghost.

Again, I really didn't want to write about this, but my sisters insisted.

Dad told my sisters, Mom, Hunnah, and me the story in hushed silence.

In fact, Dad had two encounters. The first was before the war when he was courting mom and came to meet her mother and Hunnah. Sleeping in the upstairs bedroom that later became the rental apartment, he awoke to see a woman standing at the foot of the bed.

Dad then told us about about another incident just a few years ago. Dad was walking home after closing the store at ten o'clock, as he did six times a week. It was cold winter night with the gusting winds blowing snow in the air. As he approached the house, he noticed a light in the upper attic. That was strange, he thought. He couldn't remember the last time that anyone had been in the upper attic, and he was sure that the light had not been on the night before when he came home.

When he entered the house, my mom was already asleep. So Dad went upstairs, walked into the apartment on the second floor, and opened the door in the apartment kitchen that led to the lower and upper attics. Just as he made the turn on the backstairs, he came face to face with a woman—a dead woman in a white, flowing robe or dress. She had dark hair, high cheekbones, and a pleasant smile. She just stood—no, floated—there right in front of him. Dad recognized her as the woman at the foot of his bed some twenty years earlier.

My dad is a very brave man, a war hero who survived the Invasion of Normandy, the Battle of the Bulge, and being wounded in one of the worst wars in history. No one could ever say that my dad is a coward. But that night, my dad decided that he didn't have to turn off the light in the upper attic.

When dad finished, my sweet little sister Maureen asked, "Who is this ghost?"

"Nora," said Mom, who had remained quiet while Dad was talking.

"Who's Nora?" my inquisitive middle sister Helen Kay wanted to know.

"Nora," my mother explained, "was one of my great aunts who lived here at the end of the last century. Before Hunnah and I were born. That's her in the oil painting by the front door.

In a flash, the four O'Donnell children were standing bug-eyed in front of a large painting set in an old gold-tinted wooden picture frame. I had seen this for as long as I could remember but never paid any attention to the attractive woman in her thirties with dark hair, high cheekbones, and a pleasant smile.

That had all changed with my dad's tale about Nora the Ghost.

I was never sure if my dad was kidding. He enjoyed playing tricks on us. And he had lots and lots of stories and jokes that he was always telling.

That's why he was always the Master of Ceremonies of the Annual St. Henry's Card Party and Fashion Show at the Crooked Lake Hotel. All the women liked his jokes; my mother wasn't too crazy about the attention that the other ladies gave to my father, who had all his hair and was in top physical shape because he did calisthenics in front of the mirror for an hour every morning seven days a week.

The next time I heard about Nora, the source was Mary Eileen. She's my kid sister, born in May 1948, fourteen months after me. Someone once said that children who are born close are known as "Irish twins."

Mary Eileen was different from my two other sisters—and anyone else that I grew up with.

She was a big tomboy—tougher, faster, and stronger than any other kid two years on either side of her age, including her older brother. Sometimes kids would pick on me because I was chubby and slow, and I did not like to fight. Whenever there was trouble brewing, Mary Eileen would show up and kick the crap out of the guys giving me a hard time. It did not feel good having to rely on my sister to protect me.

One more thing about Mary Eileen: she was more than a little weird. Before she made a telephone call, she would rehearse it. With her finger on the receiver, she would dial the number and start talking.

"Hello, Mrs. Morrison. This is Mary Eileen calling. May I please speak with Renee? Oh, well, that's fine. Please tell her I called. Thank you."

Then she would take her finger off the receiver, dial the number, and repeat the same conversation. This used to drive my mother crazy. No one was surprised when Mary Eileen announced one day that she wanted to be an actress when she grew up.

More than anything else, Mary Eileen was a very kind and gentle person. She used to bring home injured birds and abandoned cats. But that's not all. My sister once adopted a family—of people, not animals.

They were the Finches, and they were really poor. The dad was employed at the woolen mill, but he had to feed nine children—all dirty, hungry, and beautiful. Mrs. Finch always seemed pregnant. They rented a rickety old gray house owned by the woolen mill that the Kane family used to own. Their home wasn't much, but it was always filled with joy and love; it burned to the ground in 1960.

Mary Eileen would go down to their house, help the mom wash and take care of the kids, and assist with homework. For a couple of years, Mary Eileen also brought them food and used clothes, and at Christmas, she would bring toys.

Whenever a coat or sweater was missing in our house, we all knew where it was. No one ever complained.

Mary Eileen sometimes liked to be left alone. She read a lot, wrote stories about strange places and people, and played the flute. The only problem is that sometimes she played it in the middle of the night. My mom defended her. "She's a free spirit," Mom insisted. My dad didn't care. "If that flute wakes me up again," he would say, "she'll be a dead spirit!"

Anyway, I remember Mary Eileen claiming that she also saw Nora. It was another freezing winter evening. The wind was howling outside. She couldn't sleep. Then she heard a noise, what sounded like the apartment door opening. Her bedroom was on the second floor, fifteen feet from the front door of the apartment.

Mary Eileen got up and went into the hallway. There, right in front of her, hovering over the stairwell, was a white, ghostlike thing. She had dark hair, high cheekbones, and a pleasant smile.

"Nora?" Mary Eileen asked.

"Yes, who calls me?" the ghost replied.

"It's me, Mary Eileen."

The door to the first floor living room opened, and my father shouted up the stairs, "What's going on up there?"

The noise must have frightened Nora. She vanished. My sister was grounded for a week for again waking up Dad. I don't know if Mary Eileen really saw Nora. I was downstairs shivering in my coal bin bedroom and didn't see or hear a thing. I always kind of suspected that maybe my imaginative kid sister was rehearsing a conversation with Nora.

The most no-nonsense, down-to-earth person I ever knew was my Aunt Hunnah. She and Mom owned our house, which they had inherited from their parents. She lived in a bedroom on the second floor in the back of the house. Her bedroom overlooked the Old Mill Pond and Tin Can Alley.

Hunnah was very honest. She never lied, did not cheat at cards, and did not drink wine, beer, or whiskey. Everyone trusted her. She was always the treasurer who handled the money for the Ladies Auxiliary of the Averill Park Volunteer Fire Department, and she counted the Sunday Mass collections at St. Henry's for as long as I could remember. As the local postmaster, she was appointed by President Harry S. Truman, who wouldn't pick a liar or cheat for such a responsible position.

So when Hunnah told four kids one stormy night about her encounter with Nora, we were all ears.

"I was up in the attic one night looking for a purse in the storage chest. All of a sudden, the light bulb started to flicker…on and off…on and off.

Maureen grabbed my arm.

"Then I felt a whoosh of air…like a window was open. I turned around slowly, and I gasped."

Helen Kay and Mary Eileen huddled close together.

"Right before me, a few feet away was a…a…" Hunnah stammered.

"What was it?" I blurted out, my skin tingling, feeling like icicles had replaced the hair on my arms.

Hunnah paused, slowly looking at each one of us before she finished her sentence.

"It was a ghost!" she blurted out.

Four jaws dropped.

"She had dark hair, high cheekbones, and a pleasant smile."

"Was it Nora?" Helen Kay asked in a quivering voice.

"Yes, it must have been," Hunnah answered softly.

"Just what I saw," Mary Eileen gasped.

Maureen started to cry.

"Now, now, kids, maybe it was really nothing," Hunnah tried to reassure us, but the more she talked, it sounded like she regretted ever telling us about our live-in ghost. "Maybe I was just imagining things," she backpedaled.

But then there was the apartment tenant, Art Marden—the fourth person to report a Nora sighting. I have the hardest time dealing with what he said about Nora.

The apartment on the second floor had three rooms and a tiny bathroom with a sink, toilet, and shower. The bedroom was in the front of the house and led to the living room, which led to the kitchen and bathroom. The door in the back of the kitchen led to the backstairs, where my dad says he saw Nora. And those stairs led to the attic, where Hunnah had had her close encounter.

One night, Mr. Marden was sleeping with his wife and baby in the bedroom. The door was closed. He heard a noise in the living room and got up to investigate. Opening the door, he saw a pale woman with dark hair, high cheekbones, and a pleasant smile.

Mr. Marden always seemed like a pretty normal guy. He was a high school teacher, a serious fellow. I never heard him shout or yell at anyone, and he was always nice to me. He didn't drink too much, from what I could tell.

Well, Mr. Marden freaked out when he came face-to-face with this ghastly intruder. He ran back into the bedroom, grabbed a shoe, and threw it at Nora. The shoe went right through her and hit the wall, making a loud noise. Nora gave him a big smile, laughed, and then disappeared. Mr. Marden and his family moved out at the end of the month.

There you have it.

Did Nora the Ghost live in our haunted house? My dad, Mary Eileen, Hunnah, and Mr. Marden say so. Four people. Four sightings. The same description. But I still wasn't convinced.

After Mr. Marden and his family departed, my parents decided not to rent the apartment anymore. They told me that I could move my bedroom from the frigid, tiny former coal bin up to the apartment. It would be bigger, warmer, and quieter for my studying, and I would have my own bathroom.

I stayed in the coal bin.

3.
"ALL ABOARD!"

I HAD BEEN LOOKING forward to this day for a long time.
My dad was taking me on a train trip to New York City. I had never been on a train before. And it was the first time that my dad had ever taken me on a trip without my mom or three sisters.

A few months before we left, my mom said to Dad, "Harry, why don't you take Pierce with you on your next trip to New York?" My father wasn't too keen about the idea at first—something about, "Who will watch him while I'm gone for a few hours?" But my mom insisted.

I was so excited that I couldn't sleep that Saturday night. I had laid out my best clothes in the afternoon, polished my shoes, and taken my bath. My homework for Monday was done, and I said an extra prayer that it wouldn't snow so hard that the trains would be canceled. Where we lived, in the winter, snow was always on the ground, in the air, or a county away.

I was dressed and ready to go by the crack of dawn, waiting in the chilly kitchen for my father to finish getting dressed. My dad was always up by six in the morning, even on Sunday. He cooked breakfast for the whole family every day of the year so that my mom could sleep in until seven. On this Sunday morning, however, we just had a glass of juice.

"We'll eat breakfast on the train," Dad announced.

On the way to the train station in downtown Albany, we stopped at St. Henry's for eight o'clock Mass. Our parish church had been built around 1900. A red brick building with heavy stained-glass windows, it had wooden pews as hard as a rock and a drafty choir loft with a loud organ in the back. Like most cold winter mornings, the place was freezing.

But I didn't really care.

I was going to New York City on the train with my dad!

We caught the ten o'clock express to New York. In those days, "the train" was the New York Central Railroad. We had studied all about it in school—how Governor DeWitt Clinton built the railroad with Irish immigrant laborers in the early part of the 1800s and how the railroad opened up the state and then the West to migration and trade.

I remember waiting with excitement at the station for the arrival of the train. It was coming from Montreal, and it was a little late. People were standing around, drinking coffee, and smoking cigarettes. Newspaper vendors hawked the Sunday papers—the *Albany Times-Union*, *New York Times*, *New York Herald-Tribune*, and *New York Daily News*.

I knew all about the *Times-Union* because I had delivered that paper for six months until very recently. William Randolph Hearst Jr. owned the paper, and his father had something to do with the Spanish-American War, Teddy Roosevelt, and his Rough Riders. The *Times-Union* was the best newspaper in our area. I was lucky to get the paper route from an older boy who got a better job as a soda jerk at the local pharmacy.

Everything went okay when I started delivering in the late summer. Arising at six o'clock, riding my bike up to the village, counting my thirty-five papers, and then delivering them in forty-five minutes. I loved riding with a newspaper bag over my shoulder, steering with one hand, and tossing a paper on the porch with my other, all the while dodging a snarling dog or darting cat. My customers usually gave me a five cent tip every week—except Mrs. Loman, who was always a week late on her newspaper payment.

"I'm sorry, Pierce, I don't have any change today," she would say.

"I can make change, Mrs. Loman," I would reply.

A Boy Scout is always prepared.

"Please come back next week," she always replied as she took the paper and quickly closed the door.

So, I would have to pay for her paper to the *Times-Union* route manager. I never figured out why a twelve-year-old kid should have to loan a few bucks to a rich widow living in a big house with live-in help.

In the fall, I liked the crisp morning air as the sun rose over the sleeping town and steam floated over the Old Mill Pond. All I needed was a jacket, and occasionally a sweater, too. I remember all the bright orange pumpkins on the porches as Halloween approached. It was special to be twelve and in charge of doing something all by yourself. I had the best job a boy could ever want.

"Good morning, Mr. Everett," I often said as I slowed down and handed him his paper.

"Another glorious day," the typewriter store owner would always reply.

I can't remember him ever saying anything else. His cheerful wife was a great baker who gave me fresh baked oatmeal or chocolate cookies as my weekly tip. My sisters would be waiting at the front door for their cut of the still warm delicacies when I came home on collection day.

Then came the snow, ice, and subzero temperatures right after Thanksgiving. The eager beaver newspaper boy lasted until Valentine's Day. It got so cold that my bike tires went flat, my hands were almost frostbitten no matter how thick or how many gloves I wore, and I kept losing papers tossed in snowbanks when I missed the customer's porch.

I was afraid to admit to my parents that I wanted to quit. I was not a quitter. Thank God that my mother came to the rescue.

"Harry, it's not safe for Pierce to be out there by himself when the weather is so awful. The snowdrifts tower over him, and the sun isn't even up."

Dad thought for a moment. I knew he was proud of me for having a job. When he was my age, he was in the orphanage and never got to earn any spending money.

"All right," he said. "If he wants to earn money, he can work around the house."

That was the end of my short-lived newspaper boy days and the beginning of my weekly allowance of fifty cents for burning the trash, washing dishes, and making my bed.

The train finally arrived in Albany; it was a big, black coal or diesel burning train. (They switched to electric locomotives down south at Croton-on-Hudson before we got to New York City.) My first thought was how much the locomotive looked like the model train my parents had given me at Christmas when I was six. It was a Lionel, of course, and the locomotive came with a black coal tender and a bright red caboose. They cost fifty-nine dollars in 1953 and included a bunch of tracks and switches and a transformer. Of all my gifts, my Lionel train set was the one I loved the most.

"All aboard!" the conductor hollered as the train lunged out of the station in a big cloud of white smoke. I was seated by the window, right next to my dad, who was reading his *Daily News*. I couldn't believe it—I was really in a train that must have been moving a hundred miles an hour because the trees, houses, and bridges were flying by us in a blur.

The conductor wore a dark blue suit and a dark blue hat with gold trim and the New York Central Railroad insignia. I couldn't take my eyes off the gold watch and chain hanging from his dark blue vest. He was really nice to me when I kept asking him the time so that I could see his watch.

"Would you like to hold it for a while, son?"

"Yes, sir!" I replied, my eyes bugging out as he lifted the object of my affection out of his vest pocket. He winked at my father.

"I need your help," he said as he leaned down to hand me his prized possession.

"Tell me when it is noon, okay?"

I couldn't believe it. The conductor not only trusted me with his watch for a couple of hours—I was helping him run the train! When we got home, my mom gave me her father's railroad gold watch and chain. My dad must have told her how much I liked the conductor's.

As the train hurtled south toward the Big Apple, we ate breakfast in the classy dining car—a fancy restaurant on wheels. There were tables next to the windows covered with white linens and silverware, comfortable chairs, and friendly "Negro" waiters in crisp white uniforms. The kitchen was a tiny galley in the front of the car, but the cooks served big meals. I had scrambled eggs, bacon, hash brown potatoes, toast, jelly, orange juice, and hot chocolate. Breakfast never tasted better than the day I ate with my dad on the train from Albany to New York.

The railroad line hugged the east riverbank with stops at Hudson, Rhinecliff-Kingston, Poughkeepsie, Croton-Harmon, Yonkers, and New York City. The first settlers of the 150-mile Hudson River Valley (New York City to Troy) were Indians (today "Native Americans") long before Europeans arrived. Mostly living in peace were the Mohican, Wappinger, and Lenape tribes of the mighty Algonquins. I knew this because Boy Scouts learned about America's real founders and valued their love of nature and spiritual values.

The natives traded with the Dutch explorer Henry Hudson who sailed as far north as Troy in a futile search for the mythical Northwest Passage. The Lenape sold the island of Manhattan to the Dutch settlers for sixty guilders (twenty-four dollars) of trinkets. The settlement of New Amsterdam later became New York City when the British assumed control.

Besides the Dutch, early immigrants—seeking furs and establishing manors for farming and dairy cattle along the east bank—included English, French, and

Germans. The Irish would come later, and many would die digging the Erie Canal from the Hudson River in Albany to Buffalo on Lake Erie. Several Revolutionary War battles were waged along the Hudson River Valley.

For many Halloweens when we were kids, Mom read to us "The Legend of Sleepy Hollow" by Washington Irving. We would cringe in fear as she told the terrifying story of the Headless Horseman pursuing poor schoolmaster Ichabod Crane through the woods of this ghost-ridden, bewitched village. This paragraph set shivers up and down my spine every time I heard it:

> On mounting a rising ground which brought the figure of his fellow traveller in relief against the sky, gigantic in height, and muffled in a cloak, Ichabod was horror-stuck on perceiving that he was headless!—but his horror was still more increased on observing that the head, which should have rested on his shoulders, was carried before him on the pommel of his saddle!

The sky was overcast, and the Hudson River was partially frozen along the banks, when we passed by West Point, an hour out of New York City. There is something awesome about the high cliffs and the tall gray buildings of West Point on the other side of the river. I'd read books about the history and traditions of "The Long Gray Line" and all the famous generals (Ulysses S. Grant, John J. Pershing, Dwight D. Eisenhower, Douglas MacArthur, George S. Patton, and even the Confederate Robert E. Lee) who graduated from there.

I wanted to go to West Point and be a soldier like my dad. I read articles and books about military strategy and Allied soldiers escaping from German prisons. Whenever a WWI or WWII veteran would come into my dad's store, I would pepper him with questions about where he fought and what it was like. After a while, I noticed that most of them didn't want to talk about war.

Three hours after we left Albany, I heard those magical words.

"Next stop: Grand Central Station, New York City," my pal the conductor announced in a booming voice. "All passengers must depart the train."

It was hard to believe the ride was almost over; it had gone so quickly. But there on my left in the Bronx was Yankee Stadium—"the House that Ruth built"—and up ahead were the skyscrapers of Manhattan. Then everything went pitch black as we went underground into the railroad tunnels under New York City.

Passengers started collecting their luggage and putting on their heavy coats. My dad took my hand, and we walked to the front of the car and then the open space between the two cars. The frigid air startled me as I felt the train slowing down. My father had ridden on lots of trains.

When the Depression hit in 1929, my dad was a successful stock trader on the New York Stock Exchange—one of the youngest ever with his facility with numbers. He worked for McCafferty & Co. I once heard Dad tell Mom how he lost his job.

"Around 1935, the government put us out of business for violating some new stock trading law," Dad said. "That Joe Kennedy, the bootlegger during Prohibition, was the head guy."

Bootlegger? I had to look up the word in our family dictionary. I couldn't imagine a guy in a business suit hiding liquor in his high boots.

Dad was the sole source of support for his three sisters. He needed to find work, but so did millions of men like him. Dad took to the rails.

Out West, in Wyoming and Montana, he became what they called a "Gandy Dancer." Those were the strong men who drove railroad spikes as the tracks were laid on top of railroad ties mile after mile, day after day. The work was exhausting, but the pay was pretty good for the Depression—a few bucks a day—and he sent most of the money home to his sisters.

Then Dad ran out of work.

For a few months, he became a hobo, riding the trains as he searched for work. The other unemployed guys and he hid out in box cars and even rode with pigs and cattle. Dad kept traveling west, not finding a job and ending up in Los Angeles.

My father was so tired, broke, and hungry that he intentionally got himself arrested for being homeless. That way he could spend the night in the Boyle Heights jail and get a hot meal and coffee. But the next morning, the Los Angeles police, shotguns in hand, took him and his pals out to the city line and rudely told them never to come back again.

As my sisters and I grew up, we'd hear this story several times.

"Life teaches us lessons," he taught us. "I learned the value of money and having a good paying job, three meals a day, and a roof over my head."

That's why Dad insisted that we never waste food. I always wanted to please him. So I could blame him for my overeating and weight problem!

Once the train stopped, we were the first passengers off the train, racing up the ramp to the upper level of the station.

"Hey, Dad, please slow down," I yelled as my father took two steps at a time.

"Come on, Pierce," he urged. "We're almost there."

It wasn't easy to keep up with him. Those size fifteen feet covered a lot more territory than my size eights. Then, all of a sudden, I was standing in the Main Concourse of Grand Central Station. I was speechless. What a humongous place! The domed ceiling was so high that I could barely see it. The giant clock on one of the walls was the largest I'd ever seen. Surrounding us were small shops filled with customers who seemed in a hurry. Hundreds of people were darting in every direction. I'd never been in a place with so much energy and excitement. My mouth was wide open in awe. My father almost had to drag me out of Grand Central Station.

We caught a cab to Toots Shor's, a swanky restaurant where lots of famous people hung out. One celebrity regular was Ed Sullivan, whose Sunday night variety show was one of the few TV programs my parents allowed my sisters and me to watch. My favorite acts were magicians, ventriloquist Paul Winchell and his dummy Jerry Mahoney, Spanish comedian and ventriloquist Señor Wences, and the guy in a tuxedo who kept all the plates twirling on sticks.

"Pierce, why don't you go read that new book Hunnah gave you," was my mom's polite way of enforcing the limited TV rule. I didn't mind. The adventures in *Last of the Mohicans* or *Treasure Island* were much more thrilling than anything on TV for kids. And what black and white could compare with an Edgar Allan Poe story or an island of Lilliputians?

So, there I was in this famous restaurant and lounge with a gigantic circular bar. Just imagine how proud a twelve-year-old boy from Averill Park was of his father when everyone seemed to know Harry O'Donnell. The hat check lady, the guy who seats you, and all the waiters greeted him by his name. We went to the bar, and my dad ordered me a Shirley Temple. The bartender gave my dad "the regular"—Dewars and soda with a twist of lemon.

We were there only a few minutes when my dad introduced me to the owner, Mr. Shor and a couple of the guests—Jack Dempsey and Mickey Mantle.

I couldn't believe my eyes.

I first shook hands with Mr. Dempsey. His right hand was as hard as a rock and swallowed up mine. My dad was real strong, but I had never felt such strength. It was like putting your hand in a vice.

What was so amazing was that Jack Dempsey was sixty-four years old when I met him in 1959. He had been the heavyweight champion of the world from 1919 to 1926, my dad told me. He had not fought in over thirty years, but he still looked healthy. And his right hand was made of steel.

Mr. Dempsey couldn't have been nicer to me. He pretended that he was fighting with me.

"Take your best shot, kid," the Champ invited as he stuck out his stomach as the target.

Except I missed and hit him below the belt. It was an accident, I told him. He was polite about it, but he looked in pain for a while.

Then I shook hands with the great centerfielder and home run slugger himself. It was still a few weeks before the Yankees went to spring training. And here he was talking to me.

Mickey Mantle, like my dad, was handsome. He had light blond hair, a perfect build, and muscular thighs. He carried himself like a champion, because he was one. A few months earlier, the Yankees had just won the World Series in seven games, beating the Milwaukee Braves. Mantle had a great season himself in 1958, batting .304, hitting forty-two home runs, and knocking in ninety-seven runs.

All I remember "the Mick" saying that afternoon was: "Harry, is this the young man you're always bragging about?" Mick winked at my dad.

Well, you could have knocked me over with a feather.

I don't remember anything else Mantle said that afternoon, but I sure recall him giving me an autograph and a pat on the head. None of the kids in school the next day believed me when I told them that Mickey Mantle was my new friend.

Meeting Mickey Mantle in 1959 changed my life.

Before my trip to the Big Apple, I had always rooted for the Dodgers in the National League and the Red Sox in the American League. But not anymore. I was now a New York Yankees fan because my buddy, Mickey Mantle, played for them. Oh, I still rooted for the Dodgers, but I had a real problem when they played the Yankees in the World Series.

That afternoon, though, my dad disappeared for a few hours. All he told me was that he had some business to do. He left me with his best buddy, Tommy Romano from New Jersey. Tommy and my dad had fought side-by-side together in the war. He was what they called a "detail man" for a big drug company who went to doctor's offices and taught them about new drugs.

When my dad returned to Toots Shor's, we had a big dinner. I had lobster and wore one of those big bibs so that I wouldn't make too much of a mess of my coat and tie. My dad and his war buddy had thick, juicy steaks, onion rings, baked potatoes, and beers. It was great fun! I felt like a big shot having dinner at Toots Shor's with my father and his best friend.

I don't remember much about the train ride home in the dark. The rolling movement of the train put me to sleep shortly after we pulled out of Grand Central Station. When I woke up in the morning, I had Mickey Mantle's autograph held tightly in my hand.

4.
"BLESS ME, FATHER"

"Bless me, Father, for I have sinned," I began nervously. "It has been one week since my last confession."

Here I was again on a late Saturday afternoon. Outside it was cold, overcast, and dreary. Inside St. Henry's Catholic Church, it wasn't much warmer or brighter. What was I doing? Kneeling in a dark, stuffy confessional booth, talking through a wire mesh partition to the parish priest about the "sins" of a twelve-year-old boy.

It was embarrassing.

First: who wants to tell someone else about your failings? It's bad enough that your parents and sisters know your faults. But to admit them voluntarily to someone else? Well, it was uncomfortable, even if the priest vows that he will be drawn and quartered before he would tell anyone what he learns during the sacrament of confession.

Second, and this is the main reason that I dreaded this ritual: I didn't have any good sins to confess. Thankfully, I had succeeded in not committing any of the "mortal" sins. I hadn't murdered anybody or stolen anything or even coveted my neighbor's daughter, much less his wife. Sex was something the guys were talking about more and more, but I was clueless about "the birds and the bees" as Hunnah put it.

All my "sins" were what the Catholic Church classified as "venial sins." Fighting with your sisters, disobeying your parents, telling a little white lie—things that didn't amount to very much in the grand scheme of badness or sending you to hell. Not only were my sins trivial…they were boring.

"And how have we been since your last confession?" Father O'Connor would ask immediately after my opening statement. I don't know why he asked because

I told him the same boring things every Saturday afternoon. I had to come up with something to confess.

"Uhm, uhm...I fought with my sisters three times, ate breakfast fifty minutes before Communion—that was only once—but I was really hungry, and...uhm..."

As I ticked off my usual list of venial sins from memory, I thought I heard a yawn from the darkened space on the other side of the partition. I was stuck, desperately trying to think of something serious sounding to tell the priest, something that might shock him and take me to new depths as a sinner. I wracked my brain:

Masturbation? Not believable since I had not yet hit puberty. Heck, I didn't even know yet what that was.

Like so many painful times before, nothing exciting—much less reportable— came to mind.

"And I filched some apples from Mr. Gordon's orchard!" I blurted out.

That was a lie, too. Actually, I had only eaten an apple that Billy Glasser had stolen. I was too afraid of getting caught and stayed out on the road, pretending that I was the lookout. But I was in a pinch, and I needed a third sin. The Catholic Church is big on threes: Father, Son, and Holy Ghost; Jesus, Mary, and Joseph; Heaven, Purgatory, and Hell.

I thought the stolen apples might provoke a comment from the good Father. I waited for his condemnation. I fully expected at least a lecture on the Ten Commandments—"Thou shalt not covet thy neighbor's goods." I was ready with my profuse apology, my full declaration of remorse, and a solemn vow never to steal again. I had trained for years for this moment.

But it never came.

"For your penance, say five Our Fathers and five Hail Marys. Now make a good Act of Contrition," Father O'Connor uttered matter-of-factly.

That was it? No lecture, not even a mild rebuke. Nothing. I could have told him that I'd just poisoned the convent's drinking water, and I would have gotten the same penance.

After a few years of this ritual of meaningless Confessions, I started to develop a complex. It really depressed me that I lived such an unexciting, goody two-shoes existence. The other guys were bragging about their mortal sins while I had nothing to report. At one point, I went to my *Baltimore Catechism of Catholic Doctrine* to review the list of mortal sins.

Now the *Baltimore Catechism* was *the* authority on the basic teachings of the Roman Catholic Church. As young kids, we learned by rote all about our religion.

Starting with questions about "Who is God" and "Why does God love me?" The guide eventually discussed sin and the various degrees of sins. Consulting the *Baltimore Catechism* again confirmed one thing that I had already suspected: it was not easy to be a Catholic.

Growing up Catholic in the fifties was one test after another. It seemed like almost everything was immoral or "the near occasion of sin," which is sort of like thinking about doing something but not really doing it. Or putting yourself on the path of temptation but then resisting at the last minute. A good example would be taking a girl to the movie theatre, wanting to make out with her, but then she doesn't let you kiss or touch her.

To confuse matters even more, the Catholic Church invented "indulgences"— charitable acts and prayers used to subtract the number of days spent suffering in Purgatory after you die. You see almost no one dies in a perfect state of grace; there are always some unconfessed sins on the balance sheet. If your sins aren't too bad, you go to Purgatory and have to await your call to heaven. The nuns told us that because the wait can be long and agonizing, things like good deeds, prayers, saying the rosary, visits to shrines, and the like each merited so many days of relief from Purgatory. Throughout a lifetime, a Catholic accumulated so many days off from Purgatory—sort of like building up frequent flier miles on the airlines. By 1959, I had collected 6,250 days off from Purgatory thanks to various indulgences.

I never had any mortal sins to confess. Try as hard as I could, I didn't have too many "near occasions of sin" either. Once I may have thought about eating meat on Friday, but I didn't have the guts. Sadly, my life was an unrelenting series of venial sins, the sum total of which wouldn't equal one Class C mortal sin.

There were so many rules, and a lot of them dealt with sex. The Catholic Church was preoccupied with sex. The older I got, the more I realized how many of the rules dealt with regulating the physical relationship between boys and girls. The celibate Pope in Rome made the rules, but the chaste nuns in faraway Averill Park were the enforcers. My two younger sisters, Helen Kay and Maureen, went to St. Henry's parochial school. They couldn't sit on a boy's lap unless they had a telephone book between them, their blouses had to be buttoned at the top, and they couldn't wear teased hair, stockings, jewelry, or patent leather shoes—the latter because boys might be able to look up skirts in the reflection.

Anything remotely dealing with sex was sinful. At about this time, I discovered *Playboy* magazine. My friend Skip Vigus had "borrowed" a few back issues from his father. At first it was hard for me to look at the pictures of the half-naked women (waist up, of course) because I was overwhelmed with guilty feelings. Gradually, I got more comfortable with the notion, but I now had something worth confessing. The only problem was I couldn't understand why it was okay to look at totally naked women in great paintings but not photographs of bare-breasted women.

The National Legion of Decency dictated what movies I could see. The church's moral censors, they were a group of priests who watched every movie and gave it a rating based on its content, not its artistic merit. While profanity and blasphemy were criteria, sex was weighted the heaviest. Sophia Loren and Brigitte Bardot and their bulging breasts were automatically forbidden. Scenes of passionate kissing, petting, or a man and a woman in bed (even fully clothed) were also sure-fire guarantees of a "condemned" rating.

I remember wanting so badly to see one of those sexy foreign films. They played at a rundown theater on a side street in Troy. I used to stand outside and look longingly at the posters, wondering what it would be like to see a man and a woman hugging each other in a field of flowers or lying next to each other on a remote beach. Even if I wanted to risk my immortal soul, I was too young to buy a ticket.

"How old do you have to be?" I would ask the wrinkled old man in the tiny ticket booth.

"A lot older than you, Sonny," he replied, his gums valiantly trying to compensate for his loss of a dozen teeth.

"Well, how old?" I insisted.

He smiled. "When you start shaving."

That answer left me, for once, speechless...but hopeful. From that moment forward, I looked in the mirror every morning, praying for that day when the first peach fuzz might appear.

I wasn't in much jeopardy of committing even the near occasion of sin. I didn't have any girlfriends. I had a crush on Monica Culley, the tomboy who had horses up in Glass Lake and looked terrific in blue jeans and cowboy boots. But she was our twenty-year-old babysitter, so there wasn't much future there.

None of the girls in the village interested me. I had grown up with them—playing tag, hide-and-seek—and, as we got older, baseball, football, and war games. Most of them were much faster, thinner, or taller than me. Some of them liked to make fun of me, teasing me about my weight or clumsiness.

One older girl was always nice to me, though. She was polite, sweet, and thoughtful. Like a town crier, my friend would stop on the street to talk, telling me what bulbs Mrs. Everett was planting in her garden or that Bruno the barber, who drank hair tonic when he was low on cash, had just cut Mr. Crowley's neck while shaving him.

Her name was Daphne, and she was mentally retarded (later called "intellectually disabled"). We were never boyfriend/girlfriend, but I always liked her. When my playmates made fun of her, I would defend her. I got really upset when I later learned that an older boy took advantage of Daphne and got her pregnant. She went away, and I never saw her again. But I'll never forget her kindness to me.

My first "girlfriend" was Pam Murdoch, a blonde with a bubbling personality who lived in nearby West Sand Lake. She was my age, shorter than me, and really friendly. We sat next to each other in class, trading notes and glances. It took me forever to call her up at home.

"Hi, Pam?" I asked, gathering up all my courage one school night in eighth grade.

"Yes, who's this?" the object of my affection wanted to know.

My heart sank: she doesn't recognize my voice after two years.

"It's…it's…it's Pierce," I finally replied.

"Oh, hi, how are you?" she inquired. One thing I liked about Pam was that she never seemed nervous or unprepared.

"I'm fine. Gee, the reason I'm calling is—"

I couldn't get the words out. I panicked, frozen in mid-sentence. I started kicking myself for not rehearsing the phone call like my sister Mary Eileen always did.

"Yes, Pierce?" Pam finally asked.

"Uh, uh…would you like to…uh, uh," I stammered, paralyzed by fear.

"What is it, Pierce?" Her patience was wearing thin.

"Would you…would you please…" I chickened out. "Would you give me the pages for our math homework tonight?"

I got the assignment that I had already finished. But I didn't get a date to the afterschool Valentine's Day Dance. It would be another year before I got the courage to ask her. She accepted, and we went to the "Autumn Leaves" ball at the high school. She was radiant in her blue and white taffeta dress and high heel shoes. I wore my new Robert Hall blue suit. Her mother drove us.

Pam was pleasantly surprised that I knew how to dance. I didn't tell her that I had attended Mrs. Gouch's Dance Academy after school at the St. Henry's

Parish Hall with a bunch of other prepubescent boys and girls and had learned ballroom, square, and tap dancing.

But I quit after some of the guys teased me so badly that I got in a big fist fight on my way home one day. Blood all over my face and shirt, my right eye almost swollen shut, I stormed into my father's liquor store and announced in a booming voice:

"I'm not going back to Mrs. Gouch's ever again, and nobody can make me!"

I realized instantly how defiant and insubordinate my statement sounded. My father was not accustomed to being lectured by children. He took a long look at me. I awaited the explosion.

To my shock, however, Dad calmly said, "Come on back to the bathroom and clean up your face. I've been wondering when you would get tired of that sissy stuff."

I ran over and hugged my father tighter than ever before. He understood my feelings and supported me. Looking back, I realized that this was the beginning of my rite of passage toward manhood.

Despite weekly Mass, monthly Confession, meatless Fridays, sixteen years of indulgences, and serving as an altar boy, my Catholic childhood was not complete. Mary Eileen and I never attended Catholic elementary or high schools. St. Henry's didn't have a parochial school until I was almost in high school, and it went up only to the eighth grade.

I always felt cheated because the nuns never taught me in school. I'm told that this is a special experience, one that shapes your personality for life. Helen Kay and Maureen had the joy of nuns—so-called "brides of Christ"—instructing them in religion, sex education, and current events. Yet neither ever considered becoming a nun.

I was exposed to the nuns because of released time for religious education once a week when I was in junior high school. The Catholic kids in seventh and eighth grade were bussed from public school to St. Henry's Church for an hour of catechism classes. The nuns from the parochial school were our teachers.

My favorite was Sister Beatific Vision. That's not her real name, but it could have been since the nuns always had two first names and never a surname—like Sister Mary Helen or Sister Helen Mary. Sister B.V. was typical of the nuns: an Irish-born woman in her forties with seven siblings back in the "Home Sod," three of whom became nuns, one was a priest, and the other three were unemployed.

Sister B.V. had a saying for every occasion. The only problem was that they were always slightly off the mark. She was Archie Bunker in a habit: "A stitch in twine saves nine." "Pride cometh before Fall." "It's raining cats and hogs."

The nuns were strict disciplinarians. Usually a mere stare from one of them would silence a room. If stronger measures were required, there was the all too familiar ruler over the knuckles. I never got the ruler, so I can't attest to how it felt. Helen Kay said it hurt for only a few seconds, but the worst part was dreading the next installment. It was an effective form of deterrence.

As I grew older, I found that I had more and more real sins to confess. But by then, I wasn't too crazy about confessing them.

5.
MUSKRAT

They called him Muskrat.

His real name was Jerry Warren. He lived over on the next street with his grandmother. Their house, across from the old red trolley barn, was not in very good shape. It needed paint, the yard was messy with old cars and engines, and there were some smells that I didn't like.

But I liked Muskrat.

He was a lot older than me. When I was twelve, he had to be at least sixteen or seventeen. He was less than six feet tall, thin, and very strong. Muskrat never slept, and he didn't like to bathe much, either.

I don't remember how I met him. It was like he was always around the Old Mill Pond next to my house. You see, Muskrat was a fur trapper like the ones who came to North America in the 1600s and 1700s for beaver, mink, and other valuable animal pelts. That's how he got his nickname. Besides setting his traps for mink, Jerry also trapped for muskrat. If you've never seen a muskrat, it's hard to describe. They have fur thicker than a mink, but their fur is not as fine and soft as a mink's. Like the mink, the muskrat lives along the edges of lakes, ponds, and streams. They are mammals, but they spend a lot of time in the water.

The best time for trapping is in the fall and winter. The New York State Department of Fish and Game said that was the only trapping season. I was never sure why. Maybe it was because the animals are hungrier and go for the trap bait better in the fall and winter. Anyway, Muskrat did his trapping in the fall and winter, and he let me be his assistant.

Muskrat wasn't big on school. Even on the coldest or rainiest day, he would rather be up before dawn, hiking in his rubber hip waders along the Old Mill Pond or Fireman's Pond down by St. Henry's Cemetery, checking and resetting his traps. The school district's truant officer regularly visited Jerry's grandmother.

"Good morning, again, Mrs. Warren," he said. "Do you know where your grandson is right now?"

"Oh, he's at school…isn't he?" she always replied.

"No, ma'am," would be his response. "And when he's there, he falls asleep in class."

"Boys will be boys," she used to say, her "s" making a whistling sound as it passed through her few remaining brownish teeth.

I never knew much about why Muskrat lived with his grandma and not his mother and father. I pestered him with a lot of questions about his family when he first started taking me along on his morning and afternoon rounds, but personal stuff was out of season.

"Pierce, if you want to trap with me, we need to make a deal," Jerry told me as we walked along a partially frozen creek.

"Sure," I quickly answered. "What is it?"

"You get only three questions a day," he announced. "And they must be about minks and muskrats."

I'd never done any trapping myself. The first time that I saw a trapped mink I wasn't quite sure what to make of it. The mink is not a particularly beautiful creature—it looked like an overgrown rat. But its fur was smooth and shiny.

By the time that we got to a trapped mink or muskrat, the animal was dead either from a broken neck or a combination of bleeding and freezing to death. Jerry would put his foot on the trap, open the large, sharp jaws, and remove the deceased. I would then help him reset the trap, using as bait an apple or some concoction from his grandmother's leftovers. We'd then cover over the bloody snow with clean snow, smooth over the tracks with a pine bow, and back away from the trap. Jerry kept the traps off any trail so no human would get hurt.

The next step was the least fun.

When we got back to Jerry's house, we skinned the animals. We would first gut them and then tack them down on a skinning board. Jerry would use his big Bowie knife to make a few swift moves and remove the pelt without ripping or puncturing the fur. The pelt would then be dried and sold to a fur company for a couple of bucks. A few months later, some rich lady in New York would be showing off Muskrat's pelts.

Jerry liked to hunt, too. I never asked to go along, however. I was not keen on hunting animals. In my mind, it was one thing to set a trap and then come back to discover a dead mink or muskrat. Somehow, I didn't feel so bad about that.

And we weren't killing just for the sport of it; Muskrat trapped to help support his grandmother and himself.

I loved to fish. I never felt I was being cruel when I caught a trout or largemouth bass, cleaned it, and brought it home for dinner. Since I could walk, I had fished, and I never had any qualms about killing a fish.

But hunting an animal with a gun was whole lot different for me. One Christmas, my parents had given me a Daisy Air Rifle. Man, I loved my BB gun and practicing shooting in my backyard. I had all kinds of targets: tin cans, Coke bottles, cardboard boxes, clothespins on my mother's clothesline, telephone poles, and even tree leaves. After a while, I got pretty accurate (except when my eyeglasses fogged up); so, it was time for me to become the Great Hunter. My friend Ken "Skip" Vigus lived up on Bear Mountain Road just above Glass Lake. His dad was a hunter and had trained Skip since he was a youngster to shoot guns. My buddy was a great shot and had his own .22 rifle since he was ten.

I used to stay at Skip's on Friday and Saturday nights. His mother, Marie, was a very attractive, kind woman who let us stay up past midnight. Eating bowls of fresh popcorn, the three of us and Skip's grandmother would play a card game called canasta. Then Skip and I would go into the living room and watch the late-night movie. Our favorites were John Wayne westerns and World War II movies. We would always fall asleep with the TV on and sleep until late the next morning. This was my first real taste of independence, and I loved every minute of it.

When Skip and I awoke, we would take off into the thick woods for the day with a bag full of the best tuna fish sandwiches on white bread made by Skip's mother. Skip's father had built a shooting range for him, and we practiced shooting his .22. Sometimes, we would go hunting. Skip was a better shot, and he shot a squirrel or rabbit every now and then. I never had any luck.

One day at my house, I was shooting my sister's BB gun. Over on the telephone wire, I saw a robin. I raised my gun, took careful aim, and fired. To my amazement, the bird fell to the ground.

I had killed the robin. As I knelt over and picked up the still creature, I felt terrible. I really didn't mean to kill it; I was just having fun. A chill went down my spine as the consequences of what I had done overwhelmed me. I started crying.

I never killed another animal again.

My pal Muskrat killed only what he ate or sold. For him it was a matter of survival. He didn't have the luxury of making great moral distinctions. And his grandmother refused to go on welfare.

There's one thing about Muskrat that made him really special—he had a weird sense of humor.

One frosty winter morning, I followed him into the woods, looking for new places to set his traps. Muskrat started talking about bears, and how they sometimes get caught in his mink and muskrat traps by mistake. I was sort of surprised because I didn't think there were any bears in our area. Too many people, I had been told.

But, no, Jerry insisted, they sometimes wandered down from the Taborton Mountains ten or fifteen miles away.

"They get hungry and bored, and they go on a long trip, looking for food and excitement," Muskrat said very seriously.

If Muskrat said so, it must be so. He was the great outdoorsman. Sometimes it seemed like he spent more time in the woods than he did at his grandmother's house. I started looking over my shoulder for a wayward bear.

"Really?" I asked nervously.

"Oh, yeah, for sure," he replied in a confident voice. "You can't be too careful out here."

A little while later, Muskrat stopped on a path on the far side of the Old Mill Pond. Through the leafless trees, I could see my white house in the distance. The pond was starting to freeze over, but it was too early for hockey. Jerry instructed me to go down the path another hundred yards to check one of our traps along a mink run.

When I turned the corner just before the spot where we had trapped a mink the day before, I stopped dead in my tracks. I couldn't believe my eyes. There up ahead was huge brown bear, lying on the ground, caught in the trap.

I started yelling: "Muskrat! Bear! Muskrat! Bear!"

It seemed like hours before he arrived. I was frozen in fear. A few yards ahead was the biggest animal I'd ever seen. I knew enough about bears to know that they could outrun humans. Especially a twelve-year-old, flat footed, overweight boy whose feet felt like they weighed a thousand pounds.

"What is it, Pierce?" he asked casually.

"What do you mean 'What is it?'" I shouted, pointing my trembling finger at the reclining bear right in front of us.

"Oh that," he said in a matter-of-fact voice.

My fearless friend walked over, took out his Bowie knife, knelt with his back toward me, and thrust his knife several times with great force into the bear.

Then he stood up, cleaned off the blood from his knife, and slowly replaced it in its shield hanging from his belt.

"Another day, another bear," he calmly remarked.

By now my eyes were bugging out of my head. I couldn't believe that there was bear in my neighborhood, much less that Muskrat so bravely killed it. I couldn't wait to tell everyone in school.

All of a sudden Muskrat started laughing. Laughing so loud that it echoed off the partially frozen pond and evergreen trees.

Then it dawned on me what was happening.

I ran over to the trap. The "bear" was dead all right. The only thing was that it had been dead for a long time. I had been fooled by an old bear skin cleverly stuffed with leaves to give it the bulk of a live bear. Muskrat had put its paw in the trap.

"When did you do all this?" I asked.

"Yesterday afternoon, when I did my second rounds," he replied, still chuckling and pleased with himself.

I'd not been able to accompany Muskrat because I had too much homework. He had carried the skin, which his grandma used as a floor rug in their living room, out to the woods and rigged up the trick for his gullible young pal. The best part was how realistic it was when he stabbed the creature. Lots of real blood was dripping from his Bowie knife.

"How did you do that?" I was eager to know.

"I hid a dead squirrel under the bear rug," Jerry replied, his grin widening. "I blocked your view so you couldn't see me stabbing the squirrel and not the bear."

That afternoon, in the woods with a playful friend, a gullible boy learned a valuable lesson: things are not always what they appear to be. Especially dead bears.

6.
PETER PAN

"THE STORE" WAS IN the center of town, and the man who worked so hard there was the center of my life.

O'Donnell's Wine & Liquor Store was located at the intersection of Main Street and Burden Lake Road. In Revolutionary War days, the ancient two-story wooden building was a way station for tired horses and hungry riders on the road from Albany to Boston. Now it was the only place for miles around for thirsty adults to buy booze.

Main Street was a three hundred-yard stretch of single lane highway from the Mobil to the Texaco (later Sunoco) gas stations. Sandwiched in between were the post office, Park Pharmacy, Gouch's Bakery, Appliances and Dry Cleaners, Barnum's Newsstand and Candy Store, the A&P, the Averill Park Market & Variety Store, Zane's Market, Lakeview Hotel and Bowling Lanes, two barber shops, a beauty parlor, Everett's Typewriter Sales and Repair, and dad's store. Just off Main Street was Larkin's Funeral Home, St. Henry's Catholic Church, and the Methodist Church right next to my house on Burden Lake Road. The Fire House—an old white wooden building where we played Bingo on Friday nights—was up the hill from the Sunoco on the road to Miller Hill Elementary School where I had attended since kindergarten. As Averill Park's population grew in the fifties, we got a bank, two lawyers, a women's clothing store, and a weekly newspaper, the *Sand Lake Advertiser*.

When I was growing up, Averill Park—officially a village within the Town of Sand Lake—was smaller than Andy Griffith's Mayberry. We didn't have any local police, much less a mayor or Town Hall. A tiny dot on the map, Averill Park was the blinking traffic light at the intersection of Routes 43 and 66, the state roads leading eastward from Albany and Troy toward Massachusetts. We had no municipal park, swimming pool, or library, but we did have Crystal Lake Beach and Merry-Go-Round in the summer. More Americans died each year from dog bites than lived in my hometown. My mom told me that the census once recorded a net loss of population.

Averill Park was a cool place to hide out. There were so many dirt backroads, abandoned barns, and mountain cabins. The Irish-American gangster Gentleman Jack "Legs" Diamond lived in a field stone house on Crystal Lake. The hills were alive with moonshine stills during Prohibition. And Catholic nuns, in long black dresses and white hoods, flocked in pairs to Crystal, Glass, Burden, and Crooked Lakes to escape the city heat.

Unofficially, Averill Park did have a mayor—it was my dad, and his store was our Town Hall. No one ever held a meeting or voted to elect my father the Mayor of Averill Park. It just happened over time. You had to know my father and the role he played in our community to understand.

Most of my best pal's life was spent at his store. Monday through Saturday, he worked from nine in the morning until ten at night. Seventy-eight hours-a-week, fifty-two weeks-a-year. Few vacations or days off. Dad didn't have a clerk or help when I was a kid. He worked twice as hard as any other person around.

So, if I wanted to spend time with my dad, I'd hang out at his store.

I never missed a chance to do an errand or help him out. Of all the things that my mom would say that would please me—"Harry, why don't you take Pierce up to the store?"—was the most pleasant. I'd be cleaned up in a flash, standing at the front door like a puppy dog expecting a walk, waiting for my dad to leave for work.

In the eyes of his son, Harry Joseph O'Donnell was a bigger-than-life figure. Physically, he was built like a Greek wrestler: 6'3", 185 pounds of solid muscle. He was a physical fitness fanatic who did calisthenics for an hour every day in our front parlor. As he exercised in front of the full-length mirror, Dad listened to Arthur Godfrey on the radio or played Benny Goodman, Gene Autry, and Frank Sinatra on the Victrola. He played The Ink Spots all the time. Later, he got a fancy stereo record player for the family for Christmas. Besides shadow boxing, he did jumping jacks, body twists, toe touches, sit-ups, arm circles, neck stretches, side bends, leg thrusts, and push-ups. He also loved to jump rope.

I would get tired just watching him.

Dad did everything in life with great enthusiasm. His daily workout was no exception. Grunting and groaning, whistling and humming, he was in a constant state of motion. The furniture shook as he quickly moved his feet or hit the floor with his chest.

"Harry!" my mother would shout from the TV room or kitchen as she heard the all-too-familiar rattling of her gilded antique French cabinet, China cups, dishes, and figurines inherited from her mother, "You're going to knock the house down."

Dad had learned years ago that arguing with Mom was useless, so he continued to work out in silence, altering his routine just enough to reduce the vibrations and escape Mom's attention. Dad still exercised every day, and Mom's fancy stuff was never broken. It was like an unspoken truce.

Dad tried to teach me the basics of his workout.

"It's time you got rid of that baby fat," he announced one day.

Dad had this habit of saying things and expecting them to happen immediately.

This decree was doomed. I was worse than pathetic. What can you say about a kid who can't even get the hang of jumping jacks?

"You look like a chicken in heat," Dad barked, barely able to contain his laughter.

Even the neck stretches were a disaster. I got so dizzy from moving my neck in circles around the top of my shoulders that I almost knocked over one of my mom's vases. But the greatest indignity of all were the push-ups. My dad could pop off fifty at a time. I couldn't do one.

"Let me feel your muscle," my dad said.

I lifted up my right arm and made a muscle.

"J-E-L-L-O," my father sang to the tune of the popular TV commercial as he squeezed my limp upper arm muscle tightly. I winced in pain.

Some kids might have gotten a "complex" about their dad constantly teasing them about their physical unfitness. Not me. I loved the attention. As he got older, my father kept his youthful appearance—a full head of wavy blond hair; deep blue, alert eyes; and trim physique.

With his boyish smile, he liked to call himself "The Peter Pan of Averill Park."

My dad had other things going for him besides his good looks.

Harry O'Donnell was a man of his word. If he promised to do something, you didn't need to get it in writing. Whether it was a ten thousand dollar paint job for our house, paving the store parking lot, or an investment, his word was his bond.

"Your dad's bad for my business," Mort Shulman once told me. Mort was the friendly lawyer who rented the other half of the building from my father. "Your father does everything on a handshake. He never needs me to write up a contract, and he's never been involved in a lawsuit."

As I said, Dad was the closest thing we had to a mayor. People came to him to settle disputes. (He was a mediator before anyone used the word.) For many years, he was the President of the Averill Park Merchants' Association, our local chamber of commerce if you will. Several times, I heard him on the phone helping solve some problem between two of the Association's members who were both Dad's friends. Using his quick wit and Irish charm, Dad would quickly find a middle ground.

"Now, now, Ray. I'm sure that Zane didn't mean any harm when he said you sold horse meat," Dad reassured Ray Eastman, owner of the Averill Park Market & Variety Store, who was up in arms about some reported falsehood by Zane Bedian, the Armenian grocer who owned the rival market across the street and had an opinion about almost everything. Zane was a Republican, but my dad still liked him.

"I talked to Zane," Dad said, "and he meant to say that even horses wouldn't eat the meat you sell!"

Ray laughed at my father's joke.

Too bad. I was looking forward to the War of the Butchers.

People really liked my dad. Customers would drive fifteen or twenty miles to shop at his store. Dad always had a warm welcome, followed by a witty remark or some funny, nonsensical comment.

"We're here to help the needy, not the greedy."

"I sell liquor to buy milk."

"You don't look a day over thirty-nine."

"It's cheaper by the case."

"You can't stop progress."

"The boy stood on the burning deck, eating peanuts by the peck."

After spending so many hours at the store and listening to him deal with the public, I realized that, more than anything else, dad was a straight shooter. He told my sisters and me many times that he was in a service business and that people had choices about where they shopped. "The customer is always right" was his favorite saying.

If dad had recommended a wine and the customer later complained, he would apologize and give him a free bottle of another brand. Even though he often made little or no money on the order, he would deliver for his customers.

On too many nights after his thirteen-hour day, he would set off to deliver a pint to a remote farmhouse miles away.

My father's popularity was even harder to understand since he was a "carpetbagger" from New York City, and a Democrat in a town of Republicans. Year after year, he would serve as the Chairman of the Democratic Party. His job was to find candidates to run (always unsuccessfully) for local town supervisor while he handed out party literature at his store.

The store also served as the headquarters of the local Democratic party. In the early years, you could have used a telephone booth. Every other November, the local Democrats lost by lopsided margins. But my father never quit.

"I was born a Democrat," my father explained. "FDR saved this country and got me back to work. People have short memories."

Not my dad. The election of President John Fitzgerald Kennedy in 1960 was one of the happiest days in his life.

"He may be rich, but he's one of us," my father proudly told my sister and me as Mom and he toasted the victory of a fellow Irish-American and Catholic.

Just before the election, in a debate at school over the public address system, I had taken Senator Kennedy's side against my classmate Langdon Brown who represented Vice President Richard Nixon. My dad had helped me with my arguments for voters in the student straw poll. My biggest problem was that most of the kids' parents were Republicans "who had never voted for a Democrat and never would if their life depended on it," my dad predicted.

"It is time for a change…a New Frontier," I argued over the loudspeaker. "Forget how your parents are going to vote. Assert your independence. Vote your conscience."

They did—Nixon swamped Kennedy at my school. But my dad won his first election as a local party leader, and he got a personal thank you note from a grateful Jack Kennedy himself!

When another liquor store opened in the 1960s in the next village a few miles away, my dad's reputation for great service and discount prices allowed him to keep most of his customers. The opening of Johnny Miller's rival store in West Sand Lake was caused by the only politician that my father really hated. Whenever he totaled a bill, Dad would have to add the sales tax. His shorthand for the government's bite was "Rocky's take," referring to Governor Nelson. B. Rockefeller, the zillionaire who was New York State's Republican Governor.

My father did not despise Rocky merely because he was a Republican or tried to spend the state to death. Rocky's "sin" was persuading the legislature to authorize many new retail liquor store licenses to help pay for his spending. The flood of new licenses cheapened the value of my father's license if he ever wanted to sell it. To make things worse, it allowed large companies to own chains of liquor stores that offered deep discounts and forced little guys like my father to lower prices or go out of business. It was good for the consumers, but thanks to Rocky, my father had to work harder and made less money.

One of my earliest recollections is hanging out at the store and trying to grab liquor bottles off the shelves for customers.

"Whoa, pal!" Dad exclaimed as he caught a fifth of Imperial whiskey in mid-air.

When I was a little older, Dad let me dust off the bottles with a feather duster. I eventually learned the names, locations, and prices of every brand of liquor and wine. By the time I was twelve, I was allowed to stock the shelves and carry bags out to customers' cars. Dad also trusted me to watch the store while he did errands.

"Tell 'em to browse around," he instructed me. After telling the customers just what he said, I would run over to Zane's or the post office to report to Dad. Out of breath, I'd shout, "Dad! You've got a customer." Dad would drop whatever he was doing and hustle back to the store.

Then I graduated to shoveling snow and chopping ice in front of the store. In Averill Park, it snowed from Thanksgiving to Easter. One storm in 1958 dumped so much snow that the drifts blew up to the top of the store display window. My dad and I shoveled snow for days. It was a piece of cake compared to chopping ice, though. A storm drain was located right in front of the store. Whoever designed the stupid thing knew nothing about what happened when a thaw caused the melting snow to run into the overworked drain and a quick overnight freeze created a five-inch-thick ice rink. It was my job to get rid of the ice.

My only tool was an old, rusting iron bar with a blunt blade on the bottom. This ice chopper must have weighed fifty pounds. Grabbing it with both hands, I would lift it up as high as I could and then thrust it down toward the ice. With luck, a piece of the rock-hard ice would chip off. After a couple of dozen lifts and thrusts, my blubbery arms were aching, and I was breathless.

"Builds character," my father would shout from the front stoop of his store as the freezing wind blew the drifting snow into my face.

I had heard of middle-aged men getting heart attacks from shoveling snow. I wondered aloud about the health risks for a young boy chopping glacial ice.

"Don't worry," Dad reassured me. "The frost bite will get you first."

Frost bite, indeed. With a twenty mile-per-hour wind and the thermometer dipping into the low teens, the temperature was more like minus ten degrees! I thought that I had adequately dressed myself for any weather condition. From head to toe, I was covered in layers of protective clothing: a wool cap, fur earmuffs, red scarf over my full-face ski mask, a thermal T-shirt covered by a red flannel shirt, thick blue sweater, down-filled coat with a hood, long johns under corduroy pants, two pair of thick gray woolen socks, and a pair of rubber hunting boots. I looked like a mummy.

I also had a pair of fur-lined gloves inside thick mittens. Unfortunately, they were frozen stuck to the iron ice chopper. It got worse. Did you ever try to scratch your nose with your hands entombed in thick gloves and mittens? And good luck trying to take a pee outside when you have to take them off and risk amputation from frost bite!

With my eyes watering and my face getting more and more sweaty from chopping, I imagined that I would eventually be unable to move—my arms too numb from assaulting the ice, my legs too stiff from the bone-chilling cold, and my face immovable as my perspiring eyelids gradually froze together. Then I lost contact with my toes.

Just when I despaired of ever seeing Mouseketeer Annette Funicello on TV again, my dad rescued me with an invitation to come inside while he attacked the ice. Thawing out over a heating vent, my lips too sensitive to sip a hot chocolate, I swore that I would not live in such a cruel climate when I was an adult. If I wanted snow, ice, and freezing wind, I'd drive or fly to it. This ice-chopping ritual continued until some genius with the state highway department recognized the problem and had a larger storm drain installed.

Hanging out at the store was not usually life threatening. In fact, it was mostly a lot of fun. And one reason was listening to my dad deal with his customers.

Dad was always up. Although he had no interest in hunting or fishing, he would listen patiently to stories from old-timers (drinking Old Grand Dad) about the eight-point bucks and lunkers that just got away. He would brighten up the most depressed customer's day with his good humor.

One customer, complaining about his wife who had run away with another guy, was told, "Cheer up. It could be worse. She could have taken your camper."

"She did," he replied.

Dad flirted a little with the women who were flattered by his attention.

"Yes, Mrs. Miller, you and your sister look so much alike."

"That's my daughter, Harry."

"Oh, come on," Dad interjected as he scrambled to recover. "You must have been twelve when she was born."

My favorite shoppers were fraternity guys from RPI in Troy who would drive twenty miles roundtrip to buy their liquor and wine from Harry O'Donnell. You could tell that they liked my father's easy-going personality and jokes—not to mention the nice discount on every case. I was always impressed how "cool" these fraternity brothers looked in their khaki pants, blue Gant shirts, and Bass Weejun loafers. I would listen in wonder from the back of the store as they told my dad about their all-night parties dancing with sorority girls to a rock and roll band.

If you spent enough time at O'Donnell's Liquor Store, you could meet almost everyone in and beyond the village.

I really liked the town road crew. Those guys bought the cheapest "rot gut" wine (like Ripple or Thunderbird) and started drinking at six in the morning. They didn't have many teeth, their hair was falling out, their speech was so slurred that I couldn't understand a word (but my father could), and they all had the same limp. When I used to see them out working on the roads, they would shout, "Hey, there's Harry's son" and give me a warm wave.

My father had a great joke about the slow-moving men who fixed the potholes, cleared the snow, and cleaned out the storm drains. One summer day, one of them turned around and violently stepped on an innocent caterpillar. His buddy put down his wine bottle long enough to ask him why he had done such a cruel thing. The "killer" replied, "that caterpillar has been following me for three days."

William Kennedy was another favorite of mine. A regular wine customer, Bill was a newspaperman who had returned from Puerto Rico to write for the *Albany Times-Union*. On the side, he told my dad and me, he was writing novels.

"Well, you might strike it rich," Dad suggested.

"Or go broke like most would-be novelists," Kennedy replied. "I'm not giving up my day job."

"What do you write about?" I eagerly asked.

"Albany," Kennedy told me. "And all the Irish-American characters that have made it such a unique city."

"Great!" I replied. "I can't wait to read your novel."

"Don't hold your breath waiting," he offered, a twinkle in his eye reminding me of Darby O'Gill in the Disney movie that I had just seen.

I could stand there forever and listen to Bill Kennedy. It wasn't his silky Irish-accented voice or anything about his physical attributes. It was that creative mind and his command of language. Whether he was describing his latest encounter with the carpenter who was remodeling the old house that his wife and he had bought a few miles down Burden Lake Road, or why baseball was such a great sport, I was mesmerized. Even my father, who likes to get a word in every now and then, was in awe of Bill Kennedy's storytelling.

There were so many other memorable characters who hung out at our Town Hall. Some were local merchants like Ray Eastman, the grocer; Bill Glasser, the plumber with twenty-two children (true!); my scoutmaster, Bob Springer of our Boy Scout Troop 26; Earl Linden, my dad's accountant who liked to pop a few shots of Four Roses whiskey in the back room while he decided how generous my father should be with the Internal Revenue Service; Dr. John Reid, our family physician who had a hearty laugh and appetite; Jack Hallett, photographer and Boy Scout leader, who had a broad smile and missing teeth and knew a lot of heartache in his life; and Game Warden Jimmy Woods, who apparently thought a lot of unlicensed hunters and fishermen hung out in the back of the store.

Another regular was Bill Healey, a retired salesman who lived across the street. You could set your clock by the time (twice a day) that he came over to talk with my father. He never bought anything; he just talked and talked and talked about everything and nothing. One of my jobs when I was twelve or so was to stand in the front of the store and listen to Bill while my father escaped to the back room. The job got tougher when Bill started swearing that, as a result of a hospital visit, he had worms crawling out of his skin.

Ned Pattison was one of my dad's fellow long-suffering Democrats. A Cornell man and lawyer in his father's firm in Troy, Ned was active in civic affairs and local politics. Ned was an effective public speaker and a man of great integrity. My dad said that Ned was a "liberal."

Ned, my father, and I would have long talks about politics. Smoking his pipe, Ned would walk back and forth in front of my father's counter, debating with my father (who was more conservative) and occasionally letting me get in a question. I remember the day that my dad told Ned that it was time for him to stop talking and do something—like run for local office. Ned thought about it for a minute, and as he slowly let out a sweet-smelling puff of smoke, he agreed. "Worst that can happen is that I get my butt whipped."

Bruno was a Catholic Polish or Czech immigrant whose family fled the Communists. His son became a shoe salesman in Troy, while his daughter was one of my classmates. His wife was a short, stout woman who only grunted when you said hello. Bruno was supposedly a licensed barber, but no one was really sure from where. Most of his customers came only once. Bruno couldn't have made much money because he was always buying Band-Aids.

One day as I was walking past his small shop next to the Variety Store, I heard the loudest, freakiest scream in my life. It sounded like a herd of banshees. Suddenly, a man draped in a white barber's smock came tearing out of Bruno's shop.

"Help! Help!" the man screamed, blood streaming down his neck from a bad cut on his left ear. "This man is a maniac!"

The bloodied customer was, of course, referring to our Bruno, who stood stunned and staggering in front of his shop doorway, holding a bloodied razor, muttering "Come back! I fix ear. Come back!"

I later learned from my father that the victim was a stranger passing through town who had some time to kill. He went to Bruno for a haircut not knowing any better.

Sadly, Bruno was an alcoholic. He stood in front of his shop blitzed out of his mind at 11:00 a.m. As his business declined, he had no money to buy booze from my dad, who had promised his wife not to sell him any more liquor on credit. Desperate, Bruno turned to drinking hair tonic and witch hazel from his barber shop. His brain was fried.

I'll never forget the scene of Bruno standing in my father's store, trembling all over, his arms flailing in the air as he uttered a stream of obscenities in a heavy accent. While Dad was a compassionate man, he chased Bruno out of the store, disgusted that his lack of self-control was ruining his family.

My dad never relaxed very much. While he got his seven hours of sleep (11:00 p.m. to 6:00 a.m.), he had no real hobbies other than playing the stock market. He didn't golf, ski, hunt, fish, hike, collect stamps or coins, or play cards or an instrument. Occasionally, he would ice skate with my sisters and me, but it was not easy to find size fifteen-feet skates. Once a week every August, Dad and Mom would drive about an hour to Saratoga for the horse races, but it was only a day trip.

Sunday was Dad's day of rest. Sort of.

He would sleep in—until 7:00 a.m. After his calisthenics, he would cook a great breakfast feast of fresh squeezed orange juice, coffee, scrambled eggs,

Pepperidge Farm rolls, First Prize link sausage, crisp bacon, fresh fruit salad, orange marmalade, and butter.

Then we were off to Mass at St. Henry's. Some of the pews still had brass nameplates identifying the names of the family that once rented the pew for a monthly donation. The "Pierce D. Kane" family was represented, along with a lot of German, French, and Irish family names.

I was an altar boy and Dad was an usher and later one of the first lay lectors after the Vatican II. My father had a booming, muscular voice that bounced off the stained-glass windows donated by turn-of-the-century parishioners. Dad used to practice his Scripture readings on Saturdays. Mom bought him a book about how to pronounce all those tongue-twisting Old Testament names like Melchizedek and places like Kiriath-Jearim.

Even as an usher, Dad was the life of the party. Everyone got a warm welcome and hearty handshake.

"Good morning, Mrs. Stahlman," he greeted the wife of the high school principal who was one of my dad's horse-betting pals. "Prof. Stahlman," as my father dubbed him, hung out at the store after he retired and passed along all of his handicapping advice like they were gold nuggets.

"Top of the morning to you, Ben," Dad welcomed Ben Gauch, the roly-poly owner of the local appliance, dry cleaners, and bakery establishment and whose wife Doris taught dance lessons in the drafty wooden Church Hall. Ben Gauch had a strange way of talking out the side of his mouth. I always wondered if he had been a ventriloquist in another life.

"Well, hello, Sisters," Dad said respectfully as he bowed his head ever so slightly toward four Catholic nuns from the Convent at St. Henry's School. It was an old habit from his orphanage days, I figured. Dad and his three sisters had lived under the stern guidance of the black-and-white-clothed Irish nuns in New York City after his mother had died and his dad was institutionalized with a nervous breakdown.

"I had my share of rulers across the knuckles and beatings with a belt," Dad once admitted when I pressed him about life in a Depression-era orphanage.

Dad apparently didn't bear a grudge. He donated ten thousand dollars to the construction of St. Henry's parochial school when I was in elementary school. At the time, that was a lot of money for a middle-class merchant in a tiny town, but my dad never forgot his roots in poverty and wanted his and other children to have a better life.

Besides serving as an usher and lector, Dad was the annual toastmaster of the St. Henry's Card and Fashion Show, the biggest fundraiser of the year organized by the parish women. The spring fling was held at the historic Crooked Lake Hotel, a sprawling field stone restaurant and bar with a rustic interior (moose and deer heads mounted on the walls, Indian artifacts, and black bear rugs) and large banquet rooms. The rich and famous from around the world had been guests over the seventy-five years that the hotel stood majestically along the Crooked Lake shoreline. Whenever I entered the front doors, I thought that I was being transported back in time and that I would bump into Teddy Roosevelt, his cousin Franklin, or Thomas E. Dewey.

As the ladies showed off the latest fashions, my father cracked jokes and off-the-cuff one-liners. People would attend just to hear Dad's latest collection of humor. He liked to put his toe over the line, especially at the expense of priests.

"Did you hear the one about the Catholic priest, Protestant minister, and Jewish rabbi who were discussing how they divided up the Sabbath collection between the church and themselves? The minister said that he threw the collection up in the air and whatever landed on the oval rug in his office went to the church and whatever fell off the rug was his. The rabbi admitted that he used a similar procedure, but whatever fell outside the rug belonged to the synagogue. Finally, the priest reported that he also tossed the collection basket up in the air, but he didn't use an oval rug. 'Whatever stays up in the air is God's, whatever hits the ground is mine.'"

The audience would howl, the priest would pretend to be upset, and then my father was on to another joke. Political humor was his favorite.

"I hear that the Republicans in Congress are finally going to pass at least one of President Kennedy's programs. It's the Peace Corps. But there's a string attached. They want his brother Bobby Kennedy to be the first Peace Corps volunteer at the South Pole."

Dad also liked to flirt with sexual humor in a room full of up-tight Catholics, priests, and nuns.

"According to the Bureau of Statistics, American women live longer than American men, and they have most of the money. The government also tells us that prostitution is on the rise. I wonder if there is any connection?"

After Sunday Mass, Dad would sit in the kitchen reading three newspapers—*New York Times*, *Albany Times-Union*, and *New York Daily News*—and the *Barron's* financial publication. My parents would have a few scotches, and the kids would munch on Wrigley potato chips, cheese puffs, and nuts. I liked to watch the professional bowling TV show. Then all of us and Hunnah would have dinner in mid-afternoon, followed by Dad's nap. Dad would then do his weekly accounting, sales tax calculations, and bank deposits.

After a supper of juicy hamburgers and french fries from Pattison's hamburger stand, it was time for *The Ed Sullivan Show* at eight o'clock. This was a family ritual. Homework was done, the weekend was over, and everyone could relax and watch Elvis, the Beatles, Paul Winchell and Jerry Mahoney, comedians, opera singers, and magicians. Dad liked to sneak up behind my sisters and me in the darkened family room and scare us by jabbing his index fingers into our ribs. As Dad howled, the victim would jump up into the air off the couch. It was all so predictable—and welcome.

At 9 o'clock, the kids were off to bed, and my parents had an hour or so to themselves. From my bedroom off the kitchen, I could hear them planning the coming week or arguing about something. "Oh, Harry!" was my mom's favorite line, while Dad would usually come back with "Come on, Mary!" But there was one thing that no one could dispute: that they loved each other very much.

Dad would get to bed before Mom who was in the nearby bathroom. After a few minutes, I would hear this knocking on their bedroom wall and a soft voice beckoning "Mary" to come to bed.

"Relax, Harry," Mom would reply. That would silence my dad for a few minutes until he impatiently started knocking on the wall again, this time louder, and urging Mom to come to bed. I wasn't sure what to make of it, but Mary Eileen thought that it was some sort of mating game.

"If Dad didn't fall asleep most of the time before Mom got to bed," my kid sister Helen Kay said, "we'd be like the Glassers with two dozen kids."

SPRING

"It's spring fever. That is what the name of it is. And when you've got it, you want—oh, you don't quite know what it is you do want, but it just fairly makes your heart ache, you want it so!"
—Mark Twain

7.
SPRING TRAINING

As strange as it may seem, I may have been born with a baseball in my hand.

My mother told me that my birth was very difficult. It took hours for me to squirm out of her womb. In fact, everything about my arrival was complicated.

I managed to be born on what had been one of the worst weather days in recent memory in Upstate New York. The temperature had fallen through the mercury at the bottom of the thermometer on the front porch. It was so bitter cold and windy that my father's car tires were frozen into the snow and ice, and he had to get a blow torch to get the car moving.

The ten-mile ride to Samaritan Hospital in Troy was apparently no thrill. The country road was ordinarily bumpy, but with the addition of three months of subzero temperatures, snow, ice, and sleet, the highway was also filled with deep craters that could swallow a tire if you weren't careful. Then there were the smoother patches of "black ice" that were slippery as glass. The usual twenty-minute trip took over an hour as my mother held her stomach and moaned.

"Harry, you're going to bounce the baby right out of my stomach if you don't drive more carefully," Mom scolded my dad.

"Mary, I'm doing the best that I can," Dad replied, his patience at the breaking point as the car in front of him spun out of control and landed in a snowbank.

"Oh, God, it hurts," Mom uttered, her voice growing more and more faint as the contractions became more frequent.

Somehow, on that nasty early March night, Dad's '45 Ford made it up the icy, steep streets leading to the hill overlooking Troy, where Samaritan Hospital is perched. My mom and Hunnah had been born there, and all four O'Donnell children would enter the world at this local hospital that was the pride of the Collar City.

After an agonizing labor, I popped out in the early morning hours of March 5, 1947. I weighed about eight pounds and was pronounced healthy by the doctors. Apparently, I let out a deafening cry when they patted me on the butt.

For a while I thought that my delivery was so hard because I tried to come out feet first, but the more that I thought about the matter, the more convinced I became that the real problem was that I had a white round leather object firmly clutched in my right hand.

This makes more sense than you may think.

You see, the earliest thing that I can remember as a baby was playing with a baseball. Not just one of those little colored rubber balls that infants drool on and chase across the living room floor while the adults yell, "Oh, look, little Pierce is going to be a baseball player!" Not me. I had a real hard ball—bright white, red stitches, and "PROFESSIONAL MODEL" stamped in black on the face. I loved my baseball. I took it everywhere with me, including to bed at night. My parents would try to pry it out of my hand, but even in the deepest sleep, I held on tightly. When I had my ball in hand, I felt very secure.

As a four-year-old, I would train for hours with my baseball. My favorite drill was to wind up and throw it at the fluffy couch, run over and retrieve it, and throw it again at the couch. This could go on for hours. As I got a little older, I started throwing to my father and kid sister Mary Eileen across the living room. Every now and then, one of us would miss, breaking a window or denting the wall.

Unfortunately, my mom never fully appreciated the joys of indoor baseball.

"Pierce," she would shout, "you're going to break something else. Go outside with that thing."

"Mom, it's not a thing!" I would shout back. "It's a baseball, and when I grow up, I'm gonna be a professional baseball player."

"Really," Mom would reply, wiping her soapy hands on her green and white checkered apron and curling her eyebrows toward heaven.

"Yeah, just like Jackie Robinson, Pee Wee Reese, and Duke Snider."

Mom would come over, take the ball in her hand, and pat me on the head.

"That's very nice, Pierce, but the living room is not Ebbets Field."

I never could figure out a good comeback, so I moved Spring Training to the front yard. Unless, of course, it was the dead of winter—as it was most of the year where I lived. Upstate New York had four seasons. Winter lasted for six months, and the other seasons were rationed only two months each.

Weather reporting was hardly an exact science in 1959. We didn't have satellites or color maps on TV showing clouds blowing across the country. All we had in Upstate New York were "cold fronts." So, I never believed the balding, overweight television weather reporter on WRGB, Channel 6, in Schenectady when he announced: "Today is the first day of spring."

Right. I can't recall one March 21 when it wasn't snowing, sleeting, or freezing. Spring was false advertising. Even into mid-April, the ground was often frozen. In our front yard, an ugly mixture of frozen ice, melting snow, and sand and gravel lingered as a reminder of the town highway crew's winter assaults on snowbound Burden Lake Road. Superman couldn't push through that mess; grass didn't have a prayer.

We were one of the few homes in Averill Park with a sidewalk. Each spring, bigger cracks appeared from the months of freezing weather and ice. I was never sure why Dad built it in the first place. It was a level, concrete sidewalk that was just right for roller skating, hopscotch, and learning how to ride your new Raleigh bike, but it was only 100-feet long, and it went from nowhere to nowhere.

The other problem with our sidewalk was that I had to shovel it off every time it snowed, or I had to chip off the ice when we had freezing rain. After the first few light snowfalls in November and early December, I was able to keep the sidewalk clear and a parking space in front of the house for my dad's brand new 1959 Cadillac—the one with the long fins that the neighborhood kids nicknamed "The Black Whale" and mom dubbed "the hearse".

By New Year's Day, however, my snow shovel and I were rapidly losing the war with the weather. A few six-inch dumps of heavy snow followed by freezing rain totally obliterated the sidewalk, so I settled for carving out a space for The Black Whale. But by Lincoln's Birthday, my dad often had to keep the car up in the liquor store parking lot, which was plowed out by the local Sunoco gas station owner.

It was a hard winter on our bodies, too. Our house was kept warm by ancient radiators that circulated hot water heated by the basement coal-burning furnace. The air in the house was dry, and the whole family would get chapped hands and cracked lips from coming in and out of the bone-chilling outdoors and the dry, hot house. We would also get shocks from our clothes from the static electricity in the air. My dad delighted in his kids' screams when they were jolted by a pair of socks or flannel nightgown.

Worst of all, it was also a long, almost endless winter. The cold Arctic air blew south by mid-November, and snow sledding, tobogganing, and ice skating on Thanksgiving were not uncommon. The sun broke through a little bit in early December, but weeks before the official start of winter, a blanket of gray clouds covered the sky and cast a dreary shadow over the land. As I grew older, I became convinced that Christmas and New Year's Eve were calendared in winter to keep the people from committing mass suicide.

On days when the temperature was mild (say fifteen to twenty degrees), my sisters and I would play outdoors. It was always a major production to put on our snow clothes: long johns, corduroy pants, T-shirt, flannel shirt, two pairs of socks, snow pants and jacket, wool cap, earmuffs, and mittens attached by tiny suspenders to the jacket sleeves. Sometimes, we spent more time getting dressed in the kitchen in front of the oven than we did playing outside.

"Now, keep your mittens on," Mom would always instruct us. "And don't get snow inside your clothes."

I could never figure out what Mom meant. What else were you supposed to do when you were rolling down hills in two feet of snow, or jumping out of the apple trees into piles of snow, or having a snowball fight? Sometimes I wondered if mothers felt like they had to say nonsensical things like, "Don't get snow inside your clothes," just so they would feel good.

If you could stand the freezing cold, there were plenty of things to do. We had American Flyer sleds, a toboggan, plastic saucers, and ice skates. There were countless hills for sledding and tobogganing, and the Old Mill Pond in our backyard was a popular ice-skating rink. My sisters liked to build snowmen, and I liked to knock them over.

Not far from our house was a hill with a perfect steep run of over fifty yards. We would build jump ramps in the middle and have contests to see who could fly their sleds in the air the farthest without falling off. One of the Glasser boys dislocated his shoulder when the sled landed on him. Paul was a tough guy, though. A week later, his shoulder in a cast, he tried again. This time he landed on his head, but there was no damage.

I had a different problem: I never could get airborne more than a few feet because I was so much heavier than the other kids. I even bought a special wax for my steel runners, but I still couldn't fly off the ramp as far as my lighter playmates.

This was a source of embarrassment for me and entertainment for the other kids. They constantly made fun of my failed, oafish efforts at sledding and all other sports, calling me "Porky," "Pusser," "Fats," "Fatso," "Fatso Fogarty," and lots of other equally obnoxious things. Every time I was heckled with one of those nicknames, I would cringe, a feeling of rejection overwhelming me. I wanted to make them stop saying those cruel words, to stop taunting me when I couldn't swim as far, run as fast, or jump as high as them. More than anything else, I wanted to be accepted as one of the guys.

I found ways to avoid the name-callers, like withdrawing into my own world. There, no one judged you. Everyone was equal, welcome, accepted. My own world was friendly, warm, and kind.

And I would escape by reading books about adventure. Jules Verne, Robert Louis Stevenson, Daniel Defoe, H. G. Wells, and James Fenimore Cooper were among my favorites. In my imagination, I voyaged to the moon and 20,000 leagues under the sea; I was kidnapped by pirates; stranded on an ocean island with the Robinson family; was a Time Traveler or Invisible Man; heard drums along the Mohawk as a scout for the British army during the French and Indian Wars; and fought the Redcoats at the Battle of Saratoga less than an hour from my home. I wrote short stories and playacted with Mary Eileen, and I spent many hours with my best friend in his liquor store.

I still wanted to be one of the guys. But most of all, I wanted to be a good baseball player. The biggest obstacle to developing baseball skills was the endless winter and the delay of Spring Training. All winter, I would read books about baseball: *The Roy Campanella Story*; books about Babe Ruth, Joe DiMaggio, Ted Williams, Jackie Robinson, and Lou Gehrig; and any novel about baseball that Mom could get out of the library.

Starting in March, I would take out my baseball glove and a beat-up old baseball and sit by the window for hours, hoping that the snow would stop falling and the temperature would rise above zero. After weeks of pounding the ball into my mitt and oiling it down, I had a pretty good pocket. And as soon as the temperature broke into the forties, I was out the front door with my glove and ball.

I also took my oldest sister Mary Eileen. She and I were only fourteen months apart in age, and she was a very good athlete…and not just for a girl. She could throw and hit a baseball better than many boys in the neighborhood. And she used to beat up any boys who made fun of her or me, especially when they called her a "Tom Boy" or me "Fatty."

As soon as the thaw began, Mary Eileen and I would be standing in the front yard, melting snow over our ankles, throwing a soggy baseball back and forth. We had to be accurate because a wild toss might mean the end of our Spring

Training. There was usually a lingering snowdrift by the side of the road, and the hedges in the front yard ate baseballs. In what became a ritual for four years, my oldest sister prepped me for Little League tryouts.

Baseball was in my blood. Something about the sport—maybe the tradition or the colorful players or the gracefulness of Ted Williams hitting a ball or the power of a Duke Snider blasting a ball over the right field fence in Ebbets Field made me a fan by the time I was in first grade. I rooted for the Boston Red Sox in the American League and the Brooklyn Dodgers in the National League. I followed the minor league Albany Senators and even went to a few of their games.

One year, Elroy Face, a pitcher for the Pittsburgh Pirates, rented the apartment in our house, and I spent hours talking to him about baseball. Roger Craig grew up in nearby Poestenkill, and I was there when they had a "Roger Craig Field Day" to honor the star. I was really impressed when I learned that one of our high school English teachers had pitched for the Oneonta Red Sox.

Not only did I eat and sleep baseball, I collected baseball cards. Ever since I can remember, I would buy Topps bubblegum and baseball cards at the Averill Park Market & Variety Store. They cost a nickel a package, and you got one or two squares of brittle, pink-colored bubblegum and ten cards. By the time I was twelve, I had several shoe and cigar boxes full of baseball cards—as well as a lot of cavities from the ton of sugar in the bubblegum that I chewed over the years.

My baseball collection was the envy of the neighborhood. I kept them by season, by team, and by alphabetical order. My inventory of duplicate cards was better than most of the other guys' unduplicated collections. After all, I had mint condition cards for such players as Willie Mays, Mickey Mantle (five seasons), Ted Williams, Yogi Berra, Roger Maris (1961 season breaking the Babe's record of sixty homers), Brooks Robinson, Clete Boyer, Duke Snider, Gil MacDougal, Gil Hodges, Ernie Banks, Warren Spahn, Lew Burdette, Sandy Koufax, Don Drysdale, Johnny Podres, Whitey Ford, Herb Score, Bob Feller, Jackie Robinson, Roy Campanella, Enos "Country" Slaughter, Stan Musial, Roberto Clemente, and many others. My most prized baseball card was a Joe DiMaggio autographed by the Yankee Clipper himself!

Baseball cards were good for several things. You could trade them for other cards. For example, if I had two 1958 Mickey Mantles, I might be able to swap one of them for both Warren Spahn and Lew Burdette of the Milwaukee Braves. Now some cards were merely for collecting and would never be traded. If you had a rare Jackie Robinson 1947 card—the year I was born and he became the first

Black man to play Major League baseball—you put it in a waxed paper wrapper and never traded it.

Baseball cards were also good for playing card toss. Two or three guys would stand on the pavement and see who could throw his card the longest distance. The winner got to keep the other guys' cards.

Another card game involved kneeling a few feet away from a wall and seeing who could pitch his card closest to the wall. You would hold the cardboard card—about one-half the size of a small postcard—in your right hand, with your index finger on the upper right corner, your thumb on top and your middle finger underneath. You flicked your wrist, trying to glide the card up to the wall. There were all kinds of rules for every conceivable situation—like when your card landed on someone else's card or if you had a "leaner" against the wall and your opponent could knock it down with his card and keep it.

Not being much of a gambler, I never risked any of my good cards.

"Hey, Fatso," Matt Graves would complain, "I'm sick of winning Hank Bauer and Minnie Mimosa cards from you!"

I didn't have a lot of ways to get even with the bullies in my crowd but outsmarting them every now and then made me feel good.

As a very young boy, I fantasized about the day that I would be able to go to watch a Major League baseball game in person. Not just any old game but the Brooklyn Dodgers—MY team! The ONLY team that mattered.

One of my earliest memories is watching the Dodgers on our black and white television set. The Dodgers were playing the Giants, who had Willie Mays. Billy Glasser up the street loved Mays, and he wore a Giants baseball cap. The Dodgers were playing at the Polo Grounds. It was the bottom of the ninth, the winning runs were on second and third, and Willie Mays hit a ball deep to center field.

"It's going, it's going, it's, it's—" the announcer Vin Scully yelled excitedly. "It's caught by Snider at the wall. The Duke has robbed Mays of a long hit and clinched the game for the Dodgers."

Everyone called them "the Bums." I didn't know why, but I really didn't care. None of the other kids in the neighborhood rooted for the Dodgers. Matt Graves loved the Braves, David Barnum rooted for the Red Sox, and Jimmy Wilkins was a Yankee fan.

Finally, the day came for actually going to my first Dodgers game. I'll never forget that Sunday afternoon in July 1955. We took a chartered bus early in the morning for the four hour drive to old Ebbets Field in Brooklyn and arrived in time to watch batting practice.

We had the cheapest seats in the center field bleachers—something like a dollar for the doubleheader with the Pittsburgh Pirates and their rookie Roberto Clemente. All things considered, they were pretty good seats in the front row of the second level of the bleachers. Eating our hot dogs and Cokes, we watched Emmet Kelly, the famous Ringling Bros. and Barnum & Bailey Circus clown, entertain the crowd as the seats filled up. This clown, nicknamed Weary Willie, was a sad-faced tramp dressed in ragged clothes with a black painted beard and a swollen red nose. Before the game, Kelly would make a humorous show of dusting off home plate and tormenting the home plate umpire.

The Dodgers—"the Boys of Summer" who would beat the hated Yankees four games to three in the World Series later that year—were taking batting practice. One of my heroes, Duke Snider, caught a fly ball deep in center at the warning track.

"Hey, Duke, can I have the ball?" I yelled at the top of my lungs, expecting to be ignored. "Sure, kid," the Duke said, smiling, as he threw the ball to me, and I caught it in my glove.

I couldn't move. I was frozen in the moment, not believing that I'd been so bold as to ask the Great One for a ball, and even more dumbstruck that he had thrown it to me, and finally, more amazed that I had actually caught the thing! All the other boys and girls were so jealous. One kid even offered to trade me his entire baseball card collection of every member of the 1954 Boston Red Sox team for the Duke's ball.

Well, Mrs. O'Donnell may have had a chubby son, but hopefully he was no fool.

Now, spring wasn't entirely devoted to baseball. When I was growing up, it was also time to start selling pansies in early May. That's right, pansies. What, you may be asking yourself, was a twelve-year-old boy doing selling pansies? I know that it sounds a little wimpy, but it was really okay. You see, that was how the Boy Scouts in our troop earned money for a week or two at Camp Rotary in the summer.

For some reason, Averill Park loved pansies. Especially the old ladies. And especially if a cute kid in a Boy Scout uniform and sincere smile came to their door announcing: "It's that time of year again, Mrs. Griggs," smiling from ear-to-ear through the screen door. "Time to reorder your pansies."

Truthfully, what I knew about pansies you could put in a thimble. I didn't know where they came from, how they were grown, or even how many varieties there were. But, boy, could I sell them! I even sold them to people who didn't have gardens.

For five years in a row, I won the contest for selling the most pansies in my troop. Every spring, I sold a hundred or more flats and earned over one hundred dollars, enough for two weeks of camp and some spending money. It was great fun, and I learned a lot about people and salesmanship.

"Pierce, you could sell snowballs to the Eskimos," my scout leader Bob Springer would say.

I never could figure out why someone would want to do that, but I knew all the reasons why someone would want to buy pansies. If I'd been able to play baseball half as well as I sold pansies, my picture would have been on a baseball card.

8.
INCENSE

I MIGHT HAVE BEEN a priest if it weren't for incense.
Let me explain: in the fifties, almost every Irish American was Roman Catholic. Almost every Irish American family had at least one son. And almost every Irish American mother wanted her son to become a priest—a "gift to God," they loved to say.

I was going to be my mother's gift to God, or at least that's how it was planned. Nobody came right out and said it, but you kind of knew that was the deal. After all, I was the oldest and the only boy in a family of four children. While one of my sisters might decide to become a nun, that wasn't enough. A son had to "go into the priesthood."

There was a slight problem. We didn't have a Catholic parochial school in Averill Park. Our parish, St. Henry's, was founded at the beginning of the century but never built an elementary school. So, when it came time for me to go to kindergarten (we didn't have preschool in those days), my parents had to send me to the local public school. Every right-thinking Catholic knew that Catholic schools produce priests, but no one had ever heard of a public school kid becoming a priest.

My mother was determined to overcome the odds.

"Pierce, you can still be a priest by attending Religious Education classes at the Parish Hall."

I wasn't that keen on more schooling that would interfere with my nonexistent social life. "Okay, Mom, if you say so," I would say, trying to hide my colossal lack of enthusiasm. Young Pierce always wanted to please, especially adults. Sometimes, it wasn't clear to me whether I did things because *I* wanted to do it or because it was expected that I do it. It took me a lifetime to sort out the difference.

The nuns and priests had already prepared me for Holy Communion and then Confirmation.

But now when I was in fifth and sixth grades, I was being forced to go on Wednesday evenings for religion classes. It wasn't so much that I wasn't interested in the subject; it's just that a twelve-year-old boy has his mind on other things.

Like Pam Murdock, who sat next to me in school. She was a bouncy blonde with blue eyes and a cute giggle. She was a Protestant, but she was really nice and seemed to like me. Anyway, I told her one day about my Wednesday evening religion classes.

"Really?" she replied, giving me this weird look. "Don't tell me you're going to be a priest."

After that, I didn't want to go anymore. But my mother insisted, so I suffered through another year until I got to junior high school.

"Pierce, formation of your faith is not negotiable," Mom would always say. "God wants you!"

Then for several more years, the Catholic kids would be taken out of school once a week and bussed to St. Henry's for an hour of religious education. No one wanted to be there, and the teachers were talking about subjects that didn't seem very important in my life.

"There are seven mortal sins," Mrs. Baniak reminded us seemingly every week. She would tick them off in rapid fire. "Pride, envy, gluttony, greed, lust, sloth, and wrath."

For a young kid, some of these cardinal ("deadly") sins sounded a tad strange. For example, for me, a sloth was a cute, furry, slow-moving tropical mammal that spent most of its time hanging upside down from a tree.

They also taught us a whole list of rules.

"You can't eat meat on Fridays or Holy Days," Mrs. Redfield would begin. "You must fast three hours before taking Communion and be in a state of grace, but the elderly and sick may take their medicine."

I never quite got the meatless Fridays. Why Friday? What if you didn't like fish? Did Jesus eat meat on Fridays?

And then there were all the prayers that we had to memorize. The "Our Father" was a piece of cake after a few years. Then we graduated to the "Hail Mary" and "Act of Contrition." But the toughest one was the "Nicene Creed" and all things that we Catholics believed in.

There were some things they taught us that interested me—like the discussions about Vatican II. Now, as an altar boy, I could relate to the fact that the Mass was going to be in English instead of Latin, and the priest was going to face the people at the altar instead of hiding everything from us during the Mass.

We never got any sex education from the church in those years. I guess they figured that boys and girls learn those things on their own. All I knew was that some of the boys and girls were being pretty frisky during the hour of released time in religious education.

When I was ten, after First Holy Communion and Confirmation, I started training for the priesthood. On Saturdays, when you wanted to be outdoors playing ball or fishing or even raking the leaves, they made you go to altar boy instruction at the church. Some crotchety priest—with asthma, nasty garlic breath, and a belly so big that he couldn't tie his own shoes—taught us how to pronounce Latin for the Mass, how to genuflect, and how to prepare for, serve, and then clean up after Mass.

In those days, girls were not allowed to be altar boys. I mean, they weren't allowed to be on the altar to serve the priest during Mass.

"Mom, why can't my sisters serve Mass?" I asked one day.

"Christ and his apostles were men," she replied instantly. "So, therefore, only men can be on the altar and touch the holy chalice."

Now, I was only twelve, but that answer didn't satisfy me.

"What about the Blessed Virgin Mary?" I asked. "She was Christ's mother."

My mother smiled and replied, "That's a good question."

Years later, when the Catholic Church started liberalizing some of its ancient prejudices against women, they allowed girls to be altar servers, then to be lectors, and finally, to distribute Holy Communion just like the men. Women are still banned from the priesthood for the same reasons my mother gave me over thirty years ago. Somewhere today, a little girl is asking her mother, "What about the Blessed Virgin Mary?" It's still a good question.

The Latin was tough stuff for a kid. The last people who spoke it regularly were the Romans, and that was well over a thousand years ago. The only place where Latin was spoken was in Catholic churches and the Vatican. Someone told me that it was a "dead language," and I knew why.

"Mom, why does the church speak and write only in Latin," I asked her one day as I struggled with the most basic words.

"That's because Latin was the language of Rome which had conquered much of the world, and the church needed a universal language," Mom would explain in her most scholarly fashion.

"But Jesus didn't speak Latin," I would throw back, thinking that I had scored a knock-out blow in this Battle of the Kitchen.

"That's true, Pierce," Mom softly replied, "but he wasn't learning to be an altar boy!"

Latin was really hard for me another reason. You see, I went to public school and the other guys all went to private Catholic schools, where they'd already started learning Latin and could pronounce most of the words. I was sure that one altar boy—Bimmy Wilson, who lived over on Crystal Lake in a big house—was going to be a priest. It wasn't just his martyred saint smile like you saw in religious books. Attending La Salle High School, Bimmy knew what a lot of the Latin words meant, and his cassock and surplice were always starched and neatly pressed.

I had another disadvantage.

My mother was fluent in Latin because she had taught it in high school when she was a schoolteacher on Long Island. She taught in a high school before World War II and after my dad and she married, and he went to Europe to fight the Germans. The only problem, however, was that the way they pronounced Latin in public schools was different than the way it was spoken in Catholic schools and churches.

Take, for example, the simple two words "Julius Caesar." In public school, the "C" would be pronounced like "see." Not in Church Latin, though. The "C" sounds like "KUY-sahr."

Whenever my mother tried to help, she made it worse. Now, I don't mean any disrespect, but anything that your mom can't help you with can't be that good. You would think that after all those centuries, the least the public school and church people could do would be to agree on the same pronunciation of Latin words.

Imagine how I felt when I had to memorize and pronounce in Latin the long prayer called the "Confiteor."

> Confíteor Deo Omnipoténti,
> beátæ Maríæ semper Vírgini,
> beáto Michǽli Archángelo, beáto

> Joanni Baptístæ, sanctis
> Apóstolis Petro et Paulo,
> ómnibus Sanctis, et vobis, fratres,
> quia peccávi nimis cogitatióne,
> verbo, et ópere, mea culpa, mea
> culpa, mea máxima culpa. Ídeo
> precor
> beátam Maríam semper Vírginem,
> beátum Michǽlem Archángelum,
> beátum Joánnem Baptístam, sanctos
> Apóstolos Petrum et Paulum, omnes
> Sanctos, et vos, fratres, oráre pro me
> ad Dóminum Deum nostrum. Amen.

It was a real tongue twister, but eventually I learned—and never forgot—it. Like it was engraved onto my brain. But what torture for a twelve-year-old kid who had never studied Latin!

One last thing about Latin, and I'll let it go.

I never could figure out why the priest said the Mass in Latin. The people in the pews didn't understand what he was saying. The altar boys only memorized their lines, but we didn't have a clue what most of it meant. The only parts of the Mass that I could figure out were in English—the sermon and the collection for money.

I finally conquered Latin. But that was only the first milestone on the long road to priesthood. You next had to learn all the ceremonies and rituals. That was no walk in the park either.

The first thing that you have to be able to execute without a hitch is the simple act of genuflecting. Now, I must admit that would seem easy to do. You just drop slowly to your right knee, while your right and left hands are gently placed over your left knee. Then while perched on your right knee, you bless yourself with the sign of the cross, and stand up, using your hands to push up off your left knee. So far, so good.

Next you have to genuflect with something in your hands. At first light and small objects like a prayer book or a candle. Then, as you get more confident, the size and weight increase. There is the silver tray with two glass cruets of water and wine, then the oversized gold chalice filled with wine, and finally, a heavy Pascal candle that's taller than you.

If you can get the hang of genuflecting, you've got the right stuff for the priesthood. I wasn't so sure about my vocation, however, after the visit by the Bishop of Albany when I was twelve. I was taken out of school to be an altar boy at a Confirmation. It was supposed to be an honor to serve the bishop because he came to a parish church only every few years.

The bishop was a kindly but elderly man. He arrived in a black car with several priests. Wearing a red cassock and red four-cornered clergy hat popular in the late fifties, the shepherd of over a hundred thousand Catholic souls in Northeastern New York had a royal bearing. Smiling and slowly waving his left hand, he held out his right hand so that the faithful could kneel and kiss his ring.

"Bless you, my children," he'd say in that solemn voice like God in the movies.

Now, I could understand this blessing when he was addressing kids. But adults?

If you were an altar boy, you weren't supposed to talk to His Eminence unless he spoke to you first. This was easier said than done if you're trying to help him on the altar. I started to say something, and three priests standing guard on the altar almost erupted like a volcano. I swallowed my words and let the hot wax from a nearby candle drop onto the holy vestments of a direct descendant of Saint Peter.

Who was I to question the mysteries of the church?

Things were going pretty well that day the bishop came to St. Henry's. I handled the Latin without a problem, and I was genuflecting like a champ. I got through the entrance procession, Gospel, and sermon.

Then it was time for Holy Communion.

In those days, the priest had his back to the people, and the altar was on an elevated tier in the rear of the sanctuary. During Mass, an altar boy had to go up and down the stairs several times. Just before the consecration of the bread and wine, I was making my way from the table on the left side of the altar up the four steps to the top of the altar. I had the silver tray and two glass cruets in hand—a ritual that I'd performed over a hundred times.

Then it happened. Fate. My right foot stepped on my cassock, creating the same effect as slamming on bicycle brakes. I stopped, but my hands and their contents kept going forward. The water and wine spilled all over the bishop's shoes. The pastor was horrified as he scrambled to clean up the mess. (I thought that I heard him exclaim "Holy Shit!") The other two altar boys were snickering. The three priests with the bishop gave me very unChristian looks.

I was never invited back to serve the bishop.

Though I still might have made it to the seminary if it weren't for another, even more embarrassing incident.

It was 1959, and I had just turned twelve. One of the privileges of being a veteran altar boy was getting out of school for funerals. I'd done Saturday weddings, and the tips were pretty good. But the older altar boys always said that you did better at funerals.

My turn finally came. I went to school for an hour or so, and then my dad picked me up for the short drive to St. Henry's. I got there in time to help the priest set up the altar, light the candles, and fill the water and wine cruets. Then the priest asked me to prepare the incense holder. I was stumped for a moment because I had never done this before. But I found the gold pot suspended from three gold chains, put in the small piece of charcoal, and filled up the separate incense pot.

The funeral Mass was going fine until we got to the part where the priest walks around the casket and blesses the deceased. On Father Kay's instruction, I had earlier lit the charcoal, and it was glowing. I brought him the incense holder and incense pot, and he put a large scoop of incense on the burning charcoal.

I thought I was going to faint on the spot.

Maybe it was because I had eaten a light breakfast three hours earlier as part of my new diet and fitness program, or maybe I had a stomach bug. I don't know the reason, but the incense made me sick to my stomach as the smoke drifted up to my face. And I had to stand there holding it for what seemed like an hour while Father Kay kept reading more and more prayers.

Finally, he took the incense holder from me and started shaking it over the coffin. This was the last straw. Flinging around the holder fanned the burning charcoal and caused the incense to burn ever faster. The air was filled with a swirling cloud of nauseous incense.

If you've ever smelled incense, you know what I'm talking about. It has a pungent odor that smells like a combination of rotten eggs and sweet spices. It invades your nostrils and goes straight for your head and stomach. The strong can endure incense; the weak suffer terribly. And if you're going to be a priest, you have to be able to handle incense.

That's when I knew I didn't have the right stuff for the priesthood. God knows, I tried that spring day. I turned my head, held my breath, and even took a few gentle steps back away from the priest. But nothing worked.

I couldn't hold it any longer. I was dizzy, my knees were weak, and my stomach was convulsing. Father Kay was still swinging and praying. The stain glass windows were starting to merge into each other, with Saint Peter rushing over to join St. Paul. I was seeing the Communion of the Saints.

I dashed from the altar for the sacristy and blew my cookies into the sink. I looked up in the mirror, but I barely recognized who I saw. I swear that my face was turning green.

That was my first and last funeral as an altar boy. In fact, that was my last day serving Mass. I hung up my cassock and surplice and retired.

I always wondered how things might have turned out if it weren't for incense.

Recently, I went to the funeral of a dear friend's mother. It was a Catholic Mass for the Dead. I sat and kneeled there for over an hour. Waiting. Anticipating. Remembering.

But it never happened. The only aroma in the church was the sweet smell from a half dozen lovely flower arrangements. The priest never used any incense.

After the service, I asked the young priest about why there was no incense.

"It's now optional," he explained. "The smell bothers me."

"What happens if you have to use it?" I asked.

"There are new, better smelling forms of incense," he told me. "A variety that smokes but does not overwhelm you."

That answer sent my mind reeling.

Imagine, I thought, if on that fateful morning in 1959, Father Kay had not used incense or had been able to use the more user-friendly incense introduced in the nineties. I might have become a priest. Not just me, but maybe thousands of other young boys who couldn't stomach incense.

The church may be on to something here in increasing vocations for the priesthood. Less incense. More priests.

9.
"LOOK IT UP"

It always had a place of honor in our home.

I'm not talking about a trophy. Or an ancient relative's portrait. Or even the family Bible.

It wasn't anything like that.

But it was very valuable and cherished.

We used it every day. My mother, three sisters, Aunt Hunnah, and yours truly.

Every now and then, I would even catch my father standing over it—his six feet three inches stooped over to find something.

The "it" was our *Webster's Second International Dictionary.*

This large, oversized treasure chest of the English language was a prized possession in our family. Mom had enshrined the authoritative guide on top of the only bookcase in our family room. I can barely remember what its cover looked like because it was always open.

The mahogany bookcase was strategically located between the kitchen and my parents' bedroom, right off the only first floor bathroom in our home. I always wondered why such a huge house (fourteen rooms, a front and back porch, a two-level attic, and a basement) had only one bathroom on each of the two floors where we lived. My mom told us that when our house was built in 1850, there was no running water or plumbing for indoor toilets. People used an "outhouse" to relieve themselves. Sometime near the turn of the twentieth century, my mother explained, the house was outfitted with pipes, sinks, and toilets. I guess no one figured that the great-granddaughter of the original Kanes who settled in Averill Park would someday have four children, a sister, and a husband who had to share two toilets and two bathtubs. And when the cousins from Long Island visited every summer, we had only two bathrooms for five adults and seven children! I thought that we were roughing it until my dad and Uncle Jack Sangster, who had been an Army Captain in World War II, started swapping war stories about five hundred soldiers and one stinky latrine.

The area in front of the bookcase on the way to the kitchen was the most traveled pathway in our house—something I realized when the carpet was changed for the third time before I got out of high school. Every hour of the day, someone was going into and exiting the kitchen. The only phone in the house—for years a party line shared with several other families—was mounted on the wall as you entered the kitchen. Adults talking on the phone would pace back and forth on this threadbare patch.

The living room was twice as long as it was wide. Christmas morning when I was five, it became my Le Mans speedway. Santa brought my first bike: a shiny tricycle with chrome handlebars, red fender, and soft black seat. It also came with a braking mechanism, but I didn't know anything about stopping a bike.

With two feet of snow outside, I debuted as a daredevil by starting in the kitchen and pedaling as hard as I could, shooting over the two-inch riser separating the kitchen and family room, speeding past the bookcase, bathroom door, and couch on the left and accelerating by the Christmas tree on the right toward the far end of the room. As I exuberantly yelled, "Look, Dad, no hands!" the front bike tire hit the hot water radiator with a thud while I kept going headfirst over the handlebars. My forehead slammed into one of the blunt steel radiator ribs. Blood, tears, and a howling scream came gushing out of me.

When I recovered consciousness seconds later, my panicked mother was pressing a cold washcloth to my forehead. The accident was serious enough to require my father to take me to Samaritan Hospital in Troy for stitches. To this day, I have a one-inch scar on the left side my forehead—a distinctive mark that I wear with quiet pride in tribute to that Christmas morning sixty-five years ago when I discovered fear.

The kitchen was the place where the whole family and guests would hang out when meals were being prepared, eaten, and digested. I once figured that an average Irish-American family like ours spent at least two and one-quarter hours per weekday in the kitchen and three and one-half hours on Saturday and Sunday. This did not count the years that I spent doing my homework in the warm kitchen because there was no heater in my adjacent bedroom, a former coal bin converted into a young boy's sanctuary.

The kitchen's popularity always puzzled me since it was the smallest room in our home. The front and back parlors were the largest and most comfortable rooms with an L-shaped couch, several overstuffed chairs, a ceiling-to-floor mirror, sideboard with fancy china and crystal, antiques, stereo, and plush carpets. Yet, we used the parlors only for formal occasions like parties celebrating graduations, First Holy Communions, and Confirmations. I decided that if I ever built a house, I would make the kitchen the largest room and put the formal living room in a closet.

Other guys told me that the kitchen was also the most popular spot in their homes. My buddy Bob Campano had an Italian father and Lebanese mother. Unlike other classmates, Bob was always nice to me and occasionally invited me to stay overnight on the weekends. (He liked coming to my house to study on Sundays because my dad made an original fresh fruit salad with a touch of liquer.) Bob's parents were great cooks, and everyone hung out in the kitchen for hours as they prepared a homemade pasta feast and told stories. When his happy-go-lucky father Earl ("Hey, Skinny" was his usual greeting) built their home, he made the kitchen and seating area three times larger than an old-fashioned kitchen.

The *Webster's Second International Dictionary* was housed in what today would be called the "TV room." When my dad bought us a black and white television set when I was about five or six, he placed it in the corner of the narrow family room. It was a Sylvania, whose picture tube took up most of the space in the bulky two and one-half foot high wooden cabinet. By today's standards, that television was a primitive device. The first TVs weren't very reliable—the picture was snowy, the horizontal lines bobbed up and down, and the screen would shrink without warning, reducing the image to the size of a postcard. The clearest picture was the test pattern used by the local television station when it was not broadcasting. My favorite was an American Indian shield with eagle feathers.

The poor television reception in the mid-fifties had some benefits. I got to know George Leckonby, the ever-friendly TV repairman who spent a lot of time at our house fiddling with the back of the set and climbing up on the roof to adjust the antenna. My mother used to insist that I be home when Mr. Leckonby paid a visit.

"That man could talk the ears off an elephant," Mom would complain as she shooed me to the front door.

There was nothing unusual about this assignment since I liked to talk and listen to adults. By the time that I was in kindergarten, I would stand on the front porch and invite passersby to "come on in and have a drink." Several hobos (that's what my mom called them) came into our house for a glass of water and some fresh fruit thanks to my invitation and the kindness of Mom and Hunnah. One guy was from California, and he had hidden in box cars all the way to Albany. I told him that my dad had done the same thing during the Depression. I'm not sure that he believed me because we lived in such a nice house.

When I got a little older, I would pester the butcher, barber, and gas station owners in the village. In the "Innocent Fifties," my parents never worried about me getting in trouble or kidnapped. When it was time for me to come home, my mother would call one of the local merchants and ask that he send me on my way.

"God, Mary, your son can surely ask a lot of questions," Larry Barnum the Barber would say to my mom when she accompanied me for a haircut.

Mom would smile slightly and reply, "I know. He's inherited his father's gift of gab."

When my dad was told the same thing, he, too, would quickly agree, adding "He's inherited his mother's natural curiosity."

That's why it was my job to greet Mr. Leckonby, tell him what was wrong with the TV, and hang with him for a couple of hours until he diagnosed the problem or, more frequently, announced, "I'll have to take the set back to my shop."

Mr. Leckonby had two sons older than me, and he was proud of their athletic feats. One of them was quarterback of the Averill Park High School varsity football team. After Mr. Leckonby visited our home, I could talk to anyone about last Saturday's football game and sound like I had attended, convincingly playing back the game series by series, quarter by quarter. When I finally got to see a real game when I was older, it was nowhere as exciting as listening to Mr. Leckonby.

Opposite the TV was a long couch on which my three sisters and I would watch the limited amount of TV that my mom rationed. She believed that children should play games, play outdoors, read books, and do their homework. Long before TV was declared a wasteland or electronic kidnapper, sitting for hours in front of the "boob tube" was unthinkable in the O'Donnell family.

When we did watch TV, the O'Donnell kids would be mesmerized in the late afternoon by *The Mickey Mouse Club* on the new ABC television network. There had been nothing like it before. The singing, dancing, and staging were revolutionary. This was a TV show specifically designed for kids that did not make apologies about having fun. It didn't hurt either that Annette Funicello was one of the stars!

The couch also got a lot of use when the whole family, sitting in the dark with the room full of a white glow from the TV, would religiously watch *The Ed Sullivan Show* on Sunday evening (if our homework was done). Sullivan was "the king of Sunday night television" and presided over the hottest variety show on TV with a varied collection of jugglers, magicians, singers, impersonators, and animal acts. My personal favorites were the blindfolded Polish bears riding bicycles and the rubbery guy spinning plates on top of a stick while balancing a fishbowl on his head. I also liked the heavily accented man with the talking head that kept popping out of a box, yelling, "'S'all right! 'S'all right!" I think he was called Señor Wences.

Ed Sullivan had a great job. On his show, with his arms folded over his chest, he didn't do anything except introduce the entertainers and tell us, "Tonight, we have a re-e-e-e-ally big sho-o-o-o-o-w!"

The night that Sullivan first introduced the Beatles to more than seventy million Americans—February 9, 1964—was the beginning of the end of civilization as my mom knew it. She could not find anything redeeming about the long-haired British exports. Mom and Hunnah just shook their heads side to side as my sisters and I freaked out and jumped up and down as they played "I Want to Hold Your Hand." My dad was largely indifferent, dozing as he did most Sunday nights.

I wasn't sure about my mom's verdicts on cultural matters. Eight years before the Beatles' invasion, Ed Sullivan had featured the new singing sensation Elvis Presley. As his hips gyrated and he belted out the lyrics to "Love Me Tender," Mom dismissed the new generation's musical tastes as "vulgar." By the time the Beatles landed, she had given up any hope of understanding her children's taste in music.

My dad wasn't always napping on the couch while the family watched TV. When my sisters and I were watching a spooky movie in the dark, he would sneak up from behind and poke his fingers in our ribs, shouting, "Boo!" I would jump about two feet off the couch—like I was on top of a Titan rocket.

Dad did the same thing to my Aunt Hunnah when she was bending over. "Now stop that, Harry!" she would protest. Her lips—slightly upturned at the edges—told me that she actually enjoyed the attention.

The couch near the *Webster's* served many other purposes.

Mary Eileen and I would play King of the Hill, pushing each other off onto the floor littered with the cushions. I quickly tired of the game because my kid sister was stronger and quicker than me, and I would often miss the cushions and hit the hard linoleum or the later carpeted floor with a painful thud. The only way that I could ever win was to tickle her and hope that she laughed her way off the couch. One day she foiled me by wearing Mom's girdle around her rib cage to neutralize my tickling.

The couch was also the place where we solemnly waited for our punishment. When one of the kids misbehaved (like by fighting over whose turn it was to take out the garbage, wash the dinner dishes, or carry Dad's hot dinner tray about two hundred yards up the street to the liquor store), Mom would say, "Sit down on the couch and wait for your father to come home."

We rarely had to wait because we immediately complied with Mom's edict. You see, my dad was a "spare the rod, spoil the child" kind of a guy. I figured that during the time he lived in an orphanage after his mother died and his father was hospitalized, he must have been spanked a whole lot. My mother's upbringing must have been more gentle because she preferred the "velvet glove" approach to parenting: she spanked us a few times when we were real young, but once we were in grammar school, she resorted to the highly effective threat of making us wait on the couch (sometimes for hours) for Dad to come home and spank us.

One day I didn't even get to wait on the couch for Dad to come home. Someone had thrown rocks and broken the windows of the door to the kitchen in the back of the Methodist Church next to our house. A busybody neighbor informed my mom that I was the culprit. A quick call to my father—"Harry, you must come home immediately and discipline Pierce"—was followed by one very angry father doing the unthinkable: closing his store at midday and racing down to the house to punish his wayward son.

Mom had barely hung up the phone when the ex-boxer swept into the house, grabbed me in the kitchen, and spanked the daylights out of me for what seemed like fifteen rounds. He stopped only after "the referee" pulled him off me.

As my father was teaching me a lesson and my eyes were drowning in tears, I vainly protested, "It wasn't me, Dad. It didn't do it."

"Oh, yes it was!" he would shout back, drowning out my protests of innocence and landing another blow to my aching bare butt. A few hours after I learned my lesson, my mom's infallible grapevine reported that I was in fact not the guilty party and that the two boys who had broken the windows had confessed to the pastor, Reverend Vetter. When Mom suggested to Dad that he should apologize to his son for the unjust punishment, he sternly replied, "Never! That's for the things that he's done, and we haven't caught him."

That may have been my first inkling that life was not entirely fair.

The living room couch is also associated with some of the fondest memories from my boyhood. My dad didn't have much time for himself. In addition to the playing the stock market and the horses (which he could do by reading the newspaper and using the phone without leaving the store), he enjoyed the Friday night fights televised from Madison Square Garden in New York City and sponsored by Gillette Blue Blades and Pabst Blue Ribbon beer. He would close the store a few minutes early, rush home, put on his slippers, open a cold Budweiser (later a Michelob), and spread some Limburger cheese on saltines. Settling down on the couch just as the fight began, he would relax for an hour.

When I was about eight or nine, my dad let me become part of his Friday night ritual. My mom and I would prepare his Limburger and saltines, have his beer ready, and place the slippers right in front of his spot on the couch. Then, clad in my flannel pajamas, I would sit next to my dad and watch two men knock each others' brains out in the name of sport. My dad knew a lot about boxing, and he taught me all about Rocky Graziano, Sugar Ray Robinson, Archie Moore, and Sonny Liston. Dad had boxed when he was a kid, and he liked to stand up and reenact a punching sequence that was mostly a blur to his wide-eyed son. His favorite was a distracting left jab to the side of the head, rapidly followed by a right to the nose, left to the stomach, right to the chin, left to the chin, and a right uppercut to the chin. No opponent could withstand Harry O'Donnell in his prime!

While the fights and fighters have receded into the mists of time, I can still recall the foul-smelling, disgusting-looking Limburger cheese. I pretended that I really liked that putrid stuff. God, it tasted worse than it smelled! But when you didn't get much time with your dad, you could fake enjoying anything—even something that smelled worse than rotten eggs or your mom's hair rinse.

The *Webster's Second International Dictionary* was a silent witness to all these antics as the O'Donnell kids grew up. Firmly perched on the mahogany bookcase, the *Webster's* was like having a third parent. It educated, entertained, and rewarded you for hard work. And you were punished for not consulting the word wizard because you would never know what words like "supercilious," "flagellation," or "prestidigitation" meant unless you paused, put down your book, and looked up the word.

In fact, of all the things that my mother taught me, that may have been the most valuable lesson.

"Look it up," Mom would always command whenever any of her children asked her the meaning of a word or how to spell or pronounce something.

"I can tell you what the word means," she would explain, "but what good does it do you? The very act of finding the word, looking at its various meanings, learning its origins, and making sure that you can pronounce it correctly—that is how you learn the meaning of a word."

So, for a dozen years or so, the *Webster's* and I were constant companions. The dictionary got so much use at times that there would be a line of the two or three O'Donnell children waiting to look up their words. When I went off to college, I wanted to take my tutor with me, but it was out of the question. My sisters were still in high school, and my mom was too devoted to the *Webster's*. So my parents gave me a smaller *Funk & Wagnall's Desk Dictionary* that I used throughout college and law school.

The *Webster's* had been in the family as long as I could remember. I had always assumed that it was my mom's dictionary that she had used while attending Albany State Teacher's College (now State University of New York at Albany) in the 1930s or while she taught English and Latin on Long Island before and during World War II. This genesis fit comfortably a young boy's image of his scholarly mother who had a passion for precise use of the English language that serves her son well to this very day. Outside of a career philologist and maybe William Safire and William F. Buckley Jr., I've never known anyone who had a richer vocabulary, a deeper understanding of the meaning and origin of words, or a keener ear for linguistic mayhem.

"You are what you say," Mom was fond of saying. "A poor vocabulary is like a cheap suit."

For my mom, words were like sparkling diamonds, gems that had a proper usage just like a precious stone deserves a gold setting.

"The correct usage is 'neither you nor I are going to the store,' not 'neither you or me are going to the store,'" Mom would correct me in midsentence.

"Never end a sentence with a preposition," she often reminded us.

"The difference between 'adulation' and 'adoration' is as great as the distinction between 'like' and 'love.'"

My eyes glazed over.

"The word is pronounced 'oar-a-tory,' not 'oh-rah-tory.'"

Why didn't they spell it that way, then? I would ask myself.

"'Osmosis' comes from the Greek word."

What's with this Greek stuff, I interrupted in my mind.

It was bad enough that my mom would make me take four years of Latin in high school.

My mom enjoyed reading to us from the introduction of the *Webster's* about the history of language, the Indo-European language tree, and the evolution of written alphabets. I vividly remember her colorful explanation of the Norman Conquest of England and the resulting French influence on the Queen's English.

"Take, for example, 'last will and testament,' Mom told me one day. "The word 'will' was the English and 'testament' was the same French word for a document by which you give away your possessions and land after you die. The English and French were used together, and that usage survives today."

"Is that how we got 'Ozzie and Harriet'?" I asked my mother who shook her head in mock dismay.

Mom made these language discoveries as exciting as Columbus' landing in the New World or Newton's derivation of the law of gravity from getting hit on the head by an apple. For a young boy who did not have a computer, video games, or the internet, this was intellectually stimulating. These were worlds filled with adventure, history, drama, and humor. It may sound weird, but I delighted in just reading random words and using them in a sentence. And every month for many years, I would do the twenty definitions from Word Power in *Reader's Digest*.

When we were young, my mother would read to us for hours at a time. The house was always filled with books. Getting a book for your birthday or some other special occasion was a treat. I still remember books like *The Magic Cat*, *The Trumpeter of Krakow*, *The Cat in the Hat*, *Robinson Crusoe*, the Clare Bee novels about high school sports star Chip Hilton, Jules Verne's novels, and James Fennimore Cooper's books set in New York State. When I read about trips to the moon, voyages under the sea, or dramatic sporting events, I actually felt like I was experiencing that moment. To this very day, I know what it is like to have a gigantic octopus wrap itself around your small submarine or to make the winning jump shot or to hide from Indians in the crevices of rocks along a sylvan stream.

"What a gift," Mom would say, "what a special talent it is to take something that exists only in your imagination and put it down on paper in the form of a story that will entertain other people."

My mother also taught us that the Bible was storytelling at its best. "The inspired word of God told and retold many times by simple people," she believed. When we were kids, we would act out Biblical scenes, and all the O'Donnell kids knew that our parents met before World War II when mom played Mary Magdalene and dad played a centurion in an Easter pageant.

In our home, we were surrounded with good books. When I was a kid, the Great Atlantic & Pacific Tea Company started selling in their markets the complete *Funk & Wagnall's Encyclopedia*. But they didn't sell them all at once. Every week or so, you could buy one volume for 99 cents, starting with the A's and eventually going all the way to the Z's.

One of my regular treats was to go up to the post office just before closing time at six o'clock and walk Hunnah home for dinner. On our way, we would frequently stop at the A&P on Main Street. Our A&P had been built decades earlier, had wooden floors that were regularly oiled and covered with saw dust and smelled like fresh ground coffee. Every time we shopped at the A&P, I'd run over to the rack where they were selling the encyclopedias. I was always excited when a new volume arrived. Strange as it may seem, I would sit up at night and read entries in the *Funk & Wagnall's Encyclopedia*.

Mom believed that people had a right to read what they wanted without censorship from government. She had read James Joyce's *Ulysses* when it was still banned as obscene, and I found racy Studs Lonigan paperbacks hidden in the sideboard in the back parlor.

"Ideas should be free to be accepted or rejected," Mom told us. "The best way to defeat a bad idea is to let everyone hear it."

When Hunnah noted that this approach had not worked with Hitler, my mom would get beet red and issue a string of criticisms about the German people because of World Wars I and II and the Holocaust. Mom never forgave the Germans and hated everything German. In fact, it is the only group of people about whom I ever remember her being intolerant. So, imagine when Mary Eileen—who had a stormy relationship with mom as she became a teenager—chose German as her foreign language in high school.

"She did it to spite me, Harry," I heard mom complain more than once.

Mom was a free thinker. A faithful reader of the *New York Times* on Sunday, she dwelled in the citadel of ideas. No one delighted more in a lively give-and-take about almost anything—politics, culture, religion, art, music, and literature.

For example, Mom did not believe in nations or borders. The world's people should be free to migrate from one place to the next without restrictions like citizenship, passports, or visas.

"The institution of nation states has been the root cause of war from the dawn of time," she firmly believed. "Not just foreign wars, but right here at home where the United States cruelly massacred the Indians and stole their land." From my Boy Scout training, I was starting to understand more about the crimes against Native Americans and the false glorification of Western history.

"Pierce, you don't have to accept that something is true just because everyone says it is," she told me more than once. "You need to use your reason and logic and examine the facts for yourself."

"Does that mean I am free to decide for myself the origins of life and even the concept of God?" I finally had the courage to ask.

"Yes, Pierce, you are," she answered without hesitation, "but I would hope that you would listen respectfully to the teachings of the church."

This was a little too much for a seventh grader to handle at the time, but it wouldn't take long before I realized that history is written by the winners, conventional wisdom is just that, and faith can be a powerful force for good and bad. I doubt that I would have been as receptive to questioning authority save for the example set by Mary O'Donnell.

Homework at the O'Donnells was organized chaos. Four kids crowded around the oval, formica-topped kitchen table, covered by three-ring binders, books, and pencils, each wanting Mom to help them—and all at the same time.

"Mom, what's the capital of Montana?" Helen Kay asked.

"Come on," Mary Eileen declared. "You should know that one. It's Helena!"

"How much is thirty divided by six?" Maureen wanted to know.

"Let's look at your times table." Mom answered. "Six times what number equals thirty?"

I didn't ask as many questions as my sisters did. By seventh grade, Mom insisted that I first try to find the answer myself in my schoolbook or the *Webster's Second* or the *Funk & Wagnall's Encyclopedia*. But Mom delighted in exploring a topic once I found the answer. "Mom, the history text says that many of the colonists did not support the American Revolution."

"That's right, Pierce," Mom told me. "Why do you think that was the case?"

"Maybe they thought the revolution would fail," I answered.

"Yes," she replied, "and they still considered themselves British and had relatives and friends in the mother country."

"What happened to them when Britain lost?" I was eager to learn.

"Let's look it up together in the encyclopedia," she suggested.

Leafing through a volume with my mother, on a joint mission of discovering something new, was a delight. She harnessed my natural curiosity with research techniques and discipline, opening my eyes to the joy of exploring endless fields of learning and acquiring knowledge for the sheer enjoyment of the experience. What a priceless gift!

As I went off to college and law school, I gained a better appreciation of mom's enormous influence on my intellectual development and academic success. In this critical respect, Malcolm X was right: "All our achievements are mom's."

Before I forget, I have to reveal the origins of our *Webster's Second International Dictionary*. It turns out that my father won the dictionary as a prize. Not at a raffle or anything like that. You see, my dad, as part of promotion for Jim Beam bourbon, sold twenty-five extra cases—more than any other store in his area. The distributor offered him several prizes, but Dad picked the dictionary. So, that's how we got our *Webster's*, and as they say, the rest is history.

Mom's love of books led her to return to graduate school in her mid-forties and get a master's degree in library science with a specialty in children's books. The reeducation of Mary O'Donnell was a true labor of love because she did not have a driver's license and would have to take a public bus all the way to Albany or rely upon friends for rides. With a couple of kids still in high school, a house to run, and graduate studies, Mom studied most nights until midnight and all weekend.

Later, Mom helped organize a group of volunteers who founded a library at the local St. Henry's parochial school and a small public library in our village. After she turned fifty, Mom became the librarian of the public middle school, spreading the joy of reading to another generation of sixth, seventh, and eighth graders before she retired when she was in her late sixties. And whenever a wide-eyed student wandered into her library, wanting to know the meaning of a word, Mom would smile, lean over, and gently reply, "Come over here, dear, and we'll look it up."

10.
HIGHBALLS

Ever since I can remember, I was surrounded by alcohol.

My dad, of course, owned a liquor store. Starting at about age ten, I began hanging around "the store" as we called it. At first, I was a casual observer of the scene, watching my dad effortlessly amuse and serve his customers. He seemed to know everything that there was to know about every kind and brand of liquor, wine, liqueur, or aperitif. (In New York State, beer was then sold in grocery stores.) Whether it was new French beaujolais or Old Grand Dad whiskey, Harry O'Donnell could converse comfortably with customers ranging from engineering professors to dairy farmers.

In those days before large discount liquor store chains, my dad had the best prices around for booze and wine—especially if you bought by the case. Customers would come from as far away as Albany. Besides the low prices, Dad was very knowledgeable about his merchandise. For example, he was a connoisseur of New York State wines from the Finger Lakes.

"What's a French Bordeaux got over a good New York State red?" he would ask a Troy surgeon who had driven ten miles for a bargain.

My favorite shoppers were the hip RPI fraternity boys who had big houses on the outskirts of Troy and partied almost every Saturday night. In those days, the drinking age was only eighteen in New York State, so just about every college kid could legally drink. On Friday afternoon, they would drive out in their BMGs and Triumphs, sometimes with a hot-looking coed on their arms.

"Well, Harry, what's the special this week?" they would ask their booze guru.

A few minutes later, they would leave with a couple of cases of vodka or whiskey, and my dad would ring up a nice profit of over 20 percent. New York State had price controls on booze that guaranteed nifty profits for those fortunate enough to have a retail liquor license.

As I got bigger, I was allowed to clean the bottles with a giant feather duster, wash the linoleum floors, take out the trash, burn the papers, shovel snow, chop ice, mow the lawn, rake the leaves, take packages out to customers' cars, and so forth. Over the years, I saw a lot of people who looked like they should have been going to an alcoholic treatment clinic and not my dad's liquor store. They bobbed and weaved their way into the store, occasionally knocking over bottles and always finding it hard to spit out their order.

"Shay, Haaaaary, my boy, what's uuuuup?" Lennie the gravedigger, with the W. C. Fields red nose, would slur as he knocked a bottle off the shelf into my nimble father's waiting hands.

Now my father was very careful not to sell to anyone who was obviously intoxicated. More than once I saw him arrange for a drunken customer to get a ride home. One time, I watched the store while he drove a respected local businessman safely to his home.

Outside of the occasional and obvious inebriate, there was a class of customers who looked like they had sobered up just long enough to drive into town to purchase some groceries, to pick up the newspapers (especially the *Daily Racing Form*), and to restock their liquor supplies. These sad-looking people had a perpetual red face, drooping eyelids, and a hacking cough that could wake up the dead.

"Damn cold!" Pete Wagner would say. "Just can't get rid of it."

"Maybe you should lay off the cigarettes and booze for a while, Pete," my dad would sympathetically counsel.

"Hell, what good would that do?" the local mortician would sharply reply as his face contorted into a blinking red light while he hacked up a gallon of phlegm.

One day a regular woman customer named Mattie coughed nonstop for what seemed like an hour. Her entire body convulsed, shaking and writhing in obvious extreme pain. My father brought her to the back of the store, sat her in his easy chair, and tried to calm her down. As Mattie hacked away, her legs were trembling and sweat was poring off her forehead like Niagara Falls. Finally, Dad gave her a swig of whiskey, and her body calmed down. Later, my dad would tell me that Mattie was a binge drinker.

"She goes on tears, drinking binges, often with men other than her husband."

You could hear the stern tone of disapproval in my father's usually kind and gentle voice. "She's an alcoholic, and I won't sell liquor to her anymore."

And he didn't.

Maybe my favorite character was Farmer Brown. If he had a first name, I never heard anyone use it. Dad would barter with folks for things like paying for snowplowing the store parking lot and car repairs. A quart of Schenley's whiskey for a tire change. Farmer Brown bartered booze for eggs and butter.

The weekly ritual was a sight to behold. You see, Mrs. Brown tried to keep her husband from drinking. So while she waited outside in the banged-up truck smelling like a barnyard, Farmer Brown would take a basket of eggs and butter, covered with a red and white plaid napkin, into my father.

"Good morning, Farmer Brown," dad would say in his usual upbeat manner. "What do we have today?"

"The usual," he would always reply. "Just the usual."

Farmer Brown was a short, balding man even shorter on words.

"Okay, then," Dad would say as he took out two bottles of Schmirnoff vodka and gently laid them in the empty basket and covered the damning evidence with the napkin. "Please say hello to the missus."

Farmer Brown would then leave to return to his wife. I would look out the store window as he clandestinely took out the two bottles and hid them under some loose hay on the floor of the back of the truck. I don't know whether the missus ever caught onto this game. If she had, Farmer Brown's eggs would have been scrambled.

State law prohibited drinking on the premises of my father's store. Stiff penalties—including fines and suspension of your valuable license—were imposed for even minor violations. State liquor inspectors—looking like Inspector Clouseau with a wrinkled raincoat and rumpled hat—made unannounced inspections.

My dad was never caught, but he did have an occasional drink at the store. Who wouldn't if you worked thirteen hours a day, six days a week in a space smaller than Liberace's wardrobe? Dad enjoyed a nip or two of Taylor's Tawny Port, which he kept cold in the old refrigerator used to chill wines. As I approached age eighteen, Dad would let me have a sip every now in a small paper cup. Each time, I was duly admonished.

"If you ever want a drink, you can have it at home or here. But I don't want you hanging around bars or getting drunk at parties"

For me, wine and liquor were thus never the forbidden fruit, and I never got in any serious trouble over booze as a teenager.

Dad liked to sip his port in the back of the store with his buddies Ned Pattison, Bernie Baniak, Mort Shulman, and others. One of the regulars was Earl

Linen, my father's longtime accountant from Troy who likened a tax return filed with the Internal Revenue Service to "the opening bid" in a card game. Earl was a very smart man, and he loved to keep my father's taxes as low as possible. So much so that he failed to file the tax returns one year. When my mother found out, there was holy hell to pay.

"Earl, this is Mary," she said sharply over the phone in the house as I hid around the corner eavesdropping.

"I don't know what you were thinking, but I want those tax returns filed immediately," she said slowly in a tone that I thought was going to freeze the phone lines.

Needless to say, Earl promptly complied, and Dad didn't talk much about Earl around the house after that.

Another frequent visitor to the back of the store was Jimmy Woods, the local state game warden. Especially during the cold hunting season, Jimmy was more likely to be found sipping port at O'Donnell's Liquor Store than policing the local Taborton Mountains for deer poachers.

I really liked Jimmy because he always tussled my hair and asked me about fishing.

"Caught anything today, Pierce" he would ask in his perky voice.

"Just a few bullheads and a pickerel, Mr. Woods," I'd usually reply.

"I hear the bass are biting over at Glass Lake, Pierce," he would volunteer as I bolted out of the store, hopped on my Raleigh bike, and raced off to Glass Lake with my worms in a coffee can and fishing pole.

My dad's customers somehow could not squeeze in their shopping within the seventy-eight hours a week that his store was open. Every Sunday it seemed, a couple of them would stop by the house to buy a quart of booze. It was illegal, but Dad would accommodate them from the mixed case of liquor that he had brought home on Saturday night.

"Pierce," he would explain, "I'm in a service business. I have to give better service than my competitors, or I will lose my customers."

That service commitment extended to making deliveries to remote farmhouses ten miles away. First my father for years, and then later my sister Mary Eileen and I, would drive over bumpy, dirt roads—sometimes to deliver only a pint of vodka for a dollar. With the gas and wear and tear on his car, my father was losing money.

But far worse than losing money was losing business to any of his competitors in nearby Sand Lake or Wynantskill. Dad conducted routine intelligence gathering missions to learn their prices and specials. In his ads, my father touted: "We will not be knowingly undersold." And if a customer, even a stranger, told Dad that he could purchase a quart of Imperial twenty cents cheaper at Miller's Liquor, my father charged the lower price.

My close encounter with booze extended to my home.

My folks drank wine, beer, and drinks with alcohol. Depending on the time of year and hour of the day, their favorite liquors were scotch, whiskey, gin, and vodka. They usually drank mixed drinks—like scotch and Saratoga Vichy water or gin and Schweppes tonic. I never knew why, but they called these concoctions "highballs."

"Would you like a highball?" my father would ask a guest.

"Why, sure, Harry. Seagram's and Seven-Up, thank you," Claire Healy would reply.

My father would retreat to the kitchen where he performed his magic. Sometimes he used a jigger to measure out the liquor; other times he trusted his hand and eye to get the right combination of booze and beverage. Whichever way he poured, my dad made strong drinks.

"Wow, Harry," Claire would gush after her first generous swallow. "This is a wake-me-up drink, now isn't it?"

I could never figure out what she meant since it was two thirty in the afternoon. But as I got older, I came to realize that adults say and do crazy things when they're drinking highballs.

My mom liked scotch and soda (preferably Dewar's White Label or J&B) and Saratoga Vichy Water. Hunnah didn't drink that much, but she liked an occasional glass of scotch and soda water. Dad's drink of choice varied over the years, but on Sunday afternoons after dinner, he liked to pour creme de menthe over crushed ice. My sisters and I would sneak a sip, but we were always caught because of the tell-tale green in our mouths.

The only times that I can remember my parents arguing was after they had a few of those highballs. I didn't like to hear them fight, so I would go outside and climb up one of our three apple trees. Sometimes Mary Eileen would join me, and we would exchange a knowing look but not say very much.

My parents liked to throw parties a few times a year. The occasion was usually a birth, Holy Communion, Confirmation, or graduation. The regular guests included Gertrude and Bernie Baniak (and their daughter Camille), Dorothy and Harry Barnum (and their son David), Claire and Bill Healy who lived with the

Barnums, Rosemary and Stanley Supkis (and their two sons), and whoever the parish priest happened to be at the time.

I always hoped that my mom would invite her college classmate Gussie Biskin, a bubbling Jewish widow with a lust for life. They met in college drama classes and became friends for life. Gussie's family had been murdered in the Holocaust—one good reason why Mom hated the Germans.

Gussie told funny jokes. Gussie also whispered things in my father's ear that made him blush. As I got older, she liked to dance slowly with me as my mother pretended to disapprove.

"If I were only thirty years younger, Pierce," she was fond of saying.

Unfortunately, she never finished the sentence.

Hunnah would invite some of her unmarried or widowed friends to our family gatherings: Katherine Sowalsky (my favorite high school history teacher), Bess O'Brien (a mean card player), and Helen Paulsey (who later married a doctor and moved away). Hunnah's guests were usually the first to arrive and leave. On the whole, they were more reserved than the rest of the lively and raucous crowd.

After a few of my dad's highballs, more than one guest left feeling no pain. Over the years, I detected a departure ritual. Stanley would stand up, take Rosemary by the hand, and announce loudly to the gathering, "I'm leaving!"

The Barnums and Healys would stay until we started turning the lights out. "Oh, it's that late, is it?" they would ask in unison long after my mother had gone to bed.

The parish priests—my favorite was Father Thomas Kay and his sister Grace—never seemed to be affected, but they sometimes had trouble starting their cars. Once he actually couldn't find his car, until he realized that he walked over to our house from the rectory.

The most unusual but predictable taking leave routine was the Baniaks: Gertrude would leave before Bernie and then come back to retrieve him.

I knew firsthand that my dad made strong highballs. By the time I was twelve, I was allowed to carry the freshly made drinks from the kitchen to the front and back parlors. Along the way, I might sneak a little sip. As my eyes watered and my lips pursed, I would swear off sipping.

I'm told that I had a drinking problem as a youngster.

It happened when I was four or five, during one of my parents' parties. While the adults were in the parlors and I was unattended, I emptied part of a bottle of my father's favorite New York State red into my stomach. I haven't a clue what drove me to drink that fateful afternoon. I hadn't been to therapy, my parents treated me pretty well, and I had my own tricycle, cowboy hat, and flannel pajamas. While I had one sister already, Mary Eileen was still more than a year younger and waddling around in a diaper. She had not yet developed those annoying habits that would later drive me crazy.

So I don't know why I walked into the kitchen, crawled up on a chair, grabbed the bottle tightly in both hands, and drained part of the bottle into my gut. At first, I am told, my tipsiness went unnoticed by the dozen adults chatting and drinking far above my spinning head.

"Why are we in Korea?" one of them was probably asking another as I bumped into the furniture and guests' legs. Apparently, for quite a few minutes, I was largely ignored. Well, no self respecting little kid likes being ignored.

The tip-off that I had not over imbibed apple juice came when I threw up all over Claire Healy's new white dress in a projectile vomit that broke several indoor records. My parents were apparently not amused: I got my stomach pumped, and my butt spanked.

To this very day, I've never again tried a New York State red wine.

SUMMER

I'd give all the wealth that years have piled, the slow result of life's decay, To be once more a little child for one bright summer day.
—Lewis Carroll

11.
MR. DIBBLE

I NEVER KNEW HOW old he was or where he was born or very much about him at all. Ever since I was a little boy, he was always walking slowly up and down Burden Lake Road on his way to or from the grocery store. Or he was fishing in the Old Mill Pond right behind my house on Tin Can Alley.

His name was Mr. Dibble.

His Christian name was Aaron Dibble. I never heard anyone call him by his first name, though. Even my mom and dad called him, "Mr. Dibble."

Mr. Dibble and I were pals. We never said that we were pals, but we didn't have to say it. Everyone knows that it takes a real pal to have the patience to teach a young boy how to fish.

Mr. Dibble and his wife lived in a rundown old house down the street from us. For a long time, they didn't have any electricity, and I'm not sure if they ever got indoor plumbing. As a five year old scouting out the neighborhood, I came upon this little shack behind their house and opened the door. The awful smell almost knocked me out. I ran back to the sweet scents of my mom's rose bushes as fast as I could. Later, when I went to Boy Scout summer camp, I discovered that the stinky shack was an outhouse.

I don't think that Mr. Dibble had a real job. I never saw him going to work or anything that looked like he was working. When he was younger, he might have worked in the woolen mill a half mile down the road. A long time ago, that mill was owned by my mom's family. Maybe Mr. Dibble was retired. But when I was growing up, all Mr. Dibble ever seemed to do was go to the grocery store and fish.

Mr. Dibble was a tall, thin man with a square jaw and a ramrod straight back. He had an ancient-looking face, but a kid's love of the outdoors. He wore those OshKosh B'gosh blue jeans overalls and a red flannel shirt. When it was sunny, he had a straw hat with a wide brim all the way around. When it rained, he wore one of those floppy Boston whaler hats and yellow slickers. Snow brought out his wool hat with the handy built-in earmuffs.

Mr. Dibble was the best fisherman I ever met. Now that's saying a whole lot. I used to love to watch a guy on TV named Gadabout Gaddis whose weekly program was *The Flying Fisherman*. Gadabout knew all kinds of fishing tricks—like casting for bass under a tree overhanging the lake or the right bait for lake salmon. But, as good as Gadabout was, he wasn't as good as Mr. Dibble.

I also had a few friends, like Bob Campano, Billy Glasser, and Muskrat, who caught more than their fair share of fish. Bob was particularly skillful at catching stream trout with a light casting pole. But none of my buddies could hold Mr. Dibble's fishing pole. It has always been hard for me to understand why one person is so much better at something than everyone else.

Why can one boy run the hundred-yard dash seconds faster than another?

Why can one girl swim the length of a pool so much faster than another?

Why can one student get straight A's and his best friend flunk everything, including gym?

I don't know why, but Mr. Dibble was the greatest fisherman in the world. Most of the time, he fished with this long bamboo pole and a red and white bobber. His favorite hook was a No. 6 tied to one of his homemade leaders. He also had a net and a silver pail for keeping the bait nice and fresh.

Mr. Dibble used different kinds of bait depending on the time of the year, the weather, and his right foot. I was never quite sure what his foot had to do with it, but Mr. Dibble swore that when his foot ached, he had to use nightcrawlers. For the longest time, I wanted my right foot to ache so that I could fish like Mr. Dibble.

Mr. Dibble was the quietest human being I ever knew. I could sit with him on the bank of the pond for hours, and he would never say a word. I used to think that the only talking he did was with the fish. Whatever he said, they must have liked him because he always caught fish.

I learned mostly from just watching him. He was very patient. If a bass was playing with his bait, Mr. Dibble knew just when to snap the pole and hook the big mouth. When fishing for pickerel, which liked to swim near the top of the water, he would wait until the fish had run long enough with the bait so that the fish almost hooked itself. Once a fish was on Mr. Dibble's hook, that was it.

Mr. Dibble was what they called a "conservationist." He did not keep fish that were too small, and he never used illegal hooks or took more than the legal daily limit. The fish and game warden, Jimmy Woods, liked to stop and talk with Mr. Dibble (after he paid a visit to the back of my dad's liquor store and had a "pop" as he used to say). Mostly, Mr. Woods talked, and Mr. Dibble listened. They remained friends that way.

Mr. Dibble had something to do with the fact that the New York State Fish and Game Department stocked our Old Mill Pond every spring after the ice melted. A big tanker truck would pull up to the clearing on Tin Can Alley that had been built by the local volunteer firemen so that they could pump water out of the pond if there was a fire. The truck would funnel thousands of tiny fish into the water in only a few minutes. Within a year, Mr. Dibble and I would be catching them.

The Old Mill Pond had lots of different kinds of fish. There were the basses—large and smallmouthed and rock. We also had pickerel, perch, sunfish, bullheads, and some trout, but the trout did better in the deeper, spring-fed Crystal Lake behind my dad's liquor store. The bottom of the pond was kept clean by suckers—big, fat gray-white scavengers. They were fun to catch because they were heavy, but no one ate them—except our neighbor Charlie Moran, who also drank cheap wine and swam naked in the muddy pond when he was drunk.

The suckers were more fun to catch with spears than fishing poles. The Averill Park Market and Variety Store, up on the corner of Main Street and Burden Lake Road and across the street from O'Donnell's Liquor Store, sold these metal spears with three prongs. We used to take maple branches and carve them into long wooden poles and attach the metal spear. We would then tie a string on the end of the pole and wrap it around our right wrist.

The Old Mill Pond was fed by a stream that came from Glass Lake a few miles away. Behind the firehouse, there were a few pools in the stream where suckers gathered. Billy Glasser, Matt Graves, and I would stand on the bank of the stream and spear the slow-moving bottom feeders. I wasn't very good at this sport because I had a hard time judging when to throw the spear. When I finally speared one, I felt really bad because I had speared it in the eye.

I never spearfished again.

Mr. Dibble taught me how to catch bullheads. With what seemed like thin whiskers (called barbels) around its mouth, a broad head, fins, and no scales, the adult bullheads could weigh up to four pounds. Mr. Dibble warned me you had to watch out for the sharp fins that were like spikes just behind the head on top and on the sides. If you got jabbed, they could poison you.

Before I learned how to dig for nightcrawlers, I used small balls of white bread as bait. Bullheads were fun to catch because they were plentiful in the Old Mill Pond and did not put up much of a fight. They didn't taste that good, so I threw them back. I noticed that my pal Mr. Dibble kept his bullheads.

When I was as young as six, I had a routine on weekends, school holidays, and most summer mornings. Waking up before sunrise without an alarm clock, I'd grab an apple or orange and walk the thirty yards from our back door to my special fishing spot. I'd sit on my pail, waiting for the fish to wake up for breakfast. My favorite month was May, because the nearby lilacs bloomed on the trees overhanging the Old Mill Pond. The fragrance of purple lilacs is strong and sweet, even more so on warm, sunny days. Their season was short but memorable.

Mr. Dibble didn't pay much attention to bad weather. Fishing was fishing. When it was pouring cats and dogs, Mr. Dibble would be sitting on the edge of the pond in his rain gear. Fishing. That's what he loved to do, and he wasn't going to let a little rain stop him.

The only time that I ever saw him pay any heed to the weather was the year that we had this horrible hurricane in late summer. Mr. Dibble told me to get up in the house because the howling winds were starting to blow harder, debris was flying all around us, and the rain was coming down hard in sheets. When I protested, he silently picked up his pole and pail and started to walk home. I knew then that he was serious about the danger of staying outdoors.

I'm sure glad that I went inside. A little while later after sunset, lightning hit the electrical transformer outside of our house and set the pole on fire. My mother was screaming for all the kids to gather around her as we fled the house for fear of it catching on fire. I'll never forget my mom yelling, "Where's the baby? Where's the baby?"

Mom was referring to my youngest sister Maureen who was only one year old. Thank God that my Aunt Hunnah was always cool under fire. She walked up to my mom, tapped her on the shoulder, and whispered in her ear, "The baby's in your arms."

We all then went outside and watched the volunteer fire company put out the fire on the electrical pole. My house was saved from burning down.

Mr. Dibble also taught me ice fishing.

In case you're not familiar with this unusual "sport," let me give you a little introduction. You can ice fish only after the lakes and ponds have frozen over.

My handsome dad before going to war.   *Dad's Honorable Discharge Papers from the army.*

Mom and Dad just before he departed for England in 1942.

Dad (right) receiving a liquor delivery not long after he opened his store in 1947, a few weeks before I was born.

Mom holding me while Dad looks a tad dazed.

My mom with Aunt Hunnah, who is holding me.

Aunt Hunnah (1959).

Mary Eileen, Helen Kay, and me on the dining room table.

My Victorian boyhood home. Nora the Ghost lived in the attic.

Mary Eileen and me posing at the stump.

Spanky and his gang.

The O'Donnells heading for the beach.

My Cub Scout Pack 26.
I am on the far left.

Hamming it up with the cousins.

Me and Annie Oakley, a.k.a. Maureen.

Mighty me imitating my dad flexing his muscles.

Mom and her brood.

My hero and me.

Helen Kay, Maureen, Mary Eileen, and me.

My beloved Carmen and me at Christmas.

Where I lived, this is sometime between Thanksgiving and Christmas. The ice must be at least five or six inches thick at the deepest spot.

The real test of whether the ice is ready for serious ice fishing is whether it will hold a pickup truck that weighs a few tons and pulls an ice fishing shanty behind it. If the ice doesn't crack, it's ice fishing time. If it does give way, well, there's a whole lot of excitement as tow trucks and tractors try to pull the truck and shack out of the water.

The only way that ice gets that thick is thanks to plenty of cold weather. That was no problem in Averill Park. It was pretty routine for the thermometer to dip far below thirty-two degrees in mid-November and hardly ever go above freezing until late-February. With the wind chill factor, the temperature could dip below zero without much effort—and remain there for weeks.

While this was great for ice fishing, it wasn't so great for oil-burning furnaces, cars, or school busses. When I was about four years old, Dad "modernized" our house and his store by switching from burning coal to heavy oil to heat the place and water. But this conversion had its drawbacks.

Several times every winter, I can remember my dad getting very upset about the heavy diesel oil freezing in the underground fuel line that ran from the outdoor oil storage tank to the furnace in the basement of his store or the house. In subzero weather, he would have to use a blowtorch in an often futile effort to thaw the line. I learned my first swear word as Dad shouted, "This damn shittin' weather!"

We had at least four or five school closing days each year because of heavy snow, sleet, or frozen roads. One day, we even missed school because it was so cold that the school buses wouldn't start. That same week, it took my dad three days for his car to thaw out enough so that he could turn over the engine. Then he had to blow up the air in the four deflated tires.

The weather was rough on young ice fishermen, too. Mr. Dibble told me that I had to dress warmly, so I put on my long johns, corduroy pants, two shirts, two sweaters, a snow jacket, gloves and mittens, a wool hat with floppy earlaps, earmuffs, two pair of wool socks, and boots. Wrapped around my neck and over my face was a long wool scarf.

Now, with all that clothing, you'd think that a boy would be able to handle a little cold weather. Wrong!

As soon as I walked out the back door and headed for the Old Mill Pond, I started to feel strange. By the time that I walked the short distance to the water and greeted Mr. Dibble at one of his fishing holes, I was numb. All I could think was that I was going to freeze to death right there on the spot. The howling wind slapped my face, my nose was twitching, and my eyes were getting moist. I was miserable.

"G-g-g-ood M-m-m-orning, Mr. D-d-d-ibble," I managed to spit out eventually, my words almost forming icicles as they floated out of my mouth.

Mr. Dibble nodded slowly, pointing to a massive ice chopper by his stool.

"Choppin' ice'll keep ya warm," he said in a rare utterance.

Mr. Dibble was usually right, and this frigid February was no exception. With a leather thong around my wrist to prevent the heavy steel bar from falling to the bottom once I broke through the ice, I started chopping away. Actually, the proper technique is not really chopping so much as it is lifting up the heavy bar with a chisel-like bottom and round knob on top and thrusting downward with all your energy. The result is a flying spray of ice. It took me at least an hour, but I chiseled a hole about a foot and a half wide in the half-foot thick ice. And by the time I was finished, I was actually perspiring in ten degree weather.

Mr. Dibble was poor and couldn't afford one of those fancy ice shanties that the other men had on nearby Crystal, Glass, and Crooked Lakes. Those shacks were about six feet by six feet, with a seven-foot-high roof, a door with a window, and a stove that burned oil or wood. They also had coffee and hot chocolate, sandwiches that weren't frozen, and a corner in which you could relieve yourself without getting a vital organ frost bitten.

Mr. Dibble and I roughed it on the Old Mill Pond. He had a stool to sit on, a bucket for his live bait, and a basket for his lunch. But there was never a fire to comfort a young boy who feared that he would lose his feet and hands to frost bite. You see, Mr. Dibble burned wood to keep his little house warm and didn't waste that precious fuel to have a fire on the ice.

For ice fishing tackle, Mr. Dibble used "tip-ups," a contraption with two parallel pieces of wood in the shape of a cross that went over the hole in the ice and a spool of line with a hook.

A thin piece of metal with a red flag was bent over and attached to the spool. When twenty or thirty feet below the surface some fish would take the minnow and hook, the spool would move, triggering the red flag to tip-up and alerting the fisherman that he had a bite.

You really have to love fishing to be an ice fisherman. The worst part was sitting on the stool, waiting hours for a tip-up. The first few times that I went ice fishing, I didn't get a single bite. I liked chopping the ice and running up to the house to get some hot chocolate and sandwiches for my buddy and me. Anything that kept me moving to avoid freezing to death.

After two winters, I gave up ice fishing. I never had much luck, and I didn't have the patience to sit there and stare into a hole in the ice, occasionally getting up to skim out the newly frozen water in the various ice holes. I don't know how Mr. Dibble felt about me abandoning him in the winter. I didn't say anything about it, and he didn't ask any questions. He just kept on ice fishing by himself.

After a few more summers, I stopped fishing with Mr. Dibble altogether. I'd started high school, and I played on the football, basketball, and baseball teams. Along with my studying and chores during the school year and my summer job at Boy Scout Camp Rotary twenty miles away, that didn't leave any time for fishing. Or for Mr. Dibble.

One Sunday years later, when I called home from college to talk with my parents, my mom told me the sad news.

"Pierce, Mr. Dibble died last week. I thought you would like to know."

With tears welling up, I closed my eyes very tightly, and I saw him again like it was only yesterday. There was Mr. Dibble. Ram rod straight, blue denim overalls, and his trademark broad-brimmed straw hat. Walking down Burden Lake Road, making the turn down Tin Can Alley, and heading for "our spot" on the Old Mill Pond. A long bamboo fishing pole in one hand and a silver pail and net in the other.

And running behind him with his fishing pole and some nightcrawlers in a coffee can was a chubby little boy full of smiles and dreams about catching the Big One.

"Hey, Mr. Dibble," I shouted as I had countless times before. "Can I go fishin' with ya today?"

Slowly turning his head and breaking a tiny smile, Mr. Dibble nodded his head and motioned slightly with his right hand to follow him.

A true pal never says "no" when it comes to fishing.

12.

SISTER ACT

IN THE FIFTIES, THE rank of the oldest child in an Irish-American family was supposed to have its privileges. Nothing terribly awesome. Just a little deference—like cutting your big brother a little slack every now and then. An extra portion of tapioca pudding, first in line at the hamburger stand, or staying up later on Friday night.

Not in my family.

I was the First Child in name only. My three sisters had no respect for their elders. The O'Donnell girls—Mary Eileen, Helen Kay, and Maureen—did not recognize, much less honor, the sibling seniority system. Worse yet, there were days when they could drive you absolutely bonkers.

The most obvious problem was that I could never get away with anything. The first line of informants was, of course, my mother and aunt. If my mom didn't catch me, there was still Hunnah. It was like they had walkie-talkies in their brains allowing them to communicate between the kitchen and Hunnah's room upstairs.

"Pierce, turn down the radio," my mom would shout from the kitchen into my nearby bedroom as I tried to listen to the latest Elvis song.

"Pierce, didn't your mother tell you not to play the radio," Hunnah would yell from her bathroom when I snuck up to Mary Eileen's room and lay on her bed while I blasted "Love Me Tender, Love Me True."

There was no place to hide from them. Mothers and aunts have a sixth sense for sniffing out kids getting in trouble. Like the time one snowy day when I tried to hide in the back parlor behind the screen and read a paperback "Studs Lonigan" novel. Sneaking a peek at a "dirty book" was a whole new world for a twelve-year-old who still played with his Erector set.

"Helen, have you seen Pierce?" Mom asked her sister that fateful day as Mom stood at the bottom of the stairs in the front hallway. For forty years, this had been the usual means of communication between the two sisters. I could never figure out why they didn't install an intercom.

"No, Mary, I thought he was down there with you," Hunnah replied, a slight note of exasperation in her gentle voice.

The crisis passed for a while, and I kept on reading, turning as fast as I could the pages of this book whose color cover displayed a muscular guy in a T-shirt, a cigarette dangling from his mouth, and a foxy blonde draped all over him. Just as I was getting to a good part where Studs and the cute blonde were making out—

"Mom, we found Pierce," my two youngest sisters proudly bellowed. Standing on either side of me, peering around the corners of the screen, were Helen Kay and Maureen. The Snoop Sisters ran to Mom and informed her that her prodigal son was hiding in the back parlor. It was like having both the FBI and the New York State Troopers garrisoned in your home. You could hide but not for long.

A short time later, I was sitting on the couch in the family room, waiting for my father to come home and administer some appropriate punishment for my reading a book that I later learned my dad had bought and hid in the sideboard in the back parlor where I found it. I was rip-roaring mad at my sisters. As I plotted my revenge, I remembered something that Uncle Jack once said, "The Irish don't get mad—they get even."

Well, I got even a few months later when Helen Kay and Maureen found frogs in their beds one humid summer night. They each jumped about six feet above their beds. Everyone suspected me, but nothing happened because I rounded up the two nocturnal intruders and got them out of the house. When Hunnah came into the girls' bedroom because of their shrieking, I denied with a straight face that there'd been any frogs in their room.

"They're going nuts, Hunnah," I said flatly. "Must be the hot weather."

After that night, Helen Kay and Maureen didn't bother me for a while.

Now I wasn't the only target of their surveillance. Not long after this tattletale incident, Helen Kay and Maureen turned their attention to bigger game: my father. Unfortunately, Dad had a nasty habit: he smoked Camel cigarettes. A lot of people smoked cigarettes in those days, but that didn't stop our own little public health department.

Whenever we saw our dad at the store or he came home, we would run up and hug him. He loved to pick us up with his muscular arms and twirl us in the air over his head. We would beg him for more time—"One more time, please, Daddy. Twirl me faster!" He never tired of this ritual, and we screamed with joy and giggled as we got dizzier and dizzier on our dad's carousel.

There were times, however, when running up and hugging Dad was not so much fun. That was when he had a cigarette in his mouth. The smoke bothered all of us kids, and we complained about it privately among ourselves. But Mary Eileen and I were willing to overlook this slight imperfection in our father.

Not the Snoop Sisters, however.

Helen Kay (short for Helen Katherine) and Maureen (middle name Mary, after my mother) could not stand the smell of cigarette smoke. I don't know whether they were allergic to the gray carbon fumes, or they just found it "yucky." Whatever the reason, they did not hesitate to voice their feelings, even at the tender ages of seven and four.

"Daddy, that smells so bad," Helen Kay would start off.

"Yah, it makes me want to up throw," Maureen sputtered, her hands firmly on her thighs as she imitated Mom giving Dad a lecture about one thing or another that he did wrong.

"You mean 'throw up,'" Dad replied.

"That too," little Maureen responded.

This campaign continued for over a year. My sisters, with Mary Eileen's eventual help, would hide Dad's cigarettes and lighter in strange places—like the freezer. Dad would curse that his frozen cigarettes, even after they had been thawed out, were hard to light and didn't taste very good.

It was like having little anti-smoking terrorists in your home. If Dad started smoking at the kitchen table, Helen Kay would go get the fan out of the closet and turn it on, blowing all the smoke into Dad's face. If Dad tried to smoke in the car, Maureen would roll down all the back windows, even in subzero weather.

Finally, Dad got the message. One day at breakfast, he announced that he was going to quit smoking.

"Hooray," Helen Kay shouted.

Maureen ran over and hugged him hard around the neck. Meanwhile, Mary Eileen excused herself from the table. She returned a few moments later with twenty packs of Camel cigarettes—all of them unopened. Apparently, she had been "liberating" a pack a week from Dad's dresser and had hidden them in the Chinese vases in the front parlor.

"I wondered where all those cigarettes were going," Dad asked as he started laughing. "Here I was trying to cut down and smoking fewer cigarettes every week, but they were disappearing like I was smoking a couple of packs a day."

Dad never got angry at my sisters for helping him quit smoking. In fact, over the next few years, when he would see a heavy smoker, he would turn to the girls and smile, giving them a knowing wink—his way of thanking them again for getting him to quit cold turkey.

One good thing came from smoking. For a while, Mom, Hunnah, and he smoked Cavalier cigarettes. The king size cigarettes were sold in a circular, red and white metal tin with a cavalier on the front. One of them became "the money can," where Mom kept loose change and bills. "Take the money out of the can" or, "Put the change in the can" was an almost daily instruction from Mom.

Another problem with my three sisters was all those freckles. I don't know if it is an Irish thing or not, but my sisters had more freckles than you could count. They had them all over their face—tiny little reddish pigments that put Howdy Doody to shame. Hundreds of them!

Those freckles drove me crazy. One of my sisters would walk in a room, and there was a sea of freckles, bobbing up and down as she talked. Even though they weren't much bigger than a raindrop, they were terribly distracting. It was very difficult to pay attention to what she was saying or doing with all those freckles floating around her face.

The face was not the only home port for freckles. In the summer, when we went to Crystal Lake Beach and everyone got a good sunburn, my sisters' freckles would migrate to their arms, backs, and legs. It was like lemmings to the sea. The freckles seemed to divide like amoeba, divide again, and then another time, until their entire body looked like it had a bad case of poison ivy. I couldn't even remain in the same room with them when they were carrying so many freckles.

Now, maybe I was a little jealous. I didn't have very many freckles, and the few I had were nothing to brag about. I had a couple on my upper cheek and one on my right ear that just sort of appeared one day. A solitary freckle on my left shoulder hung around for a couple of years and then just vanished.

My sisters were famous for their freckles.

"Oh, you're the boy with those cute sisters who have all those freckles," women would say to me.

"How darling they are!" others would gush.

Perhaps the unkindest cut of all was the nun who remarked, "What a shame that you don't have freckles like your sisters."

I got so tired of hearing about my sisters' freckles that I actually investigated how to get rid of freckles. Unfortunately, at the time, there were no known cures.

It was what they called "hereditary," meaning that you got it from your parents, and there was nothing you could do about it.

Somehow, I managed to survive while living in the Freckle Capital of the World. But dealing with my sisters was an ongoing battle. Why would they hide my Cub Scout handbook or put Tabasco in my tomato juice? And what happened to my favorite Keds sneakers?

But life with my sisters wasn't all grief. We loved to play together, especially outdoors. We had three apple trees. My mom claimed that some guy named Johnny Appleseed planted them over a hundred years ago as he traveled around the countryside. My sisters and I couldn't imagine why someone would do that, but we appreciated having trees to jump out of into a pile of leaves.

The only problem with having only three apple trees was that we were one short. Mary Eileen, Helen Kay, and I had each claimed one as our own. But poor Maureen—nicknamed Bubsy because she was the youngest child in an Irish family—didn't have her own. And she wasn't happy about it.

"Cheaters!" she would allege. "It's not fair."

Bubsy asked our dad to plant another one.

"Sure, Maureen," Dad said, "but it'll take twenty years for the tree to grow up."

Disappointment seized Bubsy's face as she did the math. "By then, I'll be grown-up, too," she sighed. "It's just not fair!"

Mom had been quietly observing this scene. "You know, Maureen, apple trees are nice," she weighed in, "and I can understand why you want your own."

Taking Bubsy's hand, Mom led her out the back door into a brilliantly sunny summer day.

They stopped in front of the lone plum tree.

"Darling, a young plum tree is much prettier than some old apple tree," Mom offered as she put her arm around her youngest. "And you'll be the only person who can eat the juicy fruit."

Bubsy perked up, looking over at her three siblings.

"Thanks, Mom," she said with her adorable freckled happy face.

"Hey, guys," she said as she beckoned us. "If you're nice to me, and let me share your apple trees, you can share my plum tree."

A deal was struck on the spot as Mom beamed, and Dad looked relieved that he didn't have to plant an apple tree. A mother's wisdom is the grease that keeps the family gears turning smoothly.

My sisters and I loved birthdays. Each of us got to invite some friends over to the house for a party, and the siblings were there, too. Except the time that Mary Eileen "forgot" about my birthday on March 5 and stayed at school for a play rehearsal. I was really hurt, but Mom saved her a piece of my cake.

The best thing about your birthday was creating the menu. Mine never varied over the years: boiled hot dogs on frankfurter rolls with mustard, ketchup, and relish; macaroni salad; Wise potato chips; and Welch's grape juice. Then there was the cake and Borden's Neapolitan ice cream (vanilla, chocolate, and strawberry).

Our birthday cake was no ordinary one. Mom made a special order at the Variety grocery store a week ahead of time. Located in Schenectady and founded before Mom was born, Freihofer's was the bakery. Its cakes were legendary: three thick layers of moist chocolate cake with crème filling in between and smothered with a thick layer of vanilla frosting. The birthday boy got two slices, but I paid a price—my teeth ached for days from the ton of sugar!

I could have lived on a diet of macaroni salad. Hunnah was the macaroni salad chef. She started with Mueller's elbow macaroni boiled until it was perfectly tender but not limp. She added finely chopped onion and celery all mixed with creamy Hellmann's mayonnaise. Then she refrigerated the large bowl of this delicacy until party time.

As we grew up, my sisters and I gradually played together less and less.

Mary Eileen developed friends like Renee, a feisty foster child across the street at the Morrisons, and Bruce Covert who lived in a big house on Crystal Lake and had a large lawn perfect for croquet. Mary Eileen liked to stage dramas with her friends and siblings, ranging from cut-up comedies to corny melodramas. She wrote the scripts, and her costumes and props were anything lying around the house.

"Now learn your lines, Pierce!" the director would scold me for messing up. "I can replace you if you don't shape up."

Helen Kay never lacked for friends either. Renee's younger sister was a giggling playmate, and Valerie became a constant companion. Naturally curious, rambunctious, and adventurous, Helen Kay, along with her girlfriends, loved to explore old haunted houses and wander off into the woods looking for wild mushrooms and cute chipmunks.

"Come on, Pierce. We're going to the Latson house," Helen Kay told me.

The Latson place was all boarded up and plastered with Sheriff's notices: "NO TRESPASSING. VIOLATORS WILL BE PROSECUTED."

"No thanks," I replied. The Latsons had been brutally murdered many years before by their deranged daughter wielding a hatchet and carving knife. Dark red blotches on the kitchen floor could have been dried up blood stains.

"Scaredy-cat," Helen Kay taunted me.

It was bad enough that there may have been Nora the Ghost haunting our house. I didn't need any other spirits from the dead hanging around.

"That's okay," I replied with as calm a voice as possible. "I've got to do my homework."

"Really!" she persisted. "This is July."

Bubsy was really popular. That was not surprising because she was kind, soft-spoken, and slow to anger but quick to comfort. With her gentle demeanor and frequent acts of generosity, she reminded me of Aunt Hunnah. Miss Congeniality's favorite activity was sleepovers—both at our house and anywhere she could be invited or invite herself. Hunnah would joke that on Saturday nights, the family could make some extra money by renting out Maureen's bed.

My sisters were mercenaries. When I became a Boy Scout summer camp counselor at age fifteen, I got less than a day off. The last thing that I wanted to do was laundry, especially ironing five of my wrinkled uniforms. I asked Helen Kay and Maureen if they would help.

"Sure," Helen Kay quickly replied.

"How much are you gonna pay us?" Maureen wanted to know.

"Pay you!" I shot back. "After all that I've done for you guys lately?"

"Name one thing," Helen Kay demanded.

"Uh, uh," I stammered. "Let me think for a moment."

"We've got all day," Maureen quipped. "Take your time."

The more I thought, the more I realized that I was in a deficit position. Big time.

"Okay, you win," I finally conceded. "How much?"

My two younger sisters negotiated a hard bargain. Twenty-five cents per uniform, fifty cents for each batch of folded laundry.

"That's outrageous!" I vainly protested. "They pay me only fifteen dollars per week."

Maureen and Helen Kay stood their ground.

"Okay, all right," I reluctantly agreed. "You win."

"One more thing, Big Brother," Maureen interjected. "You pay in advance. Like Dad's store—no credit."

So much for being the First Child in the O'Donnell family!

13.
THE COUSINS

YOU KNEW IT WAS summer when the cousins arrived.

Dad had three sisters. The youngest was Louise who married Jack Sangster, a tall, dark-haired fellow with a heavy New York City accent (he poured "sear-up" on pancakes and drank "cawfee"). Uncle Jack had a good-paying job with the New York Telephone Company, and he knew something about almost everything. I mean, how many folks can tell you the population of Outer Mongolia, or why jellyfish stings hurt, or how Mark Twain got his name?

Dad's brother-in-law had also fought in World War II in Europe. An army lieutenant in the Signal Corps, he had commanded Black soldiers in combat. This was rare because the white soldiers didn't want to fight with them against the Nazis.

"My men fought with pride and valor," I heard Uncle Jack tell my dad. "They were as tough and brave as any other GIs."

"I never saw any in combat," Dad remarked.

"There weren't many of them," Uncle Jack replied, "but the ones on the front lines were fierce fighters."

Uncle Jack also told us that his Black troops were assigned to clear mine fields ahead of the arrival of the advancing GIs.

"It was immoral and discriminatory," he told my parents as his face took on a furious look. That was perhaps the first time that race "intruded" into my sheltered life in a rural village in upstate New York.

Aunt Louise was a short, reserved woman who was a little plump and quiet. I think that she was Dad's favorite sister because we didn't see much of Bernadette and only once met Marie, the oldest of the four siblings. Aunt Louise tended to defer to her husband, who treated her with great respect and doted on her. "Oh, Jack," Aunt Louise liked to say when her husband would say something that sounded strange or not believable. Uncle Jack was very well read, did the *New York Times* crossword puzzle, and loved to be provocative.

Like the time he announced that trains would someday travel at over one hundred miles per hour.

"We all know that the train cars would fly off the track at that speed," Aunt Louise would say, confident that she had for once disproven one of his wacko predictions.

"Not if they have their own dedicated tracks, sort of high-speed locomotive highways," Uncle Jack explained, proud of himself that he had a ready answer.

I think that our parents, like their kids, looked forward to our summertime visits with each other. They would sit around the kitchen table, sipping coffee in the morning and cocktails at night, talking about all kinds of things. A favorite subject was politics. Being Irish-Americans, they were lifelong Democrats.

"Do you think we can beat Ike?" Mom asked Uncle Jack the summer before the 1956 presidential election.

"I hope so," he replied, "but Eisenhower clobbered Stevenson in 1952."

"Yeah," Dad chimed in. "I don't see us winning. People have jobs, we're at peace, and Ike won the war."

Dad would turn out to be right. I remember the whole family listening to the 1956 election returns from the radio on top of the kitchen refrigerator. It was a slaughter—just like in 1952.

"President Dwight D. Eisenhower has easily won reelection," the announcer reported. "Former Illinois Governor Adlai Stevenson took only six Southern states as Ike beat him by nine percentage points in the popular vote."

That night, there was no joy in Averill Park.

The cousins were Jackie, Mary Louise (named after my mother), and Helen. Jackie and Mary Louise were twins, and they really cared about and protected each other. They shared interests in reading, sports, swimming, camping, and Italian ices.

Jackie and Mary Louise were really good athletes. Mary Louise was a fast swimmer, while her twin exceled at running. I couldn't beat them in a race even when I had a huge head start.

Helen was lot like Maureen: calm, gentle, and pleasant. Maureen and Helen Kay had to share Helen because there wasn't a fourth Sangster cousin. I think this caused some feelings of jealously because Mary Eileen and I each had our own cousin as a playmate.

"Why is it always me?" Bubsy wondered in a hurt tone. "I don't have my own apple tree, and now I don't have my own cousin."

"That's okay," Helen Kay, the diplomat, reassured her. "We can both have Helen." Thus was avoided the War of the Cousins.

We had a summer ritual of spending two weeks vacationing at the Sangsters in suburban Lynbrook on Long Island, while they spent two weeks at our house. Those four weeks of summertime joy would begin when Aunt Louise and Uncle Jack drove up the Taconic Parkway from Long Island, dropped off their kids, and stayed the weekend before driving home. Then Mom and Dad would drive the seven of us to the Sangsters' home, drop us off on a Sunday and pick us up when it was time to go home. My parents never stayed with us, even overnight, because Dad would never close his store even for a day, much less for a two-day weekend or an eternity like two weeks.

"Harry, you're a slave to your business," Mom would periodically complain, venting her frustration about the kids and her not seeing enough of Dad. "Averill Park is not going to run dry if you close for a few days."

"How do you think we pay for everything?" Dad replied defensively. "I have to sell liquor to buy milk."

This brief flare up would be quickly over with this familiar exchange. My sisters and I knew how much Mom genuinely appreciated how hard her "lover boy" (as Dad called himself) worked—six days a week, thirteen hours a day. (We were thankful that New York prohibited selling liquor on The Lord's Day.) For far too many years, Dad wouldn't hire a part-time clerk to cover for him.

"They don't know my customers and what they drink," my father would rationalize.

"Maybe, maybe not," Mom would shoot back, "but your customers do!"

Summer vacation with the cousins was the aces.

At their house, we got to stay up late, go to Jones Beach on the south shore, play stick ball and stoop ball with a pinkish rubber ball, ride bikes to the Italian deli, play pick up baseball and kickball, climb trees in the park, play cops and robbers and hide-and-seek, and pig out at the Carvel soft ice cream store. My sisters and I devoured White Castle hamburgers smothered in grilled onions,

In Averill Park, we built a huge fort under the apple trees, slept under the stars, rode ponies, played cowboys and Indians, made bows and arrows out of tree limbs and thin rope, picked wild raspberries, ate tuna fish sandwiches, and drank pink lemonade. The cousins liked to go bullhead fishing on the pond after dinner, hang out at Crystal Lake Beach (where they popped the best popcorn in the world), and explore our gigantic attic on rainy days and dodge the resident bat.

The only bummer was poison ivy. City folks like the cousins didn't have to worry much about the risks of the outdoors. But they learned the hard way. One summer, all three of them were covered, literally from head to toe, with the red, swollen rash.

"I think I'm going to die," Helen said as she cried from the endless itching that torments a poison ivy victim.

Jackie and Mary Louise tried to be brave, but the itching made them crazy, scratching the sores in a frenzy.

"It feels like my body is on fire!" Jackie exclaimed.

My mom would constantly yell, "Stop scratching!"

Easier said than done when the rash has spread to your groin and butt. Relief finally came when Dr. Reid prescribed calamine lotion. Not surprisingly, the cousins never wanted to go berry picking again.

One day, while vacationing with the cousins, Uncle Jack took us fishing in the ocean. With a long pole, we would stand on the shore, casting into the roiling surf our three-pronged, barbed hook baited with some dead fish. I never caught anything—except myself.

During one cast, I managed to bury the hook deep into my right calf.

"Oh, no!" I shrieked as I fell to the sand, writhing in excruciating pain.

As my sisters and cousins laughed uncontrollably, Uncle Jack attended to my bleeding wound. He couldn't remove the hook.

"It looks bad," he commented as if that was supposed to make me feel better. "Maybe I can cut it out with my pocketknife."

"What!" I exclaimed.

Uncle Jack piled all the kids in his car and took me to a local hospital where the doctor numbed my calf and liberated the hook. You can imagine the kidding that I got for the rest of the vacation.

"Hey, there's the Great White Fisherman!" Mary Louise would shout.

"Who are we having for dinner?" Jackie wanted to know.

"My brother looks fishy," Helen Kay chimed in, while Maureen enjoyed her big brother's teasing.

The only one who spoke up for me was my kid sister. Sort of.

"Come on, leave him alone," Mary Eileen would urge with a Cheshire cat grin. "Pierce feels bad enough that he had to throw back the one hundred and sixty pound tuna!"

More than anything, the sense of freedom and independence in the summertime was exhilarating. We could walk or ride our bikes anywhere we wanted with no fear of being snatched or harmed by some random stranger. Many days, we would take off after breakfast with a bag of sandwiches and chips and disappear until dinnertime.

"Let's go to Crooked Lake today," one of us would suggest. So off we would go, walking or bike riding the several miles on a country road to one of our favorite swimming and fishing spots. No parents or lifeguards or other adults. Just seven kids being kids.

One summer we "borrowed" the rope that Mom used to dry clothes outside. We made a rope swing to jump off a tree limb hanging over a favorite swimming spot on Glass Lake. The only problem is that I was too heavy and too weak to swing out to the deep water.

"Come on, Pierce," Jackie would urge, "you can do it."

"Jump! Jump! Jump!" the girls would chant.

So I would grab the rope, close my eyes, and take off.

Sort of.

The laws of gravity took over as I couldn't hold on to the rope and dropped straight down to the shore. Dry as a bone and mortified that, once again, I resembled more a Dodo bird than a seagull. I vowed that someday—when? I didn't know, but someday—I would be strong enough to hold my own body weight, whether I was rope swinging or doing push-ups or pulling myself up on a chin-up bar.

When you are a kid, you have heroes like Hopalong Cassidy, Jackie Robinson, and the guy who invented the PEZ dispenser. I also had Jackie and Mary Louise. They were "the cool cousins" whom my oldest sister and I desperately wanted to be like. They were a year older than me and two years older than Mary Eileen. Something about them was…well, special—in a league of their own. We imitated their mannerisms right down to eating with our left hands to drinking milk with a straw.

Jackie was a great athlete, witty, super intelligent, and knew more about history and literature than most adults. Not only did he teach me how to field a ground ball, he introduced me to so many great books like *Around The World in Eighty Days, The Last of the Mohicans, Huckleberry Finn, A Tale of Two Cities, Fahrenheit 451, Animal Farm, The Adventures of Robin Hood, Peter Pan, Swiss Family Robinson, The Call of the Wild, The Time Machine,* and all the Sherlock Holmes and Edgar Allan Poe stories.

Along with my mother, Jackie introduced me to the world of ideas, debating about anything and everything, sometimes just for the sheer fun of verbal jousting. Imagine two young adolescents, lounging under a sprawling maple on a warm summer afternoon, talking about Hobbits, Anne Frank, and the seven labors of Hercules. (Jackie's favorite was the Hydra, the monstrous, nine-headed serpent, while I preferred raw flesh-eating Cerberus with his fifty heads.)

"Do you really think that there are space aliens who came to Earth?" I asked Jackie after we read the futuristic novel *War of the Worlds* by H.G. Wells where Martians invade England.

"How do you think Dodger fans got to Earth?" he teased me.

"No, seriously," I pleaded.

"Why not?" Jackie replied. "How do we explain so many things like the Pyramids or the Parthenon with their precise engineering hundreds of years before Christ? Or UFOs? And what about prehistoric cave drawings showing strange creatures and the stone heads of Easter Island?"

I didn't have a ready answer.

Sports were always on our minds. Jackie was a Yankees fan, while I worshipped the Dodgers. Jackie didn't believe me that I'd shaken hands with The Mick.

"Give me a break!" he roared the first time that I told him. "And I dined with Jackie Robinson."

When Uncle Harry confirmed my story, Jackie slowly nodded his head.

"Neat!" is all he said, but I could see that Jackie had a newfound respect for his younger, slow-footed cousin who had a strikeout—not a batting—average on his Little League farm team.

This ritual of the cousins' exchange program lasted for about ten years until we got older and started to have other things to do in the summertime. Jackie got a summer job as a lifeguard, Mary Louise worked at an ice cream stand, Mary Eileen took flute lessons, and I became a counselor at the local Boy Scout camp. We would see each other every now and then, but we gradually grew apart as we got on with our separate lives.

Still, our hearts and minds possessed something that time would never erase. Even today, when I see kids fishing off a pier or standing at the window of an ice cream truck, I imagine the cousins, my sisters, and I hanging out together in the summers of our youth, unburdened by thoughts of getting into college, earning a living, or who we will marry. "One of the very advantages of youth—you don't own any stock in anything," Mark Twain observed.

But you do own your memories—and they are priceless.

14.
LAST PICK

WHEN YOU LIVE IN a small town, there aren't many secrets. Everybody seems to know everything about everyone else. In Averill Park, everybody knew that you didn't pick Pierce O'Donnell for your team.

I don't really know when it started, and I never figured out why. It was just something that everybody knew. Not only the kids who did the picking. It seemed like their older and younger brothers and sisters—and even their moms and dads—also understood that no one wanted me on their pickup team.

The first time I remember not being picked was when I was about seven or eight. The baseball field was near St. Henry's Church, right off the road to Crystal Lake Beach. Kids had been playing baseball for years on this makeshift diamond that had no mound, backstop, or bases. But there were well worn baselines in the grass and a small dirt patch that served as home plate. What else did you need?

One summer afternoon, a couple of kids came walking past my home with their gloves and bats in hand. I knew instantly that a game was being organized. I loved baseball, and I had been practicing with my sister Mary Eileen for several months during and after the winter thaw. And on some Sundays, my dad played catch with me in the front yard.

I had a brand new glove that my parents had given me for my birthday. It wasn't one of those little baby gloves—it was a real leather outfielder's glove, autographed by a Major Leaguer, that smelled brand new and was as big as my face. I'd made a good pocket by punching my fist and ball into the glove for hours on end.

My Aunt Hunnah had given me a blue Dodgers baseball hat and a new bat. I was ready to play ball. I ran into the house, grabbed my stuff, and hurried past my mom.

"Where are we going in such a rush?" she asked.

"To the ball field," I fired back as I bounced off the wall and careened into the hallway.

"Did someone invite you?" she inquired.

"Oh, Mom, you don't have to be invited," I yelled as I spilled out the front door.

I got to the field on my bike just as a whole bunch of other kids arrived. I was really excited, so much that I tightened the laces on my Keds, straightened out my cap, and tucked my shirt into my jeans. I was ready to play.

I'd never seen so many boys together at the field. Nor had I ever been there when they picked up teams. This was my first game. Counting heads, I determined that we had more than enough players for two full teams.

Two of the older boys were selected to be the captains. One was Matt Graves' older brother, John, and the other was Carl Wilson, a tall fellow with acne who became a high school pitcher and later a marine. John Graves got the first pick.

The picking went pretty fast. The older boys were selected first because they were better. Gary Wilson, Eddie Teal, Archie Robinson, Johnnie Albanese, and Bob Stackrow. When it got time to pick the younger kids my age, Matt Graves, Billy Glasser, David Barnum, and Harold Garstang got chosen. As they got picked, they left the group and stood near their captain.

"That's it," yelled Eddie Teal, one of the organizers who lived closest to the field and liked to play third base.

"But wait a minute," I spoke up. "I didn't get picked."

"Too bad, Fatso," someone hollered. "You can chase the foul balls."

That's how it began.

I was devastated. Everyone was staring at me. I was standing all alone, the only kid left where everyone else had been standing only minutes earlier. The chubby kid with baggy blue jeans, thick glasses, and a broken heart.

It seemed like an eternity before I could say anything. Even at that young age, I knew the futility of protesting. There was no adult there, and the kids were already starting their game. I was all alone, angry, and embarrassed. But most of all I was confused.

Nothing like this had ever happened to me before. Oh, I was used to being called names like "Fatso" or "Fatty." It came with the territory of being bigger and heavier than the other kids my age. The nicknames didn't really bother me since the kids played with me at school or in the neighborhood. I was not terribly well coordinated or fast on my feet, but there were no teams or competitions when you are five or six. It didn't really matter.

Now it did.

Rejection is hard to take at any age. As we grow older, we develop defense mechanisms to help us cope with the pain and disappointment of not being accepted, not belonging. When you are eight years old, however, you're defenseless. You don't know what's going on, and you don't know how to react.

Doing as I was told, I dutifully fetched foul balls and errant throws while my "friends" played their game. I tried to put a good face on my predicament, hustling after every ball and throwing as hard as I could back into the infield. But it wasn't the same as being picked to play.

After about an hour, I got up enough courage to ask:

"Say, can I play an inning?"

No one responded. Nothing. Just the deafening sound of silence. It was like I wasn't there—the Invisible Boy.

Then I got what I thought was my break. One of the guys had to go home early. That meant that they needed a replacement. I was the only kid on the sidelines.

"Hey, I'll take his place," I volunteered.

Then a kid on the team that still had nine players announced all of a sudden that he had to be going home, too.

"Well, that leaves an even number," decreed Johnnie Albanese. The game continued without me.

When the game ended, the kids hung around to talk about their feats.

"How about Carl's grand slam?" Matt Graves said in awe. Carl crushed a high fast ball over his brother Gary's head in center field that rolled forever.

"Did ya like that curve ball?" asked Archie Robinson, a short southpaw.

"Looks more like a sick fast ball to me," chimed fun-loving Bob Stackrow. His father was the Graves brothers' uncle, and both dads owned local bars one on Crystal Lake and the other on Burden Lake. My dad called them "The Booze Brothers."

After all the war stories from the game were told, the teams sauntered off to the Park Pharmacy soda fountain for vanilla Cokes, fizzes, ice cream sodas, and hot fudge, marshmallow, caramel, or strawberry sundaes. Someone might even be hungry enough to order a "Jerry Lewis Special." This concoction—named after the famous comedy actor who had lived in our town for a few years, attended Averill Park High School, and worked for Ben Silberg at the local pharmacy as a part-time "soda jerk"—consisted of seven scoops of ice cream, bananas, pineapple, strawberries, hot fudge, whipped cream, nuts, and cherries. If you could eat three

"Jerry Lewis Specials" in one sitting, you got all three for free. To my knowledge, no one ever managed this gastronomic feat.

I wasn't invited to the postgame party either. This time I heeded my mother's advice and went home.

"How was the game?" Mom asked in a chirpy tone as I slouched into the kitchen filled with enticing smells of roast beef, onions, carrots, and potatoes.

"Uh, great," I replied without enthusiasm.

One of a mother's innate instincts is to know when her children are lying. Indulgent fathers fall for a half-truth or lie a lot easier than mothers who are on the firing line every day. You can fool your dad, but you can't con your mom.

"They didn't let you play, did they, Pierce?" she asked softly.

I ran over to my mother and threw my arms around her. Intermittently sobbing and firing questions, I kept shaking my head as she tried to comfort me.

"Why don't they like me?"

"What did I do to them?"

"It's not fair."

Mom was too wise to try to answer her hurtin' son's questions then. Instead, she hugged and consoled me.

"Don't worry, son, everything's going to be all right."

"Your mom and dad love you very much."

"Give your mom a big kiss."

Mom helped me forget the pain, the humiliation, the rejection. She brought me back to my home where I was loved and accepted—and most of all, where I belonged.

Mom knew how much I loved baseball, how much I wanted to play, even to excel. She'd seen me sit by the window, day after day, endlessly pounding the pocket in my new glove and waiting for the snow to melt or the rain to stop so that I could go outside and play catch with anyone I could find.

No one knew better than Mom that the overgrown ball field in the village had been my field of dreams ever since I was five and saw for the first time boys and girls playing baseball there.

It was there that I wanted to learn to throw, catch, and hit.

It was there that I would be one of the guys, part of something bigger than me.

It was there that I wanted to get the winning hit in the bottom of the last inning with men on second and third—two outs, three balls, two strikes. Bang!

Yet, two hours earlier, my field of dreams had become a nightmare.

I wasn't welcome.

I wasn't good enough.

I couldn't even be last pick.

Things did not improve as I got older—they got worse, if that was possible. My sister Mary Eileen was a tomboy who loved the outdoors, animals, and sports. Besides being my regular pitch-and-catch partner, she was my pal. We fought like brothers and sisters do, but we looked out for each other. Actually, she looked out for me a lot more than I could look out for her. Mary Eileen always had my back.

Mary Eileen was one tough cookie. Falling out of an apple tree, scrapes, scratches, and bruises, and brutal cold weather—nothing fazed my kid sister. She was a triple threat to boys a year or two older than her: She could run as fast, throw as far, and punch as hard as any of them.

That was good for her but bad for me.

I was raw enough that I didn't get picked for baseball games when all the players were boys. Then they started picking Mary Eileen instead of me. That was the most embarrassing thing that could ever happen to a guy my age.

"Can't even beat out your sister," Billy Glasser would taunt.

"Pierce is a weenie," David Barnum would add.

"Go home to your mommy, little Piercey," Matt Graves would pile on.

This was the low point of my existence. My playmates preferred to play with my kid sister than me. After all those years that I taught her how to catch a fly and throw the ball to home plate. My seven-year-old sister was better and more popular than me.

At first, I took it out on Mary Eileen.

"Why don't you play with the girls?" I would ask.

"'Cause I like playing with the boys," she would answer in defense of herself.

"Well, you're taking my spot," I'd fire back.

"That's not your spot," she'd reply, her chest swelling. "You don't have a spot. No one wants you on their team."

That was it! I rushed upstairs to my Aunt Hunnah's room in a rage.

"What's wrong?" my gentle aunt asked.

"It's...it's...it's Mary Eileen. She's stolen my spot on the pickup teams."

"Come here," she said as she held out her soft arms and smooth hands to hug me.

Hunnah was resting by the window next to the bed, in what she called her favorite "sitting chair." She was watching one of her programs on her black and white TV set with the floppy rabbit ears. Hunnah liked the variety shows, but most of all she adored Jack Benny. From hours of laying on her bed and watching that show, I can still hear Benny, the cheapskate master of understatement, say in his distinctive, shrill voice, "Oh, Rochester!"

Nestled on Hunnah's lap, I quickly forgot my sister's betrayal and my playmates' rejection.

"Don't worry about it," Hunnah reassured me. "You're a good boy. Those other kids are jealous of you."

I'd never thought about it that way before.

"What are they jealous about?"

Always thoughtful, Hunnah paused a little longer than usual before answering.

"I don't know but believe me. You're a nice, friendly boy. Stay that way and don't worry about those kids."

Somehow I survived being eight years old and last pick.

But making a baseball team that I wanted to be on was never easy for me.

When I turned nine, it was time to try out for Little League. We had two levels of play—Farm Team and Majors—and each team had twelve players.

When I was a kid, I thought that there were only two ways to watch a baseball game: from the bleachers behind a chain link fence or from the bench in the dugout.

That's because I was never "good enough" to make my hometown Little League team. Oh, I tried out every year from the time I turned nine until I was twelve. And every year was the same old story.

"Sorry, Pierce, not this year," the Major League manager would tell me at the end of tryouts.

Trying to make me feel good, he would add, "But good news. We have a uniform for you on the...Farm Team.

Every year, that was like thrusting a dagger in my heart. The Farm Team was the dumping ground for misfits who were too young, slow, uncoordinated, or pathetic to be one of the twelve players on the Majors. Now, understand that I lived in a small town, so there weren't a lot of boys who were between nine and twelve. Not making the Majors when the competition wasn't too tough added insult to injury.

But it was worse than that for me.

I was the only kid who didn't make the Majors for four years in a row! I had the dubious distinction of being on the Farm Team throughout my Little League playing years. It hurt more than I could tell anyone at the time.

It was also embarrassing for me to play. They didn't have any baseball pants that fit me. My belly and thighs were too big for my age. But they found a solution for their permanent Farm Team catcher: I wore blue jeans.

Every year, I would wait to be called up to the Majors. Inevitably, someone would get injured, move away, or go on vacation before the end of the season. It was traditional to call up one or two Farm Team players to give them a chance in the Majors. We were told that if we hustled and played well, we Farm Teamers might have a shot at the Majors.

It never worked out for me though. I would come to practice early and be the last player to leave, help prepare the field for games, and lug the equipment bag from a coach's car to the dugout and back again after the game. I hustled, hustled, and hustled some more. But what good did it do me?

Other kids got promoted every year. But not the fat, flat-footed, awkward, bespeckled O'Donnell kid. I was the Rodney Dangerfield of young baseball players.

It wasn't because I lacked desire. I wanted nothing more than to succeed at baseball. It was by far my favorite sport. I ate, slept, and worshipped the game. My glove was always under my pillow, and my bat was at the foot of my bed. My old Brooklyn Dodgers cap was stained, dirty, and misshapen. If they ever gave a prize for wanting to be a good baseball player, I would have run away with it.

My problem was that my talent lagged a mile behind my ambition.

One coach, Angelo Patti, summed it up: "Pierce has only three problems with his game: hitting, catching, and throwing." Coach nailed it.

I couldn't hit a fast ball, curve, or change up.

My fielding left a lot of room for improvement. Ground balls eluded me—hopping over, under, or to the side of my glove like Mark Twain's celebrated jumping frog.

My throwing was suspenseful. You never knew quite where my rubber band right arm, loosely attached to my right shoulder, would send the ball.

One Farm Team game was particularly humiliating. I was catching with a runner on first base. When he took off, I caught the pitch, jumped up to throw to second, when the crotch of my blue jeans blew out, leaving yours truly exposed in his jockstrap. They say that some people there that day never returned to watch me play again.

The other kids constantly made fun of my failed efforts at baseball and all other sports. They let me play touch football, but only if I agreed to be "permanent center," whose only assignment was to hike the ball for both teams.

(I never got to run with the ball or throw or catch a pass.) When it came to ice hockey, I was always the goalie, because I was the slowest, least agile skater.

One thing never changed—calling me "Porky," "Pusser," "Fats," and lots of other ugly names. Every time I got hit with one of those dreaded nicknames, it was like getting poked with a sharp stick, the emotional equivalent of a mugging. I would cringe, a familiar feeling of rejection overwhelming me. I wanted to make them stop saying those cruel things, to stop taunting me when I couldn't swim as far, run as fast, or jump as high as them.

More than anything else, all I wanted was to be accepted as one of the guys. That never happened when I was a kid. I found ways to cope by building up a lot of defense mechanisms. Like pretending that these guys who taunted and picked on me were really my friends; never telling my parents about my true, constant feelings of alienation; and withdrawing into my own world. I think that's where I first learned about avoidance.

My own world was friendly, warm, and accepting. I read books about adventure. Jules Verne, Robert Louis Stevenson, Daniel Defoe, and James Fennimore Cooper were among my favorites. Escapist fantasy novels were also a staple of my reading diet. In my imagination, I voyaged to the moon and twenty thousand leagues under the sea; I was kidnapped by pirates; I was marooned on an ocean island with the Robinson family; I traveled back and forward in time; and I heard drums along the Mohawk as a scout for the British army during the French and Indian Wars.

I was not without playmates. Mary Eileen and I wrote stories, and I acted in her plays. My sisters Helen Kay and Maureen were nice enough to sometimes share their friends with me. And I spent many happy hours with my best friend in his liquor store.

But I still wanted to be one of the guys in our village. I endured beatings; had my money, baseball cards, and food stolen; received countless strawberries (someone grinding his middle finger knuckle into your skull); and got painful punches to the upper arm—not to mention weathering a steady stream of insults. It seemed that the more I tried to be friendly and accommodating, the more they taunted and rejected me.

I didn't get invited to their birthday parties either. Just David Barnum, another outcast, and I went to each other's party. I wasn't asked to sleep over at their homes—except by Skip Vigus, who didn't live in the village and was a ruggedly independent boy who loved the outdoors. And, of course, for years

I wasn't welcome to play pickup sports with the village boys, either. I had to play with my sister Mary Eileen and the other neighborhood "rejects" like Billy Normandin, who was a sweet, intellectually challenged older boy whose father had a 1930-something car in the garage that Billy and I used to pretend to drive.

I don't want to convey the impression that all the time I walked around, head down, feeling sorry for myself. The rejection hurt and probably a lot more at the time than I presently can (or want to) recall. But I didn't let the petty nastiness take over my life. More than any other reason, it was probably because my Aunt Hunnah gave me some wise advice.

"Pierce, they are behaving immaturely," she would tell me after I confided in her the latest indignity—like stealing my clothes when we were skinny-dipping in Crystal Lake. "They want to feel superior, so they have to have someone to pick on. Someday, they'll regret how they treated you. You're a good boy. Ignore them as best you can; you have many better things to do with your life than worry about Matt Graves, Jimmy Wilkins, and Billy Glasser."

THE KANES AND O'DONNELLS were as Irish as you could be on the American side of the Atlantic Ocean. When I was a boy, I'd hear adults talk about how the English were brutal conquerors of Ireland. With courage and pluck, the Irish managed to outlast their occupiers, and after centuries of subjugation, my ancestors eventually won their freedom. Ireland became a prosperous, democratic nation with the best educated people in the world. This triumph gave rise to the saying about surviving The English Hell: "The best revenge is a good and long life."

By the time that I got to high school, a lot of things had changed. The older kids who didn't let me play on their sandlot teams went on to the varsity baseball team at the local high school. But Stackrow, the Wilson Brothers, Albanese, Teal, Robinson, and the others never had a championship season.

Billy Glasser, David Barnum, and Harold Garstang never played on our high school team. Matt Graves played for a year or two but dropped out. They didn't make the cut, so to speak.

Averill Park didn't have a freshman or junior varsity baseball team. So, as a freshman, I tried out for the varsity. I was pleasantly surprised to be picked—until I realized why. For an entire season, I was relegated to functioning as the permanent, third string catcher, handling batting practice, warming up pitchers, and keeping track of all the equipment. As Yogi Berra said, "It's déjà vu all over again."

This was not a championship season either. The team was weak, leaderless, and divided. The only thing that everyone seemed to agree on was that they could torment Pierce. It was more than freshman hazing—it was mean-spirited, malicious, and unremitting. My spikes disappeared, my jock strap had hot muscle balm rubbed in it, and I was forced to take a lot of cold showers—in my uniform. It was clear to me that I was being pressured to quit the team.

But I was either too stupid or too stubborn to get the message. I had finally been picked for a baseball team (forget the reason!), had a regulation uniform (no more blue jeans!), and I was slowly learning to be a better player (even if I never played in a game!). The last thing that I was going to do was quit.

When the season ended, I made a vow to myself: next spring, I will be a starter on the varsity baseball team. That would be a daunting challenge for a guy who never made the Majors in Little League, much less got one at bat or played an inning for his entire freshman year.

I traded my catcher's mitt for a fielder's glove. All fall and winter, whenever I could steal the time from homework, class activities, and JV basketball, I'd spend hours in the high school gym, throwing a rubber-coated baseball against the concrete wall, fielding the ground ball, and throwing out the runner. The Polish immigrant janitor would throw pop flies to me all around the basketball floor. Mary Eileen pitched me Wiffle balls for batting practice. And I conditioned like a maniac, running several miles every workout, doing my father's strenuous calisthenics regimen, and lifting the few weights that I could find in the school storage room.

Finally, the first day of spring tryouts in 1963 arrived. About twenty-five guys surrounded Coach Earl Retzlaff, one of our PE teachers in his second season. With no foundation to build upon, he had to start fresh. His first spring in our competitive league was rough. Prospects for this season didn't look too promising given the number of graduating seniors, and the unproven crop of freshman and sophomores was a big unknown.

A short, balding man in his forties with a broad smile and brilliant white teeth, Coach was a tough taskmaster. With his beagle named Baseball always hanging around, Coach barked orders, bellowed his dissatisfaction with an error or lack of effort, and incessantly paced back and forth in front of bench to the point of creating a six inch ditch. When a player took a third strike, protesting

"I thought it was a ball," Coach would stare him down, shouting, "I'm the only one paid to think around here, and I'm not paid enough to suffer fools like you!"

"Okay, let's get started," Coach announced. "O'Donnell, put on the catcher's gear for batting practice."

"No, Coach," I replied. "I'm not a catcher anymore."

Well, if looks could kill, I was a dead sixteen year old.

"What did you say?" Coach shot back.

"I'm trying out for third base," I answered, having rehearsed this act of defiance in my head all winter. "The position is open."

His brow furrowed. Coach just stood there motionlessly, hands on his hip. The silence was deafening.

"Third base?" he incredulously inquired.

"Yes, sir," I responded. "All I want is a chance to prove myself."

A small grin broke the tension. Coach walked over to me, put his hands on my shoulders, and said in a voice that only I could hear, "Okay, Pierce, show us what you've got."

The rest is history as they say.

That spring, my sophomore year, I made the team, started at third base all season, and batted over .300. We had a winning season. I won the Coach's Award as Most Improved Player.

Opening Day was my inauspicious debut, however. Just before game time, the groundskeeper had finished mowing the tall grass in the infield, but he didn't have time to collect the considerable clippings. In the first inning, a batter topped the pitch, sending the ball slowly dribbling toward me. This was my very first play.

Imitating my hero Brooks Robinson, the nimble Baltimore Orioles third baseman, I rushed toward the ball and swooped down, effortlessly sweeping the ball up with my right hand and throwing under arm to first base. Perfect form. A bang-bang play.

Not quite.

You see, I'd gracefully picked up a large clump of grass that had covered the ball. The grass didn't get very far as it blew back in my face.

Safe at first. Mortified at third!

The next year, when I was a junior, the team performed even better and had a winning season—Coach's first ever. I played every game, made some double plays, and improved to a .330 batting average.

In my senior year, not only did the Averill Park Warriors baseball team win the Central Hudson Valley League championship, we went undefeated! 18–0. Our team was loaded with terrific talent; guys like Bob Campano, Paul Allen, Bob Bowman, Bill Hotaling, Jim McNamee, and Harry Kachadurian—former Twin Town Little League all-stars. All except one player—me!

My buddy Bob Campano saved our perfect season. With us losing 5–2 in the bottom of the seventh inning (we didn't play nine innings in high school), bases were loaded. Bob took a low pitch on a 2–2 count. Ball three. The pitcher then threw a heater right down the pike. Bob launched the ball into sub orbit over the center fielder's head. Grand slam!

At the awards banquet in the high school cafeteria, Coach couldn't contain his glee.

In a startling move, he took out a pair of really dirty baseball socks and put them on the table. Amazingly, they stood up by themselves.

"When we won the opening game," Coach started to explain, "I told myself that I wouldn't change my socks until we lost. Well, we never lost, and here's the proof!"

Toward the end of the joyful evening, filled with celebratory speeches and various awards for the players, Coach took out a large trophy and put it on the table.

"As I've said all evening, there are so many reasons why this team had a perfect season," he began. "But in my mind one really stands out."

Parents and players looked quizzically at each other.

"One player typified this exceptional team's unrelenting desire to be their very best every at bat, every play, and to win no matter what the odds," Coach continued. "And we all know who that player is."

Smiling from ear to ear, his brilliant white teeth flashing, Coach walked over to my table and handed me a beautiful golden trophy with a batter on top. The inscription said:

Averill Park High School Warriors
1965 Undefeated Season
Batting Champion
.385 Average
Pierce O'Donnell

The Irish were right.

15.
THE METHODISTS

The Methodists caused me a lot of trouble.

My family was Roman Catholic, and we attended St. Henry's Church. My father was an usher, Mary Eileen sang in the choir, and I was an altar boy. My father had donated lots of money to build the parish's new elementary school; my two youngest sisters, Helen Kay and Maureen, were taught there by the nuns, whom we called the Penguins. We were on good terms with the pastor, Father Thomas Kay, who shopped in my father's liquor store. His sister Grace and he came to our family functions like parties for Holy Communion, Confirmation, and graduations. My parents served stiff drinks at the house. Maybe that's why their parties were so popular.

Protestants outnumbered Catholics in our town. They had five churches—the Baptists, Presbyterians, Congregationalists, United Church of Christ, and those Methodists. I didn't really pay much attention to people's religion, unless they were Methodists.

Let me explain.

Our house was right next to the Methodist Church. Only ten feet separated the two buildings. My bedroom window looked out onto the side of the church, which kept sunlight from coming into my room.

Our house was there first—many years before they built the Methodist Church. On Sundays, the parking lot in the back would fill up long before the service. Catholics were always rushing to get to Mass on time, but those Methodists were always early.

My parents warned my sisters and me that if we ever went into the Methodist Church, we would be in a lot of trouble. They said we would be "excommunicated." We weren't sure what that meant, but it sounded really bad.

You can't tell kids that they can't do something that is next door. It's just not fair. My folks should have told us that we could go in there anytime and even become Methodists if we wanted. Then we would have ignored the Methodist Church.

But they didn't. And we didn't.

My friend David Barnum was a Methodist. He lived with his parents up in the village on Main Street. The front of their house was Barnum's News & Candy Stand. They sold newspapers, magazines, and candy. That's where I first started reading comic books. My favorites were Superman and the Green Hornet.

I used to ask David lots of questions about what it was like to be a Methodist, but he didn't have any real good answers. They were baptized with water, and so were we. They had Communion, and so did we. They had an organ just like we had. The only difference I could see is that their minister was married and had kids, and our priest was single and had a sister.

One summer day, I couldn't stand it any longer. I had to go inside and check out the Methodist Church for myself. I went and got David, and we started scouting out the place. The front door was locked, and so was the back door that led to the kitchen. Then David tried the cellar door, and it was unlocked.

I paused for a minute at the first step, David yelling, "Come on, scaredy-cat! Let's go." I couldn't help but think about going to hell if I stepped even one foot inside the Methodist Church. "You're a sissy, Fatso," David was now shouting. Those were fighting words. I ran after him into the church basement and forgot all about my immortal soul.

It was pitch black, the only light coming from behind us through the open cellar door. David made his way to a light switch, and we quickly climbed up the old wooden stairs. I was scared. My heart was pounding.

There we were, in the main part of the Methodist Church. It was really bright and cheery with a lot of dark red carpets and drapes. They had wooden pews, an elevated altar area, and a choir loft. It could have been a Catholic Church if someone had put a different sign out front.

I expected at any moment that some loud voice would scream from up high, "Pierce O'Donnell. You have disobeyed me. You are damned forever!"

When I didn't hear that voice the day I broke into the Methodist Church, I started to wonder about a lot of other things that I had been told about God, Catholicism, and all the other religions. As we left, my heart was no longer pounding.

Only a few months after I made peace with the Methodists, their church was gone.

It was a cold, fall day. The leaves had turned, and the first hint of winter was in the air. You knew that winter was coming when you could see your breath and the grass cracked under your feet from the night's frost.

I was coming home from school on the bus. When we tried to make the turn off Main Street and down Burden Lake Road, the road was blocked. As we got out of the bus for the short walk home, I heard someone yell, "It looks like the O'Donnells' house is next!"

I ran like a bat out of hell down the street.

I couldn't believe my eyes. There must have been eight firetrucks parked all around the Methodist Church and my house. The church was on fire, flames shooting out the windows and up into the cold air. Volunteer firemen were running around with long hoses and axes. The water was being pumped from the Old Mill Pond on the other side of our house.

The church was a goner. The firemen were now focusing on our house, throwing all the water they could on the side next to the church. I ran over to our front lawn and found my mother and three sisters all huddled together. They were in shock but otherwise okay.

"Where's Dad?" I asked.

"He's fighting the fire," my mother answered in a weak voice. I ran over to one of the captains, a man who ran one of the funeral parlors.

"Have you seen my dad, Mr. Larkin?"

"He was fighting the fire in the basement."

I ran around the right side of our house and doubled back to the rear of the church. There was my dad, huddled over another fireman. I would learn later that the man had gone into the smoke-filled basement, but he didn't put on his gas mask the right way.

My father threw on a gas mask, one like they used in World War II, and dashed into the basement. Finding the man on the floor, unconscious, Dad carried him on his shoulder outside to safety. The man was starting to breath all right just as I arrived.

"What can I do to help, Dad?"

"Pierce, take your mother and sisters up to the store right now."

I obeyed, and for the next two hours, we didn't know whether our house had burned down. All we could see from the liquor store was dark smoke and flashing red lights. My sisters and I talked about where we would live if our house was destroyed. Nobody had any bright ideas.

Finally, my dad returned to the store. All covered with soot and shivering from the cold and being drenched by the water poured on the house and church, he was exhausted.

"We couldn't save...the church," Dad told us. "Our house will need a new coat of paint, but it survived."

They caught the guy who started the church fire. He had broken in the same way David and I had, through the basement door. The police say that it was arson. What was weird is that the arsonist was one of the volunteer firemen who then came to help extinguish the fire. The guy was a crazy man sent to a state mental hospital in Poughkeepsie..

After the Methodist Church fire, they tore down the torched remains and removed all the debris. But they left the field stone foundation, and over the years, grass, shrubs, and trees grew up. It was a mess.

My father tried to buy the lot so that he could expand our side yard. Dad was going to level the foundation and plant a lawn. It would have made a neat practice field for baseball and the greatest touch football field. But the Methodists wouldn't sell it to the Catholic O'Donnells. My dad made a generous bid, but the church sold it to one of their parishioners (Elsie Loker) who lived behind us. She bid only one dollar more than my father after she was told my father's offer.

Within a couple of years, the Methodists rebuilt their church on another lot up in the village, right next to the new post office building. By then, Vatican II had reformed many old-fashioned rules of the Catholic Church. Something called "ecumenism" among the various Christian religions became popular. I wasn't quite sure what that meant. What I did know was that I could now walk through the front door of the Methodist Church and attend their services—without fear of losing my immortal soul.

Things change if you just wait long enough.

FALL

"Whether it's the best of times or the worst of times, it's the only time we've got."
—Art Buchwald

16.

"YES, MISS GEHLE"

EVERYONE'S HAD THE TEACHER from hell. You know the type: tough as nails, no nonsense, heard every excuse, and thinks you're a cocky, lazy bones who needs to be whipped into shape.

And she is just the teacher to set you straight.

My problem was different.

In the seventh grade, when I was turning twelve, I had the teacher from heaven.

Her name was Miss Gehle (pronounced like "eel" with a hard G in front of it). A flinty spinster who presided over the first year of my passage from grammar to junior high school, Marcelle Veronica Gehle was no ordinary teacher. She was highly intelligent, perfectly polite, and totally dedicated to teaching. Now don't get me wrong, she had all the attributes of the teacher from hell, except she smiled all the time and spent more time in church than most priests I've known.

Town legend had it that Miss Gehle once joined a convent but didn't become a nun. No one ever said why. It didn't make any sense to me because she spent so much time praying, going to church, and helping other people. No one could be more holy than Miss Gehle, my three sisters and I always said. Not even the Pope himself.

There was another, more intriguing rumor about Miss Gehle; she was once engaged to a handsome young man, but for some unknown reason, they never married, and she had a broken heart. This mystery romance seemed possible, too. She was a very attractive woman in her late forties, with her slightly graying hair pulled back tight from her forehead, a tall, slender frame and an angelic face right out of a Michelangelo painting.

My mother and Aunt Hunnah knew Miss Gehle very well. Mom and she had both graduated from State College for Teachers in Albany. They all went to St. Henry's Church, and I think that they may have even grown up together in our small town. Hunnah's best friend, Katherine Sowalsky, was close to Miss Gehle—all three of them being unmarried female college graduates in a town that had more gas stations than single men with college degrees. I once asked Hunnah why she never got married. She ducked the question, but I asked again.

She gave me a sad look and said, "I never met the right man."

Even though I was young, I could understand. You see, I knew all the so-called "eligible bachelors" in Averill Park, the village that mapmakers forgot. Most of the available men—when they weren't working in the woolen mill, driving a school bus, delivering mail, or fixing potholes on the town highway crew—spent their time hunting deer, playing darts, bowling, and drinking Genesee or Utica Club beer for ten cents a glass up at the Lakeview Hotel run by the parents of my friend Matt Graves. Come to think of it, that's what a lot of the married men did, too. I guess it's no wonder that the women had their own auxiliaries and spent so much time with PTA and church activities. Bingo must have been invented by lonely women.

I always thought Miss Gehle looked unhappy. You get to know somebody watching her five days a week only a few feet away. It's hard to explain, but she had this pained expression and misty sadness in her eyes. She often seemed to be staring off in the distance, her body present but her mind absent.

My oldest sister had Miss Gehle the year after me and was very perceptive about these things. Mary Eileen thought that our Miss Brooks lived in another world. Not that she was a space cadet, but rather that her mind was filled with visions of Jesus, Mary, and the Holy Saints. The strain on her face, my sister believed, came from having to suffer through the idiocy and evil of this world. (Teaching seventh graders like me certainly exposed her to the idiots.) Mary Eileen actually thought Miss Gehle might just be a saint.

There sure was plenty of evidence to support Mary Eileen's theory. During the school year, she went to Mass on Saturday and Sunday, and vacation time and summers meant daily morning Mass. Just watching Miss Gehle in church was a religious experience. Whether she was kneeling or standing, her eyes were squeezed tightly shut, and her hands were always perfectly pressed together in front of her like a motionless praying mantis. She knew all the people's responses in Latin and sang all the hymns in a light, clear voice. When she received Holy Communion, her body seemed to swell with joy.

Miss Gehle was always helping out people. There was nothing conspicuous about her virtue. Day in and day out, she quietly collected used clothes and food for poor families. She also took the infirm, elderly, and carless to church on Sunday. Good deeds were second nature to her.

If Miss Gehie wasn't a saint, she was certainly the most pious person I ever knew. I was dying to ask her lots of questions about her life. It was strange because I never had this curiosity about any of my other teachers up to then. Miss Gehle, however, fascinated me.

I never had the courage to ask Miss Gehle anything personal. Actually, as the year went by, I learned that she did most of the asking, and I was supposed to do the answering—both in and out of class.

That's one of the disadvantages of having a teacher who knows your family so well. You can't get away with anything in a small town. Not even the slightest little mistake. Everything gets reported and distorted.

I remember the time I was late for class one morning because I couldn't get my locker opened. I had to go to the principal's office, and the secretary had to find the janitor who was out on the football field fixing something. All this took only about fifteen minutes. Well, given the icy reception that I received from Miss Gehle when I reported late for class, you'd think that I'd burned down the library.

"Pierce had a little trouble at school today," Miss Gehle casually mentioned to my Aunt Hunnah at the post office later that day.

"Oh!" said Hunnah.

"Nothing too serious, but it bears watching," she added in a hushed tone.

There are no secrets in a family. Hunnah immediately called my mother at home who called my father at the store. By the time I arrived home on the school bus, I'd already been tried, convicted, and sentenced. It took my best powers of persuasion to convince the jury that I was the victim of a gross misunderstanding.

For the rest of the year, I got to class early.

There's something else about Miss Gehle that I have to mention: her strange voice. Actually, it wasn't so much her high-pitched voice—it was the way she talked. First, everyone in the class was "Mister" or "Miss." Second, we had to respond, "Yes, Miss Gehle." This ritual was so routine that kids said that their seventh grade teacher's name was "Yes, Miss Gehle."

Miss Gehle spoke in long words and short breaths. If she were saying "Holy Roman Catholic Church," it would sound like "HOOOOly ROOOOman Cathhhhholic ChUUUUrch." It took her minutes to recite the first page of *A Tale of Two Cities*.

Miss Gehle didn't suffer fools gladly…or at all. She expected that her students would be respectful, attentive, and prepared. The greatest sin in her book was to be discourteous.

I remember a day in the fall when a senior—a big, hunky football player named Al—gave her some lip during an assembly in the auditorium when she told him to stop talking. Al shot back, "Yes, Miss Gehle," in a sarcastic voice. Everyone turned to watch this confrontation between the tough guy on the aisle and Ichabod Crane's sister.

"Mr. Rogers," she replied as she walked over and stood directly over him.

"Yes, Miss Gehle," he repeated in his mocking way as he stood up to his full six feet two inches of height, towering over her.

"Either you will sit down, be quiet, and behave yourself," she began, every word hanging in the air for a few seconds and floating over the auditorium, "or you will spend the remainder of the football season with me after class."

The thought of reliving seventh grade with Miss Gehle was like threatening to kick him in the groin. When Big Al slumped to his seat, a defeated bully who had met his match, the assembly erupted in applause for her spunk. We didn't hear much from Big Al after his near-death experience with the meek lady in the gray suit with the gray hair who drove a gray Chevy and lived in a gray house.

Miss Gehle believed that school was a place where you learned. Not only basic lessons in math, reading, history, science, etc., but also something she called "values." She was an unflinching, old-fashioned educator who believed that the nation's youth must be trained in Americanism.

Miss Gehle made no bones about where she stood at times when the United States was being tested at home and overseas. She was a patriot, a dyed-in-the-wool, rock-ribbed Republican. I was kind of surprised that Miss Gehle didn't disguise her political views in the classroom more. Sometimes she got a little carried away and couldn't help herself. Like the time that she told us that President Herbert Hoover was misunderstood, and Franklin Delano Roosevelt was the Antichrist. Mary Eileen was required to write a paper "Better Dead Than Red."

Of course, in our town of overwhelming Republican registration, there were few Democrats to raise their voices in protest over the introduction of partisan politics in the classroom. My family was all Democrats, but I never complained to my parents because I liked Miss Gehle and figured that she was entitled to her opinions, so I cut her some slack. Anyway, I sat there for an entire school year, listening to her conservative political ideas, but didn't get brainwashed.

This was the height of the Cold War. The Soviet Union had launched Sputnik and was believed to be ahead in the race to space. The Korean War had ended in a disgraceful draw at best, and communism held Eastern Europe, China, and parts of Southeast Asia in a vice grip. FBI Director J. Edgar Hoover warned us of "The Enemy Within," and *I Led Three Lives* was a popular TV show about the American Communist double agent Herb Philbrick and the infiltration of communists into legitimate organizations in our society.

Miss Gehle was at her rhetorical best when she railed against communism.

I wasn't even a teenager yet, but I remember her talking about the horrible situation in a faraway country called Laos. She assigned a book called *The Night They Burned the Mountain* written by Dr. Thomas A. Dooley, a brave American doctor had devoted his life to saving and improving the lives of Laotian villagers in the high mountains. Dr. Dooley wrote movingly of his patients' plight and atrocities by the communists who were waging a guerilla war to seize power.

Dr. Dooley was Miss Gehle's hero. Her eyes misting and her voice cracking, she would stand there in front of the class, swaying ever so slightly from side to side, as she spoke of his courage and faith in God.

"This man believes in something greater than fame or fortune," she told us. "Dr. Tom Dooley is the living embodiment of Christ's mandate that we should love and care for one another. And he is an American who is serving his country by showing the world that we will not sit idly by and let the unfortunate people of the world die from disease and malnutrition."

Miss Gehle was also a tough grader.

When I was ten, the school district reopened the old high school and made it the "middle school" for fifth and sixth graders from the several towns that had their own elementary schools. I'd done well up through the fourth grade at Miller Hill Elementary School, and I was put in the A track class when I got to middle school. I thought I was an academic hotshot, getting grades in the low and mid-nineties.

Then I hit seventh grade and Miss Gehle.

It was like trying to breathe in a tornado.

Miss Gehle wasn't very impressed with my scholastic achievements. My spelling was no good, my writing composition lacked clarity and structure, my math building blocks were shaky, and worse of all, my penmanship sucked. Getting my first report card from Miss Gehle was the worst day of the first twelve years of my life—far worse than the day that the doctor told me when I was six that I had spots on my lungs.

Upon opening my report card, I froze in horror, in bone-chilling disbelief, my hands trembling as I read down the column: English 79, Math 78, Science 81, History 83, Social Studies 80, and Handwriting 65.

It was my academic Waterloo.

I didn't know whether to cry, scream, or run away with the circus. The last option was the one I favored, but I didn't know how to find the Ringling Brothers. So I went home, gave the report card to my mother, and went to my bedroom to await the inevitable.

But the inevitable never happened.

We got through dinner without any comment from Mom, and when Dad got home from work, Vesuvius didn't erupt. I started to worry. Why weren't they going bonkers about my terrible grades? Maybe they were still compiling the list of my punishments and lost privileges.

I didn't sleep well that night. After breakfast, my parents asked my sisters to go into the other room. Okay, I figured, here it comes.

"We read your report card, Pierce," my mother opened calmly, more calmly than I had thought the occasion deserved.

"Needless to say, son, we're disappointed," my dad added, his face remaining quiet.

"You can do a lot better, don't you think?" my mom asked.

"I think so," I answered meekly.

"We know you can," Mom replied. "You're in junior high school now, and it's going to get a lot harder from here on."

"We want you to come home right after school and do your homework and then your mother will go over it with you," my father said in a soft voice, but there was no mistaking that it was a direct order from my commanding officer.

Dad then signed my report card, my mother kissed me, and they sent me off to school.

That lesson in the power of positive thinking as a motivator has remained with me the rest of my life.

Miss Gehle gave me a wake-up call, and my parents had the wisdom to turn it into a learning experience for their son.

That was the last time that my parents ever had to sit me down about a report card. From that day forward, I was driven to succeed in school, to live up to my potential, and, frankly, to please my parents who believed so much in me. That spring, my parents took the family to Florida during spring break for a rare vacation, but I stayed home to work on a term paper for Miss Gehle and to get my "lifesaving" merit badge, which I needed to qualify for Eagle Scout.

Miss Gehle became one of my favorite teachers, and I became an A student for the rest of junior and senior high school, graduating as the valedictorian. For the next ten years, whenever I would return home to Averill Park and go to Mass at St. Henry's, I would run into Miss Gehle.

"Mr. O'Donnell," she would say.

"Yes, Miss Gehle," I would reply.

Some things never change.

17.
HAPPY THANKSGIVING

It was my favorite holiday. I looked forward to it for months, recalling the distinct smells and unique feelings that I associated with this extraordinary day. Of all the days of the year, this was always my happiest.

It wasn't Easter or the Fourth of July or even Christmas, I had nothing against those holidays.

Easter was a special day, more religious than secular. It was an odd holiday, the only one that never came at the same time every year. We always ate baked ham and sweet potatoes for our main meal, and Hunnah would cook one of her special desserts.

The candy in the Easter basket was a nice touch, but I got really sick once on the marshmallow stuffed chocolate Bunny. Ham, sweet potatoes, tapioca pudding, marshmallow, and chocolate all mixed together are not a pleasant sight—especially when they decorate your mother's best oriental rug.

Independence Day meant a great parade along Main Street, picnics, and an adult softball game up at the old high school. The weather was usually warm enough to go swimming at Crystal Lake Beach or Tifft's Beach on Glass Lake. The bass started to bite then, too.

Christmas was an exciting time. The fun of decorating the house and Scotch pine or Douglas fir trees with ornaments that my mother and her mother had used, the frenzy at my father's liquor store, and buying and exchanging gifts for family and friends. As I grew older, I got to help out at the store during the Christmas season, dusting off shelves, shoveling snow, chipping ice off the sidewalks, carrying packages and cases of liquor to the customer's car, washing the floors, burning the trash, fetching the mail, getting change at the bank, and delivering orders. It was hard work, and I was always so exhausted that I could never stay awake on Christmas Eve for the midnight Mass at St. Henry's.

As much as I enjoyed those other holidays, they were nowhere as special as Thanksgiving. My dad was home all day because state law required that liquor stores be closed. He was well rested (unlike Christmas) and in good spirits. The weather was usually crisp but not subzero. With any luck, the pond was frozen enough to go ice skating, and Dad would come down and help us shovel off the light snow.

One Thanksgiving, my father, three sisters, and I went ice skating at a small pond not far from my friend Skip Vigus' home on Bear Mountain Road. We had to walk about a mile on a steep trail to the pond, but it was worth the trek because the pond was as slick as glass and ours alone for the afternoon. It was cold—about twenty-eight degrees—but the wind was still. A light snow powder covered the trail.

The past Christmas, the kids had given Dad size fifteen ice skates as his present. "Just what I always needed," he joked at the time.

But he had been too busy to use them until this fateful Thanksgiving Day. We left Mom in the kitchen with Hunnah fixing our Thanksgiving feast.

Her last words still echo in my ears: "Harry, be careful. You're no spring chicken anymore."

To the man who called himself "the Peter Pan of Averill Park," those were almost fighting words. But Dad sloughed off her warning. "Don't worry, Mary. We're only going ice skating. What can happen?"

Dad was in his late forties and in excellent physical shape from his daily calisthenics regimen and hard work at the store. In his youth, he had been an accomplished roller and ice skater. The fact that he hadn't been on skates in more than a quarter of a century was apparently of no concern to him.

For us kids, it was a rare treat to have our father out playing with us on something other than the occasional Sunday afternoon. Maureen, my youngest sister, was about six and not yet a skater. Helen Kay, then nine, was a good skater and instinctively helped Maureen.

Mary Eileen, my kid sister who was eleven, wore men's black figure skates and brought her hockey stick and puck with her so that she could play with Skip and me. She was a formidable foe because she was such a good skater and tough as nails. I knew guys who steered clear of her body checks.

I was an okay-but-not-great skater by the time I had reached a dozen years of age. I still bent my ankles too much, and I was not very good at skating backward. I could sort of stop, but I had been known to take out a line of skaters in my day.

When I got out of control, I was no stranger to the large snowbanks on the side of our rink on the Old Mill Pond.

On this Thanksgiving Day in 1959, we got to the pond without incident, and everyone was doing their thing. Skip was a great skater, and Mary Eileen and he were doing jumps and twists. Helen Kay was trying to guide Maureen as she slipped and fell around the perimeter of the slick pond. Out in the middle, I was struggling to stay off my ankles and skate with the bottom of my feet.

Dad had to put in the laces for his new skates and was rising from the bank with his shiny skates tightly fastened to his mammoth feet. He was wearing gray wool pants over thermal underwear, a red woolen cap, a plaid scarf, and a winter jacket. He looked like a character out of a Norman Rockwell painting.

Dad hesitated for a moment as he stood on his skates for the very first time. He tested his laces, bent his knees a little to get the feel of being on skates, and then off he went. It was not what I had expected.

Dad was tentative, inching his way onto the ice, his knees bent, and his butt hanging low. Gradually, however, he gained confidence, stood up more, and put one foot in front of another. After a few minutes and trips around the pond, he stood tall, moving with tentative grace.

"How's it feel, Dad?" I yelled.

"Great," he replied as he playfully stole Helen Kay's wool hat and threw it to Mary Eileen.

Dad was having the time of his life. Smiling, laughing, cracking jokes. It was the best side of him, and this Thanksgiving Day he was letting loose.

Then disaster struck.

Dad was getting bolder and bolder, skating faster and faster around the pond. I don't really know what happened. Maybe he turned his head to say something to Skip or maybe he got distracted by the hawk that had been circling for the past few minutes. Whatever the reason, Dad met with a great fall.

It happened suddenly. One moment Dad was skating up a storm, grabbing at our scarves and tickling us, and the next moment his feet came out from underneath him, sending him crashing to the hard ice. It almost looked like he was fooling around. That's obviously what little Maureen thought, as she yelled, "Do it again, Daddy! Do it again!"

But Daddy wasn't laughing. In fact, he wasn't moving. He lay still, flat on his back.

I rushed over to his side, and I could see that he was in pain. He had landed squarely on his butt.

"Are you all right?" I asked nervously.

Dad didn't answer.

"Dad, where does it hurt?" I followed up.

Still no response.

"What can I do for you?" I shouted at close range.

Dad slowly lifted his capless head off the ice, looked around to get his bearings, and raised himself to his elbows.

"You can stop yelling in my ear for starters," he finally replied.

Skip, Mary Eileen, and I helped him to his feet. His rear end was sore, but his pride was far more wounded. We called a halt to our skating, helping him down the trail.

When we got home, Dad tried to make light of his mishap, but by the next morning, he had a huge black and blue bruise on his left butt cheek, and he walked with a noticeable limp. During the next two weeks, the clotted blood moved slowly down his leg and finally settled in his big toe. The sight of Mom lancing his dark blue toe and the dead blood draining out was the most disgusting sight I'd ever seen.

Dad never went ice skating again.

Not all Thanksgivings were as eventful as Dad's Great Fall.

Most of the time, after morning Mass at St. Henry's, the family hung out in the cramped kitchen as my mom and Hunnah prepared the feast and dad caught up on his newspapers, sipping a strong Dewar's and Saratoga Vichy with a lemon twist. My sisters would be helping, setting the dining room table and grinding up the fresh cranberries and orange rinds for our special O'Donnell/Kane family holiday concoction.

I had various duties, ranging from lifting the turkey out of the oven to cleaning up after Dad carved the bird. Unofficially, I was the turkey dressing taster, and it took me several heaping spoonfuls before I could be sure that my mom had once again triumphed with her pork sausage stuffing.

What I remember most about Thanksgiving are not the sights or sounds but the smells.

When a turkey first starts cooking, there isn't much to smell. After about three hours, however, the kitchen is filled with the most wonderful aroma as the bird begins to sizzle and the dressing starts to bake. When Mom opened the oven for the basting in the last hour, I would almost be knocked over by the beckoning aroma of sausage, onion, and sage drenched in turkey fat drippings. A turkey never tastes as good as it smells just before your mother takes it out of the oven.

When Maureen and Helen Kay were young, my dad helped Mom avoid the hard work of cooking on Thanksgiving by ordering a turkey and the fixings from Mrs. Ormsby. But it didn't feel like Thanksgiving because the kitchen didn't smell like Thanksgiving. Even though Mrs. Ormsby was a fine cook, Thanksgiving dinner doesn't taste the same without those familiar smells.

By the time I was twelve, however, Mom was back cooking Thanksgiving dinner, and Thanksgiving was restored to its rightful place as the first holiday.

I also liked Thanksgiving because I got a chance to hang out with the adults. As the potatoes were boiling, the butternut squash was simmering, and the turkey was being carved, the three adults would engage in spirited conversation.

"Say, Helen," Dad fired at Hunnah in an accusatory tone, "what's this about another postage stamp increase?"

"Look, Harry," Hunnah shot back, "we have the cheapest and most efficient postal service in the world. The problem is that third class mail gets such a cheap rate. First class subsidizes all that junk mail."

"We ought to allow private companies and the post office to compete against each other," Dad rejoined. He never let up when he could tweak his opponent.

"Sure, and you'd end up with a mess like the phone companies," shot back the experienced defender of what she proudly told her nephew and nieces was one of the first Cabinet departments established by the new federal government over 150 years ago.

"Can't you two ever argue about anything else?" Mom asked, as she lit her Kent cigarette and nursed her Grant's Scotch and soda.

If it wasn't the performance of the post office, the three of them debated politics (whether John Fitzgerald Kennedy would win the Democratic presidential nomination), religion (the reason for the sharp decline in Catholic vocations), meat quality and prices (Miller's versus Zane's Markets), and, of course, the weather (snow predictions and the need for a new furnace).

I sat transfixed, absorbing every word while snacking on handfuls of Planter's mixed nuts, Wrigley's potato chips, and cheese puffs. Sometimes I would sneak into the living room and watch some of the Detroit Lions football game. I'm sure that this isn't true, but I could swear that the Lions only played football on Thanksgiving in a blizzard.

As I watched the game, I would sip eggnog. I loved the rich, creamy feel and the cinnamon and nutmeg taste of this drink. I often wondered why it was served only between Thanksgiving and New Year's Day. It's a good thing that you couldn't get it year round because I would have weighed twice as much as I did.

We usually ate around four in the afternoon. For some reason I never knew, the family always sat in the same places every Thanksgiving. Dad and mom were at the heads, mom closest to the kitchen. Hunnah sat to mom's right, Helen Kay to mom's left. In between Helen Kay and Mary Eileen was Maureen. I sat opposite Mary Eileen, to my father's left and Hunnah's right.

These were the preordained positions, and any attempted change was met with loud resistance. When my father's Aunt Katie O'Shea, who raised two of his sisters and him when they left the orphanage, came to live and die with us, there was a lot of hushed conversation in the kitchen about where she would sit for the Thanksgiving meal. (She ended up between Hunnah and me.)

Once the table was brimming with the food, Dad would lead us in the blessing—the "Bless Us O'Lord" grace that Catholics mumble by rote. Mom and Dad washed down their food with a bottle of Dad's best champagne from the store. Hunnah might take a sip or two, but she wasn't much of a drinker.

The kids got to drink milk or water, although I remember one year that Dad surprised us with fake champagne—some bubbly apple cider drink. My sisters and I all thought we were grown-ups, toasting each other, clicking our glasses, and pretending to be tipsy. Little Maureen giggled so much that she got a bad case of the hiccups.

Mom insisted that we eat all the food on our plates. "Remember the starving children in India" was her favorite slogan, followed by "Waste not, want not." When one of my sisters claimed to be full, Hunnah would chime in, "Your eyes are bigger than your stomach." She never said that to me, though.

The truth was that I liked to eat. There was nothing on the Thanksgiving table that I didn't really enjoy. For that matter, I can recall very few things that my mom or Hunnah ever prepared that I didn't like. Oh, maybe lima beans, but even they tasted pretty good when mixed in with your mashed potatoes and gravy.

No one thought much about dieting when I was young. The fact that my "baby fat" lingered into the second decade of my life did not seem to trouble my parents. Cutting back on fatty and fried foods, sugar, beef, or total calories was hardly discussed. The Kane family tended to be overweight, and my fit and trim father never harped on me losing weight.

Dieting and Thanksgiving at the O'Donnells were never mentioned in the same breath. I was good for at least two rounds of everything on the table—except the stuffing, which I might eat alone for a third helping. Then came Hunnah's homemade delights: pumpkin, apple, and pecan pie topped off with whipped cream or Sealtest vanilla ice cream. Dad had a sweet tooth and was always good for seconds on the ice cream. Mom and Dad would then top off the meal with crème de menthe over crushed ice that made their tongues turn green.

After all that Thanksgiving feasting, there was only one thing left to do: take a nap. Just as soon as we had cleared the table and finished our chores, I headed for the front parlor, closed the partition and shut out the world. By now, it was after six o'clock and dark outside. My stomach was full, and I'd quickly become drowsy reading a book.

I'd fall asleep for several hours, usually awakening after the rest of the house had gone to bed. But I couldn't sleep, so I'd sit in the parlor, surrounded by paintings of Nora (the resident ghost!), monks hoisting beer mugs in a medieval monastery, and a late nineteenth century winter scene of a horse drawn sleigh gliding down a starlit country road.

My mind would drift back to a simpler time. Averill Park in the mid-nineteenth century when the Kanes settled in a sleepy hamlet with a one-room schoolhouse, a glass factory, blacksmith, and woolen knit mills. Electric lighting, the automobile, and the telephone had not yet been invented. One year, I imagined that I was a driver of a horse-drawn carriage, another a farmer, and a third a bartender in a country saloon.

As I got older, went off to college and then started a family, Thanksgiving continued to be my favorite holiday. I became my dad, carving the succulent turkey, leading the blessing, and toasting everyone around the dining table laden with the same gastronomic delights from my boyhood. The one thing that I didn't do, however, was go ice skating with my kids.

18.
"WHAT DID YOUR MOTHER SAY?"

Most kids, if they're lucky, have a mother when growing up. The O'Donnell kids were super lucky. We had two moms…at the same time. Let me explain.

My mother had a younger sister, Helen Theresa Kane whom I nicknamed "Hunnah" by mispronouncing her name when I started talking. Mom and Hunnah were raised in our home that dated back to 1850. They grew up middle class and happy in the 1920s.

I never knew any of my Irish-American grandparents. My mom told me that Grandpa Pierce Daniel Kane, her dad and my namesake, had several different jobs. Besides selling insurance, he was a "Railroad Dick"—a detective or guard or something like that for the New York Central. Grandma Helen Elizabeth Kane, their mother, worked for a while in the accounting department at Frear's department store in Troy. For a long time after the first Kane emigrated from Ireland during the Potato Famine in the late 1840s, the Kane family had owned and operated woolen knit mills in the area, making uniforms for the Union Army.

My sisters believe that mom's parents brewed their own beer during Prohibition, and they made dandelion wine in the bathtub. Grandma Kane was frugal; she taught her daughters the art of leftovers. Mom told us that her father wanted to buy a car, but her mother killed the idea and instead used the money for indoor plumbing and toilets.

Grandpa Kane had a hard time finding work during the dark days of the Great Depression. That was before President Franklin D. Roosevelt in 1935 appointed him postmaster of our little "Third Class" post office in Averill Park. The job, with good pay for the times, was a coveted patronage position, a reward for being a loyal (and lonely) Democrat in an overwhelmingly Republican town. Hunnah and mom always had a roof over their head, good food on the table, and loving parents who raised their daughters in the Catholic faith and instilled a commitment to responsible citizenship and charity.

When Grandpa Kane died in 1938, President Roosevelt named Grandma Kane the postmaster, and when she died in 1944, my mom's sister, Helen Kane, got the job from President Roosevelt. A Kane was postmaster in Averill Park for forty-five years. I always wondered if that meant that one of my sisters or I would be postmaster someday.

Hunnah and mom were always close, sharing a dog and playmates as kids and hanging out together at the beaches on Crystal, Glass, Crooked, and Burden Lakes, sledding, ice skating, and local dances. They loved to read and trade books back and forth. Their tastes ran from classics like *Huckleberry Finn*, *Little Women*, and *The Secret Garden* to historical novels like *Ivanhoe*, *A Tale of Two Cities*, and *The Three Musketeers*. Hunnah particularly liked stories about the lives of the saints, while mom was into anything Shakespeare and O'Neill.

One day I found a copy of *Ulysses* by James Joyce in the back parlor bookcase. "What is this book about?" I asked mom.

"Well..." she paused longer than usual in answering some of my questions. "The author is a famous Irish writer."

"Okay, I figured that out," I replied, "but what does he write about? What is the story?"

"It's...it's about three people in Dublin and what they do and say in one day," she answered.

"Man, that must have been one long day," I fired back. "The book is over seven hundred pages!"

"*Ulysses* is one of the greatest novels of the twentieth century," she explained.

"Well, maybe I should read it," I suggested.

"Uh, uh," mom stammered, "let's wait until you're a little older."

What I later learned explained everything: *Ulysses* had been banned as obscene by the government until 1933 and could not be legally imported from Ireland to the United States. My mother's copy had been smuggled into the country after the ban but years before it was lifted. Mom was a literary rebel.

When I was growing up, the kitchen was the epicenter of our home; cooking and eating were central to an Irish-American family. My sisters and I would often gather in the kitchen—the smallest room in the house—with mom and Hunnah, drawn there by the irresistible aromas of slow-roasted beef and pork or brownies and rhubarb pie.

My mother had some terrific specialties: pork chops with Spanish rice and tomatoes; baked ham and sweet potatoes; roast leg of lamb, onions, and potatoes; and liver, bacon, and onions. Her turkey stuffing, a recipe that went back to Ireland, was to die for. The smell of dinner cooking greeted you at the front door, luring you deeper into the house, your nose leading the way. If I was lucky, I would be mom's taster.

"Excellent, mom," I always said as I sampled one of her delicacies. "But, you know, I better try another taste just to be sure that it's done."

"Get out of here!" mom would playfully say. "You'll ruin your appetite"

"Mom's the cook, and Hunnah's the baker," Helen Kay told us one day. "We have to eat what mom cooks, but we WANT to eat what Hunnah bakes."

Hunnah had a magic touch with a mixing bowl and oven. Using handwritten recipes in a card file box handed down from her mother, who got many of them from her mother, Hunnah could bake and cook almost anything. She perfected apple pie (with apples from our three apple trees), corn bread, tapioca pudding, fudge, lemon bundt cake, chocolate cookies, penuche, and my sisters' birthday cakes. My sisters drooled when Hunnah baked chocolate cake with mocha frosting, made by adding leftover morning coffee and chocolate to vanilla frosting. I was a hold out, still preferring my Freihofer's special order birthday cake.

During the week, we would put in our order for what we wanted Hunnah to bake on the weekend.

"I want oatmeal cookies," Maureen would announce,

"No, it's my turn," Helen Kay would interject. "I want rice pudding."

Then Mary Eileen and I would shout our demands. I always went for the tapioca pudding, hot off the stove with sprinkled cinnamon, while Mary Eileen loved blueberry muffins made with fresh blueberries picked by us.

"Okay, okay," Hunnah would finally say. "What do you think this is—a bakery?"

Four kids vigorously nodded their heads.

Monday through Friday, our family ate dinner together—except Dad, who ate the same meal that the kids brought to him at the nearby store on a tray covered by aluminum foil to keep the food warm. We always waited for Hunnah to get home from the post office a few minutes after six o'clock. If the weather was bad, I'd walk the quarter of a mile and accompany her home.

Our dinner conversations were lively. Before we dove into the salad, baked chicken, roast, or creamed cod fish (my favorite Friday dish), vegetables (broccoli, green beans, and steamed carrots were regulars), potatoes (baked, boiled, mashed, browned), and rolls and butter, we would say the traditional grace: "Bless us, O Lord, and these Thy gifts, which we are about to receive from Thy bounty, through Christ our Lord. Amen."

Mom would go around the table and ask the kids and Hunnah to name one thing for which we were grateful that day. Sometimes I would get stumped.

"Uh, you know—Mom," I'd start.

"No, Pierce, I don't know," she'd fire back. "Please share with us."

My sisters would start giggling, enjoying the sport of Big Brother on the hot seat.

After a long pause, I'd go to my default answer: "I'm so grateful that…the sun came up this morning."

Hunnah would scowl, while Mom just shrugged her shoulders.

My aunt always had something thoughtful or kind to say. One of the most memorable was: "I thank God that I can live in this country, town, and home with the people who I love and who love me."

Sometimes Hunnah was more practical: "I'm grateful that we found the missing package of bird seed for Mrs. Hunt. She was driving me nuts."

"Where did you find it?" Mary Eileen wanted to know.

"On her front porch, where my mailman left it!" Hunnah replied with a look of annoyance on her face.

Hunnah and mom were the food police. If any of the kids did not finish everything on our dinner plate, we'd hear: "Eat all your food. Children are starving in India." Sometimes they'd issue this order in unison.

I always thought that I had a weight problem because I had to eat what I was served. Then one day Hunnah set me straight about portion control.

"Your problem is that you're a pelican," she'd say. "Your eyes are bigger than your stomach." Now that was saying a lot about a kid whose belly hung over his pants.

Dinner was followed by the evening rosary. All of us would gather on our knees around mom's bed and say the rosary. Hunnah was really good at the rosary, often leading us in the repetitive praying. I didn't lead much because I had a problem with my chubby fingers and the little beads on the string, causing me to miscount.

"That was only nine," Bubsy loved to correct me. "When are you going to learn to count?"

"When are you going to learn to shut up?" I shot back, sometimes elbowing her in the side.

"Mommy, Pierce hit me!" she would cry out.

"Leave my little sister alone," demanded Helen Kay as she comforted "the victim."

"You're a troublemaker, Pierce," Mary Eileen interjected, never wanting to be left out of a good sibling brawl.

"Stop it! Stop it!" Mom would shout. "All of you, and be reverent. This is the same as being in church."

My mother was a very smart woman, but I always thought comparing her bed to an altar was a stretch.

Everyone in town said that Hunnah was a terrific postmaster. It helps that her parents had once served Averill Park as postmasters, and that Hunnah had an awesome memory.

"Excuse me, ma'am," I once heard a man ask Hunnah at the post office counter. "Can you tell me where Mrs. Weatherwax lives?"

"Which one?" Hunnah asked. "Harriet, Cynthia, or Marjorie?"

"I'm not sure," he responded.

"Well, let's see," Hunnah replied. "Harriet is a widow, Cynthia is her daughter, and Marjorie is Harriet's deceased husband's sister."

A lost letter or parcel triggered a manhunt. Hunnah prided herself on the quality and efficiency of service offered by the post office. In those days, the mail was hand sorted with some put in mailboxes in the lobby and the rest delivered by a rural mailman in a car. Usually, the letter or parcel wasn't lost forever—just "misdirected" in Hunnah's words.

Every now and then, Hunnah let me sort some of the mail. I had to stand on a wooden box to reach the slots on the top of the sorting rack. My career as a mail boy didn't last long.

"Hunnah," I'd shout across the room. "Mr. Jones is in Miami visiting his son whose wife just had a baby."

"Pierce, how many times do I have to tell you not to read people's postcards?"

My next job was putting envelopes through the machine that canceled the stamps at a fast pace. Taking a handful of envelopes, I'd feed them into the feeder. One day, I was wearing a shirt, the sleeves of which were longer than usual. As I turned to say something to Warren, one of the mailmen returning from his delivery route, disaster struck: my shirt cuff got caught in the feeder, yanking me toward the machine, envelopes flying in the air.

"Oh my God!" Hunnah yelled as she ran over to turn off the sorter.

"What happened?" I asked, startled but unhurt.

"You tried to mail yourself," Warren joked.

"Why don't you go over to your dad's store," Hunnah suggested. "I'm sure he could use some help."

That was the last time that I was allowed behind the counter. Hunnah canceled my budding postal career, "promoting" me to sweeping the lobby floor, burning the trash, and getting coffee for her clerks, Claire Healy and Jeanne Wilkens, and her.

As a friend of the post office, I was entitled to buy first edition stamps for my stamp collection. In 1959 alone, I bought Oregon Statehood (four cents), Abraham Lincoln (one cent), Jose de San Martin (eight cents), and Arctic Explorations (four cents). For one of my birthdays, Hunnah gave me a catalogue for holding my stamps, and she would give me old stamps for my collection. I couldn't believe my eyes one birthday when she gave me an 1894 Ben Franklin (one cent) and a 1922 Teddy Roosevelt (five cents).

No one loved the postal service more than Hunnah. She was a cheerleader, never missing an opportunity to praise the men and women who delivered the mail. Framed on the wall next to her desk was the post office's motto: "Neither snow nor rain nor heat nor gloom of night stays these couriers from the swift completion of their appointed rounds."

Hunnah wanted to impress upon her nephew and nieces the post office's awesome history.

"Benjamin Franklin was the first postmaster general when America was still thirteen colonies," Hunnah liked to tell us, beaming from ear to ear, her lovely brown eyes aglow.

"And guess which president was a postmaster in his early life?" she asked us one day.

"George Washington," I blurted out.

"Nah," said Mary Eileen, "he chopped down a cherry tree."

"Why would anyone kill a poor cherry tree," Helen Kay wanted to know.

"President Abraham Lincoln ran a post office for a while," Hunnah proudly announced.

No one defended the postal service more than Hunnah. Always protective of the oldest federal government agency, she did not appreciate any criticisms or teasing.

"Helen," Dad would begin. "I heard the post office just delivered Japan's surrender."

"Harry, that's not funny," Hunnah would reply, taking the bait every time.

"I'm so sorry," Dad responded, pretending to be sincere. "I was mistaken—it was Germany's surrender."

On the same day every month, my *Boy's Life* magazine arrived at the post office. I lived for that day, eager to explore the world outside Averill Park and progress as a Boy Scout. When it didn't come on the usual day of the month, I'd run up to the post office.

"Hunnah! Hunnah!" I'd yell at the counter, out of breath from the short run from my house. "Where's my *Boy's Life*?"

"It's obviously late," she'd patiently reply.

"Gee, why is it always my magazine that's late?" I'd want to know, believing that everyone else's mail in the country was always delivered on time.

"I'm sure there's a good reason why your *Boy's Life* isn't here yet," she'd calmly explain. "Did you ever think that maybe it was delayed at Boy Scout headquarters in New Jersey and not in the mail?"

The problem with Hunnah was that she was so reasonable.

When I was a little kid, the post office occupied a portion of the first floor of an old building next to the Park Pharmacy. It was the same location where Hunnah's parents had served as postmaster. The building was run down, badly insulated, and unimpressive. The floors creaked, the roof leaked, and the lobby was only slightly larger than a confessional.

Hunnah vowed to get a new post office. For a long time, she got nowhere. The men who ran the post office didn't pay attention to a rural, third-class post office—especially one run by a woman. That was a mistake!

Using her network of long-time friends in the state and national postmasters' associations; persistently lobbying local, state, and national public officials; and making a trip to Washington, DC, at her own expense, Hunnah finally got her new post office. I think they agreed to build a new one just to get her off their back. Don't mess with a first-class postmaster protecting her precious third class post office!

I'll never forget the dedication ceremony. I was an eager Cub Scout, and our Pack was invited to be part of the celebration.

"Pierce, I spoke to your leaders," Hunnah told me the day before, "and you have been selected to carry the American flag tomorrow."

"Really? Really?" I wanted to know. "For sure, Hunnah?"

"Yes, Mrs. Dick says that you've earned the honor with your hard work and leadership."

I ran over and hugged Hunnah for what seemed like an hour. I couldn't believe my ears. Nothing as awesome as this had ever happened to me in my entire life…of ten years.

I didn't get much sleep the night before the big day. But I was ready. I had walked around the house practicing being a flag carrier. Dad gave me some pointers, and Mary Eileen helped me get my yellow kerchief rolled up correctly.

They say that it was unusually cold that day, even for Averill Park. You couldn't prove it by me. All I felt was the warmth inside of me knowing that I was doing something special in front of over one hundred people and helping Hunnah celebrate her brand new post office.

Hunnah didn't travel much, but twice a year she went to the conventions of her postmasters' associations. She'd go to places like Boston, Cleveland, Chicago, New York City, Saratoga Springs, Philadelphia, Miami, Washington, DC, and Denver. Hunnah had good friends who were postmasters all over the country, and they looked forward to these business trips that were more like reunions. My sisters and I couldn't wait for Hunnah to return because she always brought us lots of "swag" such as pens, coffee cups, pencils, glasses, bowls, flashlights, note pads, and hats—all inscribed with her organizations' names and logos.

One summer day, my sisters and I were hanging out in the kitchen while mom was shucking corn. I asked a question that we'd been debating among ourselves for quite some time.

"Why hasn't Hunnah gotten married?"

My mother didn't answer right away. You could see that she was thinking hard about her answer.

"Oh, I don't really know," mom finally responded. "I guess that she wasn't lucky like me and never met the right guy."

"Did she ever have a boyfriend?" Helen Kay wondered.

"Well…I know one boy who was crazy about your aunt," mom told us.

"Who? Who?" Maureen was eager to learn.

"You know who Jerry Lewis is, right?"

We all nodded our heads. Who didn't know about the funniest actor on TV and in the movies!

"Didn't he used to live across the street for a while?" Mary Eileen asked.

"Yes, indeed," Mom answered, "and he had a real crush on Hunnah, but my sister was so shy. When Jerry frequently came to the front door asking for her, she'd run out the back door."

When I asked Hunnah about Lewis, she'd shake her head. "He scared me, Pierce. He was crazy."

What a shame, I said to myself. If Hunnah had married Jerry Lewis, he'd be my uncle, and I could have gotten free movie tickets.

Hunnah would have made a terrific wife for a lucky guy. We know what she would be like as a mother…because she was a mother for four very fortunate children. I don't mean that she supplanted our mother—no one ever could. Hunnah supplemented Mom in so many ways that enriched our childhood.

If I had to sum up my Aunt Hunnah in only one word, I'd say "kind." Hunnah was nice, but she was so much more than that: kindness personified how she lived her life. *Webster's Second* draws a noteworthy distinction between nice ("pleasing, agreeable, delightful"), but she was much more—she was kind ("having, showing, or proceeding from benevolence").

Hunnah would do anything for her sister's children—from helping Helen Kay and Maureen pick out their outfits for parties or school dances to helping with homework to consoling me when I was down in the dumps because I had been bullied or didn't make a team or get picked to play touch football or sandlot baseball. Mary Eileen would have Hunnah help her with the lines for some school play. (Mary Eileen was very talented even as an eleven year old). It is impossible to recount all that Hunnah did for us, but the most lasting memory is that she never turned us away.

When any of us needed comforting or just a good hug, Hunnah was always there for us. Her room was a sanctuary of serenity. Our beloved aunt had this indescribable calmness that radiated all around her, healing our distress and uplifting our spirits. Mom stimulated our minds, while Hunnah nurtured our souls.

Not every night but often enough, we would retreat to her second-floor haven when my mom and dad were having some quiet time together or they were arguing downstairs (often about one of us) or when we wanted to watch TV after finishing homework. While Hunnah sat in her easy chair gently rocking back and forth, four rambunctious kids would flop on her bed, jockeying for position and arguing about which show to watch on her black and white TV with spotty reception.

"Hunnah, can we watch "Dobie Gillis?" Helen Kay asked.

"That Maynard G. Krebs is a wacko," Mary Eileen chimed in. "I want *The Twilight Zone*."

"No, please!" Maureen pleaded. "That's too scary. I like *The Flintstones*."

I didn't really care. While I preferred shows like *Gunsmoke, Alfred Hitchcock Presents,* and *Perry Mason*, I was outnumbered. TV was just an escape for an hour or so, and I preferred to read a book.

My sisters loved to play "dress up" with Hunnah. They'd put on her dresses, scarfs, furs, sweaters, hats, and jewelry—all way too big for them—and parade around the room like mini-adults.

"Hello, Mrs. Boobyhead," Mary Eileen would say to Hunnah, falling out of her shoes and tripping on the flowing gown."

"Excuse me," Maureen would interject as she kept trying to get the oversized plumed hat off her eyes and bumping into the door.

Helen Kay was more cautious, preferring oodles of jewelry, mink stoles, and colorful scarves.

Hunnah would laugh her head off.

"Just think," Hunnah would say, not able to contain herself. "I don't have to go to New York or Paris to see the latest fashions!"

Hunnah was shrewd. At various times, each of us would run up to her room and ask her for permission to do something, like sleep over at a friend's house or buying a new baseball bat or spend a summer night outdoors in a makeshift tent under the apple trees. Every time, Hunnah would reply, "What did your mother say?"

That would be the end of that matter because she knew that mom had already nixed the idea. No appeals from her sister's decisions. The last thing that Hunnah would do is contradict her sister.

But every now and then, she would come to our aid if mom had not already ruled on the matter. I remember one instance, when I was only ten, and I wanted to go up to the firehouse.

"Hunnah, what do you think about me checking out that brand new Mack fire truck that just arrived," I asked.

"What did you mother say?" Hunnah asked as usual.

"I haven't asked her yet." I answered. "I'm afraid she'll say 'no.'"

"Why?" Hunnah wanted to know.

"Because she'll probably think I'll be a pest and get in the way," I explained.

"Tell you what, I'll call my friend, Chief Logan, to see if it's okay," she offered. "And then if he says 'yes,' I'll tell your mom that you have permission."

Mom let me go, Mr. Logan gave me a ride on the Mack, and he allowed me to blast the horn. That was one of the happiest days of my young life. Even at that age, I realized that Hunnah was not only kind—she was one clever woman.

Hunnah was also funny. She subscribed to magazines with jokes, and she would read with us the Sunday comic strips. We loved "Peanuts" (adorable Snoopy), "Dick Tracy" (with his two-way wrist radio), and "Dennis the Menace" (poor Mr. Wilson!). On my own, I read "Beetle Bailey," set on a fictional Army base (Camp Swampy) and inhabited by a bunch of misfit soldiers like lazy private Beetle Bailey, his bossy Sergeant First Class Orville P. Snorkel, and frustrated boozer Brigadier General Amos T. Halftrack. I would often tell my dad about the characters' zany antics.

"Dad, was Fort Dix like Camp Swampy?" I'd tease him.

"No, Swampy has running water, heat, and toilets!" Dad would joke.

Having a second mom had other benefits. Like presents. Whenever we had a birthday, First Communion, Confirmation, and graduation, Mom and Dad gave us a present. And Hunnah would always attend and also give us a present! Sometimes they didn't coordinate the gifts. One birthday, I got two fishing nets!

Hunnah was a devout, old-school Catholic who attended Mass every Sunday and Holy Days of Obligation, didn't eat meat on Friday, read her prayer book daily, and regularly went to confession. She freaked out if one of us "used the Lord's name in vain" or balked at saying the family rosary. She rarely missed the witty Bishop Fulton J. Sheen on TV. ("Hearing nuns' confessions is like being stoned to death with popcorn.") Priest and nuns were entitled to great respect, and Hunnah could not tolerate any criticisms of Holy Mother Church.

Hunnah lived her faith, supporting an assortment of charities, both Catholic and nonprofit. She donated money for the construction of the K through fourth St. Henry's parochial school, the Averill Park Volunteer Fire Department, eradication of muscular dystrophy (Jerry Lewis's cause!), CARE, literacy, and her alma mater Russell Sage College (a women's college founded in 1916 by a suffragist). Anonymously, she fed, clothed, and bought medicine for the poor.

Hunnah may have been the most trusted person in our town. During World War II, she distributed ration books to local families. The ration books contained removable stamps needed to purchase certain scarce items such as sugar, meat, canned goods, and cooking oil. Hunnah was the person who counted the Mass collections on Sunday (assisted by Helen Kay), and she handled the money at Friday night bingo at the firehouse. (Sometimes, she'd take me with her, introducing me to lemon meringue pie and fried chicken.)

If Helen Kane was your friend, you could count your blessings. She had her high school classmate Katherine Sowalsky, coworker Claire Healy, Dorothy Barnum, and Helen Pausley.

These lifetime friends got together on weekends for lunch in Troy or Albany or a day trip to Saratoga or the Berkshires. The conversation was lively—lots of talk about fashion, food, births, and deaths. Given the mix of party loyalties, the political debates could get rough.

"That Kennedy fellow is too young to be President," Dorothy Barnum, a devout Republican and Methodist claimed.

"You mean too Catholic!" Katherine Sowalsky, a devout St. Henry's parishioner, said.

"Ladies, ladies," Helen Pausley intervened. "Let's not spoil a nice lunch talking about all this political nonsense."

Hunnah kept her own thoughts.

"No one is going to persuade anyone," she told me. "After years and years of voting Republican or Democrat, people don't change."

Hunnah was a card player (she taught me gin rummy), and she had a regular card game with her friend Bess O'Brien. A smoker and scotch drinker, Bess seemed to have endless energy. We weren't sure about her age.

"Ninety going on thirty," Dad suggested. "Don't let the wrinkles on her face and cane fool you."

Whatever her age, Bess was young at heart—a regular party girl.

"I never turn down a social engagement," I heard her tell Hunnah once.

"Don't you get tired of going out all the time?" Hunnah asked.

"Sure, Helen," Bess responded, "But, you know, if you don't say 'yes,' they stop inviting you."

When I got older, I thought about Hunnah's friend's philosophy. It was nice to be wanted, but at what price? Hunnah had it right all along: be yourself and your friends will be your friends because of who you are and what you stand for.

19.

EATING MY WAY ACROSS TROY

WHEN YOU LIVE IN Averill Park, Troy is the big city. Going to Troy was easy for most kids. Both their mother and father had a driver's license. But not the O'Donnells. Mom never learned to drive, Hunnah refused even to try, and Dad worked Monday through Saturday, thirteen hours a day, leaving little time to ferry his kids here and there. And Troy was closed tighter than a drum on Sunday, open only for church-going and stopping at the corner Italian bakery for sweet rolls for breakfast after services.

So, other than the occasional kindness of neighbors, the United Traction Company bus was our only means of getting to Troy.

Some of my earliest memories involve going to Troy with my mother on the bus. It always seemed like an adventure, especially when mom had all four kids in tow, it was twenty degrees above zero, Mary Eileen wanted to sit by herself, Helen Kay wanted to know why she couldn't stay home with a girlfriend, and six-year-old Maureen wanted to crawl all over the bus.

One of the bus stops was right in front of my dad's store on Main Street. As the bus arrived, we would get a warm send-off from my father, including fifty cents each for spending money. The bus fare was sixty-five cents each way (we used prepurchased tokens), and there were never more than a dozen people on the bus until we got closer to Troy.

This bus was the only means of public transportation to Troy. Years earlier, there had been a trolley—called the Troy and New England Railway—that ran between 1895 and 1925. I always thought its name was curious since it didn't go all the way to Troy and never made it to New England. The large red trolley car barn, a stone's throw from my home, now housed Tremont Lumber.

Compensating for not being able to drive a car, Mom became a veteran bus rider. She memorized all the schedules and never missed a bus in all the years that my sisters and I traveled with her to Troy. A few times, we ventured on the bus all the way to Albany, the state capital, which had the great state library and museums.

The bus traveled a serpentine route of about ten miles from Gifford's Market in Glass Lake to downtown Troy. Along the way, it proceeded down Route 43 through Sand Lake, past Nash's Store and post office and the old High School, into the Averill Park Village, continuing on Route 43 at the junction with Route 66, past Lake Pharmacy and Mobil gas station, Fireman's Pond, St. Henry's Cemetery, the new high school, and my friend Bob Hill's house, into the West Sand Lake Village, right onto Route 150, past St, Mary's of the Wood's Chapel, through Snyder's Lake, into Wynantskill, past Albia, the Miss Troy Diner, St. Jude's Catholic Church, and Vanderheyden Hall orphanage, and then down into Troy on the east bank of the Hudson River. The trip took about an hour, with the bus making about twenty stops along the scenic route.

We seemed to have the same bus drivers year in and year out. Friendly, and usually overweight, they were addicted to coffee and cigarettes. Cheerfully, the men—with names like Louie, Al, and Ray—gave directions, helped old ladies on and off the bus, and reassured young passengers traveling alone for the first time. I always felt safe and welcome on those big, smoke-spewing red and silver buses.

The bus drivers must have been among the most patient men in the world. I liked to sit up front, across from the driver, right next to the forward door. From there, I had an excellent vantage point to see what was happening up the road and back in the bus. It was also a perfect spot from which to talk the bus driver's ear off. I had no trouble sustaining a conversation from Averill Park to Troy, peppering the driver with countless questions.

"Did you have to go to school to learn to drive a bus?"

"What's diesel fuel?"

"Have you ever had an accident?"

"Pierce, you're an amazing kid," one driver once remarked. "I've been driving you for two years, and you've never repeated the same question."

I wasn't sure if he was complimenting me.

One of the drivers was an amateur local historian. I remember him telling stories about several the houses and buildings along the route; some events dated back to the Revolutionary War and the days of the first Dutch settlements three hundred years earlier. He was particularly knowledgeable about murder scenes. One remote house on a hill, he reported, had a gruesome double murder.

The victims were tied up in the basement, hanging by their feet from the beams, their throats slit like pigs, and their lifeless bodies reflected in the pool of blood a few feet below their heads. For months afterward, I would dream about that grisly scene, each time waking up as I walked into the basement and discovered the horrifying scene.

The buses were sturdy vehicles that rarely broke down. One time, however, during a driving snowstorm (that's one where you shouldn't be driving), the bus slid off the road into a ditch. We were several miles from Averill Park, it was dark outside, and there were only a few passengers. But the driver kept his cool.

Another passenger and I lit a flare and diverted traffic around the accident scene. The driver managed to commandeer two tow trucks, which—after several attempts—miraculously pulled the heavy bus out of the ditch. I got home an hour late that night, but I had a great tale to tell my family and friends.

Troy was a mid-size city of some fifty thousand people whose forebears came primarily from Italy, Ireland, Germany, France, the Netherlands, and Great Britain. The city prospered for a while. In the mid–1800s, Troy was the sixteenth largest and fourth wealthiest city per capita in young America. For almost a century, the city was booming with manufacturing iron, steel, shirts, shirtwaists, collars, and cuffs, earning it the moniker "The Collar City." One notable local industry was the Burden Horseshoe Factory, where fifty-one million horseshoes—one every second—were manufactured; a blacksmith could make only four horseshoes per hour.

By the late 1950s, Troy's once distinct neighborhoods were transitioning from ethnic enclaves to being a melting pot. The housing stock was old. With a declining and less affluent population, Troy was already in the midst of an economic slide that would eventually destroy the city's shopping district along the Hudson as consumers flocked to suburban shopping centers and city dwellers exited to new suburban communities. The telltale signs of a dying city surrounded a young boy as he walked the downtown streets: closed shops; lots of "going out of business" sales; long-abandoned, decaying manufacturing buildings along the Hudson River; and a gloomy atmosphere.

You could hear dejected people at the lunch counters and bus stops:

"Did you hear that Earl's Knitwear closed?"

"Yeah, another abandoned store and ten more people out of work."

"They laid off seventy-five people at the Watervliet Arsenal."

"I heard. What's happening to this city?"

Each year that I went to Troy, the decline and despair became more evident. By the mid-1960s, much of downtown Troy looked like a ghost town with more and more boarded up shop fronts, closed department stores and movie theatres, rising unemployment, and a defeatist attitude among the people. The post-World War II surge of jobs and consumer income that most of America experienced bypassed Troy—the city that prosperity forgot.

The situation got so bad that in the 1960s, the city fathers tore down a large portion of historic downtown in anticipation of receiving a Great Society urban renewal grant. The city center looked like Dresden. The only problem was that the federal funding never materialized. Troy lost its great old buildings and its soul.

In my early youth, the bus trips to Troy were for the purpose of visiting Dr. Cavanaugh, my pediatrician. A friendly Irish-American with the patience of Job, he had offices in a brownstone on tree-lined Fifth Avenue, one of the posher neighborhoods. He had real lace curtains—a symbol of having arrived for the Irish—and his waiting room had a distinctive smell of cabbage from the kitchen in the back of the house. Dr. Cavanaugh always gave me a pat on the head and a lollipop.

As a young boy, I also traveled to Troy for chest X-rays at the Rensselaer County Health Department. I had a bad cough, and Dr. Cavanaugh sent me to the red brick building on the hill overlooking the city. The X-ray found some tiny spots on my lungs. All I remember is that I had to make periodic visits to this bleak place with its white walls, cheerless staff, and frigid x-ray machine that made my skin crawl when it pressed against my husky chest. After several years of this torture every few months, the spots disappeared, and I gladly never returned.

Most of my visits to the Home of Uncle Sam—where JFK and Nixon campaigned in 1960 and Kurt Vonnegut wrote several of his novels—were happy occasions.

History fascinated me. Our gifted teachers taught much more than memorizing wars, dates, and the boring succession of presidents and monarchs. We also explored causes and lasting effects of famines, revolutions, and migration. We discussed the rich diversity of heritages, understanding the formative blend of ethnicity, religion, race, family, and place. We identified ourselves as Irish-Americans or African-American, an O'Donnell from County Donegal or Asante from Ghana, and Catholic or Jewish. History was the chronicle of how people lived, died, and worked, as well as entertained and governed themselves.

I walked my way across Troy.

Troy became my living history lesson, a journey back in time when immigrants, yearning for a better life for their families, flooded the Upper Hudson River Valley, and education, hard work, and pluck were the essential rungs on the stepladder out of poverty. During my frequent Saturday visits, I walked through different old neighborhoods and commercial districts, parks and cemeteries, trying to visualize the people and daily life based on my understanding from studying the city's rise, prosperity, and decline. Troy's celebrated architecture—sprawling Victorian homes and belle époque buildings—were treasures from a bygone era when Troy flourished during the Industrial Revolution.

My walks featured imposing memorials to fallen warriors in Monument Square, elegant brownstones on Fifth Avenue, Rensselaer Polytechnic Institute up on the hill, rotting wharves and the Terminal Warehouse on the polluted Hudson River, a long-shuttered Fitzgerald Bros. Brewery, and Thomas's Tavern, Hendrick Hudson Hotel, Troy Music Hall, W. & L. E. Gurley Building, F. W. Woolworth Co., and the Army-Navy store (where I bought Army patches, fatigues, and a surplus canteen). As I strolled through this outdoor museum, I imagined scruffy, boisterous children dodging horse-drawn liveries on cobblestone city streets; elderly war veterans, wearing their uniforms with justifiable pride, marching on Memorial Day; and trains delivering wool for the knitting mills and iron and coal for the steel mills. I could hear the hustle and bustle of trolleys and pushcarts, smell the manure offset by roasted chestnuts, and climb aboard an antique fire truck, pretending to take my crew to a burning tenement.

One aspect of Troy in the late fifties I did not have to imagine. In the early days of my Saturday walks, I'd go down River Street and then walk along the Hudson River banks. The sight was disgusting: dead dogs, cats, rats—and human feces—floating in the murky water. The nasty, putrid smell, especially on a hot summer day, was overpowering. The Hudson River was unfit for swimming, fishing, and drinking. After a while, I took the river off my route.

I talked my way across Troy.

No walk would be complete without engaging all kinds of fascinating people in conversation. I was Harry O'Donnell's son, and I had an unnatural curiosity about the world around me. Whether it was a German cobbler's shop, Miller's music store, or an Italian peddler sharpening knives and scissors, my youthful inquisition never ran out of questions.

"Son, you could talk the hind legs off of a donkey," a fruit and vegetable stand owner with a heavy Irish brogue told me one Saturday morning while I was interrogating him about his watermelons and squash on display on the sidewalk in front of his store. I wasn't sure what he meant. So, I asked him.

"Mr. Flaherty, what do you mean by that?" I wanted to learn. "How could a kid like me, asking a few questions, make that happen?"

"Forget it," he said, in a tone that made me think that perhaps I should buy an apple and get on my way.

"What kinds of apples do you have, Mr. Flaherty? I asked.

At that point, he threw up his hands and went back into his store.

Cops on the beat were always around. Two of the regulars—Officers Romano and Kaminski—were friendly. And bored. Maybe I imagined it, but I got the sense that I helped relieve a little of the monotony of patrolling on foot in downtown Troy, where the only crime was a jaywalker or a drunk vagrant mistaking a fire hydrant for a urinal.

"Hey, Leo, here's our man Pierce," Romano announced to Kaminski.

"Where were you last Saturday?" Kaminski asked me as I strolled up Congress Street after a stop at Famous Lunch for a juicy cheeseburger. "We missed you."

"Hi, fellows," I cheerfully replied. "I had a Boy Scout weekend camping trip at Lake George."

"Sounds like fun," they both said.

"Anything exciting happen?" Romano wanted to know.

I launched into a five minute answer about everything about the weekend—from the pancakes that I burned to getting lost while collecting firewood not far from our campsite. Officer Romano eventually took a look at his watch about the time that I was describing Dutch oven cooking of peach cobbler.

"Sounds great," he said. "See you soon."

As they walked away, I realized that I had forgotten to tell them about the bear who visited during the night. "Oh, well," I told myself, "I'll tell them next Saturday."

One person didn't seem to mind my endless inquiries. A stocky woman with brunette hair, long fingers, and a kind face, Mrs. Carlson was one of the librarians at the Troy Public Library on Second Street across from Russell Sage College, where my Aunt Hunnah got her degree. No Saturday trip to Troy would be complete without a stop to check out several books and wander through the stacks. My mom had taught me how to use the Dewey Decimal System, the method of categorizing books by subject from 000 to 999.

"Mrs. Carlson, where are the nine hundreds?" I asked early one Saturday afternoon.

"What are you looking for?" she asked in a kind voice.

"Biographies of American Revolution generals," I unhesitatingly replied. I had a paper due for American History class.

"That would be in nine hundred and twenty on the second floor to the left," she swiftly answered. "Just past geography and travel but before ancient world history."

"Thanks, ma'am," I said, as I bounded up the steel stairs in hot pursuit of a book about Horatio Gates. My history teacher had mentioned that this former British officer in 1777 commanded the Continental Army soldiers in the pivotal, winning Battle of Saratoga—a historic town an hour's drive from my home. Sitting down in the aisle, I took down several biographies, losing track of time as I consumed them all afternoon. At some point, Mrs. Carlson gently tapped me on the shoulder.

"Pierce, we are closing," she told me in that whispered voice that is required of a librarian.

"What time is it? I wanted to know.

"Five o'clock," she said.

"Oh, no!" I exclaimed, as I grabbed the books, bounded down two steps at a time, and checked out the books. The last bus to Averill Park left at 5:15 in front of Stanley's Department Store. Hardly a sprinter, I "raced" down the sidewalks, trying to hold the books under one arm while I carried my gym bag in the other. Twice I dropped a book, realizing each time that I made it even more impossible to get there on time.

"Wait! Wait!" I breathlessly yelled as the bus pulled away. My only hope was the next intersection. As the bus encountered some traffic, I ran alongside. At the stop light, unable to waive my occupied arms, I repeatedly shouted at the top of my voice: "Yo! Over here!"

My voice was drowned out by the din of city life. As the bus pulled away, my heart sank. I was in Big Trouble. There was nobody to come fetch me: Dad was working, Mom didn't drive, and I didn't have money for a taxi, much less know how to find one.

This was the day that I learned how far it was between Troy and Averill Park. With a combination of walking and hitchhiking, I got home well after dinner.

"You scared me to death, Pierce," my mother greeted me when I arrived.

"I'm sorry, Mom," I apologized. "I missed the bus because I stayed too late at the library."

Because my mother raised her kids to love books and she had personally introduced me to the Troy Public Library, this was probably the only excuse that would get me off the hook. It also had the virtue of being true.

"Okay," she replied, "but your dad and I are getting you a watch for Christmas."

That was the last time that I closed the Troy Public Library.

My favorite hobby was eating. Any type of cuisine. If they put it on my plate, I ate it—and usually a second serving. It took a lot of effort to be overweight at age twelve.

I ate my way across Troy.

The food in Troy was so much better than in Averill Park. I had a ritual. I'd get off the bus at Charlie's Hot Dogs on Congress Street. This small diner was famous for its delicious three inch hot dogs in a steamed bun for only fifteen cents each. The cook could line up to ten on his hairy left arm as he used his right hand to slather them with mustard, onions, relish, and meat sauce in that order. At least half of them would be sold to the young pelican whose stomach was larger than his eyes.

"How about a Coke, please?" I added to my order.

"Would you like ice, kid?" the heavily tattooed, bald counterman gruffly asked. His soiled white apron hadn't been washed since the Korean War.

"Sure, if it's no extra charge," I inquired, trying to save money for the long day ahead.

"Not today, kid," he replied, a thin smile exposing his good nature.

I liked to go to Jack's Drive In (double cheeseburger with extra cheese and smothered with fried onions), Ted's Fish Fry (best French fries around), Manory's (the city's oldest restaurant), and Verdile's Italian restaurant (lasagna to die for). One of my favorite eateries was Callaghan's, a fancy restaurant where Hunnah and her friends Claire Healy, Dorothy Barnum, and Helen Paulsley would occasionally take me along with Dorothy's son and my pal David. Callaghan's waiters wore heavily starched uniforms, and I devoured the irresistible hard rolls and sweet butter. I always ordered the hot turkey sandwich with dressing, cranberries, and french fries instead of mashed potatoes. This feast was washed down with a Shirley Temple and culminated in a dessert of hot apple pie á la mode.

There was also the Fountain not far from Stanley's Department Store on State Street where I would have my second lunch after my walk or Troy Public

Library visit. The food was all-American. This more informal eatery was lined with booths, and the waitresses were efficient if not always cheerful.

"Whataya want, kid?" Rosie would say in her nasal voice. Rosie could have been a stop sign with all her dark red lipstick.

"The usual," I always replied.

"Turkey club on white toast, extra mayo, slaw, and chips," Rosie yelled to the short order cook who smoked a Camel without ever touching it. I always inspected my sandwich for fallen ashes.

"Vanilla milkshake?" Rosie knew to ask.

After all those Saturdays, I'd become a regular.

No meal was complete without the best hot fudge sundae with strawberry ice cream this side of heaven. The menu also featured a huge banana split with three large scoops of ice cream, three toppings, two fresh bananas, whipped cream, nuts and cherries. But I usually managed to resist.

I had to save room for the treats at the movie theatre.

That was the reason I went to Troy most of the time. At the end of the fifth decade of the twentieth century, the Rensselaer County seat had two remaining movie theatres—the Troy and Proctor's. At least one Saturday afternoon a month, I would travel by bus to Troy for the double feature at one of the theatres.

The double feature was as American as apple pie when I was a boy. The price of admission was fifty cents, and buttered popcorn, candy, and a soda cost about the same. The theatres were cavernous buildings with orchestra and balcony seating. They were spotless and well maintained.

Built in 1914, Proctor's—with nearly 2,300 seats—was the largest theater in New York State. A five-story structure with a brick, marble, and terra cotta facade, it was originally a vaudeville hall, hosting such stars as Bob Hope, Jack Benny, Fred Astaire, and Jimmy Durante. Above the stage is a mural depicting the Marquis de Lafayette's visit to Troy in 1824.

My taste in movies, like food, was nearly universal. Westerns were one of my favorite types of movies. My heroes were John Wayne, Robert Mitchum, and Jimmy Stewart. I ate up *The Alamo*, *Rio Bravo*, and *The Man Who Shot Liberty Valance* (featuring both Wayne and Stewart!). The stories didn't vary much: a lone marshal takes on a town of criminals and cowards, a star-crossed cowboy and girlfriend find themselves in harm's way, Indians threaten a wagon train heading west, and so forth. A kid with an afternoon to kill, popcorn in his mouth, and twenty degree weather waiting for him outside didn't care too much about the predictability or triteness of the plots.

I also liked the zany caper. I couldn't get enough of Dean Martin and Jerry Lewis, maybe because I identified with the goofy outsider. My favorite movies were *Around the World in Eighty Days, It's a Mad, Mad, Mad, Mad World, The Pink Panther,* and anything with Zero Mostel, Jonathan Winters, or Sid Caesar.

The other popular genre of the time was, of course, horror. I never really liked horror movies. However, I vividly remember *The House of Usher, The Curse of Frankenstein,* and *Psycho,* but they didn't scare me that much. And all those mutant insects and vegetables that ate Japanese cities made a budding movie critic out of me.

I wasn't big on romance movies, but I ate up anything with Julie Andrews. I thought she was very pretty, and I loved her singing. I faithfully saw *The Americanization of Emily, Mary Poppins,* and *The Sound of Music.* To this day, I get a tad nostalgic when I hear "The Hills Are Alive."

My absolute favorite movies were anything involving World War II. I was mesmerized by *The Bridge on the River Kwai* and the heroics of the captured British Officers tormented by their Japanese captors. I couldn't get enough of *The Longest Day,* starring Richard Burton, John Wayne, Henry Fonda, and Eddie Albert or *The Great Escape,* starring James Garner, Steve McQueen, and Richard Attenborough. These were heroes just like my father who I imagined invading Normandy side-by-side with John Wayne. I would come home after a war movie and ask my father all kinds of questions about his own experiences.

"That's a movie, Pierce," he used to tell me, suggesting that the movies romanticized war and minimized the human suffering.

I could always count on my dad to give me straight talk.

20.
CHIN-UPS

I ALWAYS WANTED TO be an Eagle Scout. Not just a Cub Scout or a Boy Scout. An Eagle Scout.

No one in my family had been a Boy Scout, much less an Eagle Scout. Scouting in the United States began about the time that my father was born, and he had too hard a time—surviving as a poor orphan and supporting his three sisters and himself—to spend time earning merit badges. My cousins Jack and Freddie on Long Island weren't scouts. Neither was Uncle Jack. Nobody I knew was a Boy Scout.

One day, when I was eight, my mom told me about Cub Scouts and a den that was forming in the village. A nice lady in her fifties, Mrs. Jean Dick, was going to be the Den Mother. Her kids were grown up, but she really liked children.

My mother told me a few things about Cub Scouts. They met once a week during the school year, played games, made things, earned awards, and marched in parades. Best of all, Cub Scouts went on hikes, cooked outdoors, and, when they were ten, got to go on a weekend camping trip with the Boy Scouts.

I was only eight, and I hadn't gone many places or done lots of things yet. This Cub Scouting sounded too good to be true. I had to check it out.

The first thing you have to do to become a Cub Scout is buy a uniform. That meant going to Troy. Troy claimed to be the "Home of Uncle Sam," the familiar bearded figure in red, white, and blue outfits who came to symbolize the United States of America. Local historians claimed that a Trojan named Sam Wilson supplied the United States Army during the War of 1812 with Great Britain. Wilson supposedly stamped "from Uncle Sam" on the boxes.

My dad never had time to go to Troy or anywhere else because he worked Monday through Saturday, from 9:00 a.m. to 10:00 p.m. in his liquor store. Without a second driver in the family, the O'Donnells had to be resourceful.

We walked and rode our bikes to lots of places, bummed rides from friends, hitchhiked, and took the public bus to Troy and Albany.

After mom quickly quit professional driving lessons due to sheer terror, my father took over. But not for long.

I remember my father trying to teach my mother to drive when I was in elementary school. They never got out of the front yard.

"Harry, you're too bossy," my mom yelled at my exasperated father, who was merely trying to teach her how to start the car and change gears using the standard shift.

That was my mother's last driving lesson. When it came time for me to learn to drive, I didn't want to start World War III between my parents. I could just hear my mother, "You had the patience to teach your son, but not me!" So I took lessons from my younger sister Mary Eileen, who already had her license thanks to a driver's education course in school.

One Saturday, in 1955, Mom and I took the United Traction Company bus from Averill Park to Troy to buy my Cub Scout uniform. The red and silver bus ran every couple of hours, and it cost only about a dollar round trip. Up until World War II, there had been a trolley that went from Troy to a car barn a hundred yards from our house. I had seen pictures of the open air cars at the turn of the century, filled with men in their three-piece suits and women in bonnets with large, fluffy skirts. City dwellers loved to come out to the country for day trips and enjoy the swimming and the old merry-go-round and games at Crystal Lake Beach and Amusement Park. By the mid-1950s, however, the only remnant of the trolley was some rusting track and the red car barn, which would become a lumber yard. The private passenger car and the public bus had killed the trolley.

Stanley's Department Store was a Troy institution. You could buy almost anything there, except a car and a shotgun. Different departments on the several floors sold houseware goods, men's, women's and children's clothing, toys, and so forth. My family shopped there a lot, and I loved to roam around the aisles looking at all the merchandise. My mom would go crazy when I wandered away from her. In my explorations, I noticed lots of things like a well-dressed man slipping a pair of socks in his pocket, and little old ladies in the bargain basement carrying raggedy-looking cloth shopping bags that never had very much in them.

Up on the second floor, tucked away in the back, was the Scouting Department. There boys and girls—Brownies, Cubs, and full-fledged Girl and Boy Scouts—could buy their uniforms, books and pamphlets, badges, and camping equipment. My eyes bugged out that first time I entered this magic kingdom. I didn't know much about what I saw, but it captivated my imagination.

In one section, a rack contained the booklets for each of the Boy Scout merit badges. Subjects like cooking, camping, hiking, swimming, woodcarving, first aid, athletics, and cycling. My mind reeled at the possibilities.

Another rack had the Cub Scout materials, and I picked up the Wolf book. Sitting on the floor while my mom waited to order my uniform, I flipped through the pages, mesmerized by all the fun and activities awaiting me.

As I sat there on the floor, I overheard the salesman talking to my mother. I couldn't get everything that was said, but I did hear him say, very politely: "I'm sorry, but we don't stock his size. I'll have to order it."

I was used to this problem of not being able to find clothes that fit me. Getting pants was particularly difficult. I was a chubby little kid with a large belly, flabby chest, chunky legs, weak arms, and no butt. When I tried on pants at the store, they were either too tight in the waist, too baggy in the seat, too confining in the thighs, or too long. I was a tailor's nightmare. My mother always had to alter my pants. I did better with shirts, although I sometimes popped the buttons around my navel.

Boys with odd-shaped bodies like mine could not buy clothes like other guys. We wore sizes with the tough-sounding name "huskies." Until I was old enough to go shopping on my own for my clothes, I thought that huskies were dogs that pulled sleds in the Yukon. Then I learned that there were other boys and girls with the same weight and shape problem. I also noticed that the selection for styles and colors were much more limited for "huskies" than "regulars." At an early age, it embarrassed me that I could not buy clothes like other kids.

It seemed like months as opposed to the actual few weeks, but my Cub Scout uniform finally arrived. I pestered my mom for days about when she was going to alter the length of my pants so that I could wear my new blue uniform. Finally, she adjusted the length, and I put it on and ran to the mirror in the front parlor.

Well, you could scrape me off the ceiling! I was so proud of myself. What a neat uniform—blue shirt and slacks, yellow kerchief with a brass wolf head kerchief ring, a web belt with a shiny brass buckle, and a blue baseball cap with the yellow Cub Scout insignia. Later, I had my Den 1 patch for my right shoulder, and as I earned badges, my mom or I would sew them to my breast pocket.

This was my very first uniform of any kind. When I was younger, Santa Claus had brought me a Lone Ranger cowboy outfit. One of our earliest family pictures shows a dazed-looking four-year-old boy with a cowboy hat, a shirt with silver buttons and leather fringe, a red bandana, chaps, boots, and a double holster with two six guns. I wore it for days, running around the house killing outlaws and fighting off wild Indians. My sister Mary Eileen cooperated by letting me tie her up to the front hall banister. My mother was not amused.

As much as I loved my Lone Ranger costume, it couldn't compare to my Cub Scout uniform. There's something special about a uniform. For me, it signified belonging to an organization that has millions of other members whose secret handshakes, codes, and traditions instantly bond you to total strangers wherever you met them.

Scouting also meant acceptance, a fellowship that did not exclude me because I was chubby or awkward or slow-footed. Unlike the school playground, neighborhood ballfields, or Little League, it was a place where I was welcomed and not ridiculed or beaten up. When other Cubs made fun of me, Mrs. Dick would scold them in her heavy Scottish accent.

"Now, David, you're no prize either with those floppy ears," she would remind the Barnum boy.

"And you, Billy Glasser," she would add, "since when are you one to criticize others, what with your nose runnin' all the day?"

After a while, the other Cubs didn't make fun of me anymore. Without making speeches, Mrs. Dick taught us tolerance at a very tender age. It's a shame that there weren't more den mothers like Mrs. Dick.

When you joined Cub Scouts, you subscribed to a magazine called *Boy's Life*. The official magazine for the Boy Scouts of America, it was chock full of exciting stories about adventures in the wilderness, animals, crafts, and hobbies. I read it from cover to cover and couldn't wait to get the next issue.

One of the first *Boy's Life* issues that I read as a Cub Scout had an article about a heroic Eagle Scout who had saved the life of a child. The Eagle had risked his own life to crawl out on the fragile ice and rescue the drowning girl.

In the article, they described how hard it was to become an Eagle Scout. You first had to achieve Tenderfoot, Second Class, and First Class, then Star and Life, and, finally, Eagle with twenty-one merit badges, a community service project, and an interview with Scout leaders and other Eagles. Few Boy Scouts ever became Eagles, and it was a distinction that stayed with you for the rest of your life.

I know it sounds corny, but the day I read that article about the brave Eagle Scout, I set my sights on achieving that goal for myself. In the first eight years of my life, I had never done anything like that before—saying that I would accomplish something in the future. I remember announcing to my parents that I wanted to be an Eagle Scout.

"That's nice, Pierce," my mom replied, "but don't you think you should see how you like Cub Scouts first?"

"Sure," I answered, "but I know what I want to be when I grow up. An Eagle!"

"That's good," my dad said, "but in the meantime, would you please take out the garbage and burn the papers? Even Eagle Scouts have chores."

I raced through Cub Scouts. Earning Wolf, Bear, Lion, and Webelos as well as lots of gold and silver arrows, I was a Tenderfoot just a few months after I became a Boy Scout on March 5, 1958, my eleventh birthday. Most of my Cub years, when I was eight, nine, and ten, are a blur. I do recall, however, splitting coconuts from Hawaii with an ax in Mrs. Dick's garage and rigging up a primitive walkie-talkie with string and tin cans.

And, oh yes, I remember ripping the crotch of my Cub Scout uniform pants right before a Fourth of July parade watched by hundreds. Try marching in step for an hour, holding a flagpole, while you are pressing your legs tightly together.

In Boys Scouts, I belonged to Troop 26. We met one night a week, from seven to nine, in the gym of the old high school. The floor was concrete, the walls were made of brick, and the stage was about four feet off the ground. When you were horsing around and fell off the stage, you were glad that they taught first aid to all Boy Scouts.

Our Scoutmaster was Bob Springer, a butcher at the local Averill Park Market & Variety Store. Bob was a veteran outdoorsman with a cheery disposition and sharp sense of humor. While he didn't have a son in Scouts, I think that he had been a Boy Scout. Anyway, he was a great Scoutmaster.

Bob Springer was an original. Plain speaking, he inspired by example. He was always punctual, knew everything about Scouting, practiced positive thinking in teaching, and never used swear words—at least in public. Bob had been in the navy and told funny stories about boot camp and his ship duty.

I personally know that he had the patience of Job. For some reason, Bob took me under his wing. He cared about my development as a Scout and person. I reciprocated by stopping by the meat counter almost daily to report some progress on a merit badge or to ask some question about an upcoming activity.

Grinning out of one side of his mouth as he always did, Bob would turn from his butcher block, wipe his blood-stained hands on his soiled white apron, and say, "Well, Pierce, what do we have today?" By any objective measure, I was a pest, but Bob was never short with me.

I have tried to understand what made Bob (he insisted that he be called by his first name) such a terrific adult Scout leader. It wasn't his extensive education—like my father, he may not have had a high school diploma. It wasn't his great public speaking skills. Bob shunned the limelight and let other adults do the talking whenever he could. And it wasn't any desire on his part to be promoted to higher level positions in the Scouting movement. No, Bob Springer just wanted to be a Scoutmaster in a rural town, where he could train young boys how to survive and enjoy the outdoors and learn valuable life skills along the way. And maybe, just maybe, they might be better citizens someday.

For most of its history, our troop did not have a single Eagle Scout. The book on Troop 26 was that we were among the best trained Scouts, superb outdoorsmen, and fierce competitors at District-level Scout-O-Ramas and summer camp rallies. However, we weren't much into earning merit badges or advancing beyond First Class or Star. We probably had more blue ribbons on our troop flagpole than any other outfit in the Uncle Sam Council, but no Eagle Scouts. When Bob took over the troop, he set out to change that.

By the time I graduated to Boy Scouts when I was eleven, our troop had finally installed a couple of Eagle Scouts. One guy I recall was Phil Worrell, a muscular, hardy fellow who was at least seventeen or eighteen years old. Phil had mastered the skills of Scouting the same way that Sandy Koufax learned to pitch. He knew the ins and outs of everything from advanced knot-tying to subzero camping and cooking. Phil was a tough taskmaster who gave no slack to a tenderfoot like me.

"O'Donnell," he would yell, "you're a sorry excuse for a Boy Scout. Look at that tent. Your mommy's not here to clean up after you. Shape up or ship out, you hear me!"

I heard him. Loud and clear. The more crap Phil dished out, the more I wanted to improve. When I would fall behind on a hike, struggling under thirty pounds of gear and sweating like a waterfall, Phil would come back, give me a verbal kick in the pants ("You're slower than molasses going uphill in January with snowshoes on"), and then take some weight off my back and carry it himself. I would then strain to walk faster and catch up with the rest of the troop.

I didn't realize it at the time, but Phil had also taken me under his wing. Maybe it was because I was such a sad sack.

"O'Donnell, this troop would freeze its ass to death if it had to rely on you to cut firewood and tend the fire!"

Maybe it was because Bob Springer told him to look after Harry's son.

"Make sure that we don't kill the kid or lose him somewhere."

Or maybe he saw the desire written all over my chubby face. Ambition unmatched by ability but compensated for by sheer determination.

Whatever the reason, Phil was like the big brother that I never had. He wasn't beyond an occasional hazing, however. I got my share of hot feet, collapsed tents, urine in my canteen, and missing boots on a freezing morning. I got picked on a great deal by the other scouts, but it was usually good-natured. One time, however, things got a little carried away. Literally.

It was my first summer at Camp Rotary, the camp for our District located in the mountains above Poestenkill about twenty miles from my house. Back in the early years of Scouting, the Troy Rotary Club had donated the land and helped build the camp on Davitt's Pond. I was eleven years old.

My very first night, I went to sleep on the cot in my tent located in the Tuscarora campsite a half mile from the water. The next morning, I woke up and stepped out of bed and fell into the pond. It seems that the older guys thought it would be a cute prank to move my cot to the edge of the dock. When Bob Springer heard about it, he grinned and playfully told me that he had received complaints from the other scoutmasters about my snoring on the dock and waking up the other troops.

I only had one real disaster. We were on a freeze-out in the middle of January. It was so cold that your breath turned to snow. I was out getting water and managed to spill the two buckets all over my hiking boots. Not only did I soak my boots and socks, but I drenched my leather arch supports that had been made specially for my flat feet. Not thinking, I put the arch supports in front of the cabin fire along with my boots and socks. Everything dried quickly, except the arch supports crinkled up and became hard as stone. My father was not amused at having to pay another fifty dollars for new arch supports.

On that same mid-winter camping trip, I found another way to be a klutz. We were sleeping on bunkbeds, and I was on the top. Somehow, in the middle of the night, I rolled over too far and fell eight feet to the floor wrapped in my sleeping bag. I hit the floor with such a thud that I woke up the whole cabin. As

I lay on the floor more in shame than in pain, Phil Worrell stood over me, shining his flashlight in my face.

"You have to watch it, Pierce," he said. "That first step is a bitch."

By the time I turned twelve in the spring of 1959, I had managed to reach First Class. One day, I went to see Bob at the meat counter.

"Bob, do you think I could be an Eagle?" I asked.

"Gee, I don't know," Bob replied. "It's real tough, you know? But anything is possible."

Bob must have been able to see the disappointment on my face at his less-than-encouraging response.

"Look, Pierce," he quickly added, "it will take a lot of hard work and dedication. You'll have to lose a lot of weight, get in much better physical shape, and earn the confidence of the older Scouts. And I will help you."

That's all I needed to hear.

The next twelve months changed my life. I threw myself into earning merit badges. You needed five for Star, ten for Life, and twenty-one for Eagle Scout. The first ten came pretty quickly. I worked hard at skills for cooking, camping, hiking, swimming, citizenship, first aid, and safety. Merit badges were awarded by merit badge counselors, usually parents or former Scouts with expertise in an area. We had to read the merit badge pamphlet published by the National Headquarters of the Boys Scouts of America and then show our proficiency in all of the required skills or knowledge. The counselor would then certify that you had earned the merit badge.

By the winter of 1959, I was well on my way to Eagle Scout. In fact, I had earned twenty-one merit badges (including Sheep Farming), done my community project, and passed my oral examination. But I was still not eligible to become an Eagle.

I had not yet earned Lifesaving and Personal Fitness merit badges, both of which were required for promotion from Life to Eagle. There was a very good reason why I had not yet collected these badges. I was a 150-pound weakling.

I had not really understood, much less heeded, Bob's admonition to get myself in better physical shape if I wanted to become an Eagle Scout. But as I looked out my bedroom window at the drifting snowbanks in the dreary, snow-socked winter of 1959, I was painfully aware of what he meant.

And time was running out.

There were six of us in the troop who were working toward Eagle at the same time. Four were several years older than me, but two of us, Gary Tonnies and I, were still twelve years old. Making Eagle when you are thirteen—about the earliest possible age given the challenges and waiting periods between ranks—was considered a super achievement. I wanted desperately to be in the group of six that made Eagle in the spring.

That winter I started a diet and conditioning program. In those days, long before Pritikin, Diet Center, and Weight Watchers, dieting meant deprivation. I cut back on all my food, swore off ice cream, candy, cookies, soda and all desserts, ate a lot of grapefruit, and took extra vitamins. My "baby fat" started to fall off me. After only four months, I was able to go shopping and buy regular pants, instead of huskies. It was one of the happiest days of my life.

I also started doing strenuous calisthenics with my father every morning. His hour-long regimen included jumping jacks, body twists, toe touching, sit-ups, shadow boxing, running in place, and other tortures. My father was in superb physical shape for a forty-five-year-old man; indeed, a man twenty years younger would love to have been in half as good shape. My dad was fond of calling himself "the Peter Pan of Averill Park."

I also began road running. It was tough to get any traction on icy, snow-covered streets, but I nevertheless made the effort. If I could run and build up wind in freezing weather, I might be able to meet the speed and distance running requirements of Personal Fitness. No one was happier to see the spring thaw than me, as I gleefully traded rubber fishing boots for sneakers.

My father also installed a chin-up bar in the backyard. Personal Fitness required that I be able to do twelve pull-ups in a row without stopping. My first attempt, I barely could do one. Every day, however, I went out to the bar and worked at my chin-ups.

That winter I also signed up for Lifesaving merit badge taught at Troy High School by the athletic director, Mr. Cooley, who lived in my town. At first, it seemed hopeless. While I could easily pass the written test and perform CPR, I was inept to say the least when it came to lifesaving in the water. Time after time, Mr. Cooley or another Scout would play the drowning victim, I would swim to the rescue in the Olympic-sized pool, and they would nearly drown me.

Mr. Cooley never gave up on me, however. He would stay after hours while I swam extra laps to strengthen my strokes or worked on my technique. He lived in Averill Park and drove me home after the lessons.

"Pierce, this Eagle Scout thing means a lot to you, doesn't it?" he asked one day as we rode home in darkness.

"Yes, Mr. Cooley," I replied. "More than anything else in the world."

"Then keep at it and never quit."

I passed Lifesaving merit badge a couple of months later. Despite his best efforts to drown me, I fought off Mr. Cooley in the final rescue, grabbed his hair to get control, threw my right arm over his chest, and furiously swam to the other end of the pool.

"Congratulations, Mr. Eagle Scout," Mr. Cooley said as he pulled me out of the pool.

As much as I loved the sound of those words, Mr. Cooley was premature. I had one more challenge ahead of me before my mother could pin the Eagle on my chest. And the last hurdle appeared insurmountable.

Not only did I have to do twelve chin-ups, I had to run a mile in a certain time to earn Personal Fitness. The Eagle Scout Court of Honor had been scheduled for late spring. I had two months.

My parents had planned a Florida vacation for Easter break.

This was a big deal because our family had never gone on a vacation together for longer than a weekend drive to Long Island. This was going to be great fun, especially after one of the worst winters in the history of the Upper Hudson River Valley.

But I stayed home with Hunnah.

Not only did I have a term paper for Miss Gehle, I wanted to work on my Personal Fitness merit badge. For the two vacation weeks, I took the bus to Troy and worked out at the old YMCA gym. Sit-ups, chin-ups, weightlifting, throwing the medicine ball, rope climbing, and running. Six hours each day.

When my family returned from vacation, no one noticed that I appeared to be trimmer and fitter. I went over to my dad, proudly made a muscle with my right arm and thrust it in front of him. As he had done so many times before, he squeezed my muscle and sang the words of a popular TV commercial, "J-E-L-L-O, Jello!"

Finally, the day came. The test for Personal Fitness merit badge. The Boy Scout motto is "Be Prepared." I hoped that I was.

Everything went pretty well at first. Sit-ups, rope climb, and push-ups. But running the mile in under six minutes was a killer. I'd never made it in my practice runs.

After five minutes, my pace was not good enough. It was make or break time. I looked ahead, mentally mapping the rest of the course. Using all the energy left in the tank, I crossed the finish line two seconds short of six minutes.

Then came the dreaded, final event.

Chin-ups.

With my feet not touching the ground and holding on to the metal bar with my two hands, I had to pull myself up and thrust my chin over the bar. Twelve times without allowing my feet to touch the ground. In all my practicing, I had never done more than nine.

The first six usually came pretty easily. Seven and eight were a strain. By nine, sweat was pouring off my brow, into my eyes. I couldn't see, but I couldn't stop. The tenth drew a warning from the monitor: "Make sure that your chin goes above the bar!" The eleventh required every bit of energy left in my body. My hands were perspiring, my grip was loosening.

It was now or never.

One more. One more chin-up. One more time.

I don't really remember anything after the twelfth, final one. I'm told that I grunted, uttered a terrifying, primordial scream, and pulled myself up over the bar. All I recall is lying on the floor, soaked in sweat, totally exhausted, my mind racing as I heard, "You did it!"

And I had.

A few weeks later, surrounded by five sets of other proud parents, I was invested as an Eagle Scout. With my father standing on one side of me, Bob Springer handed my mother the beautiful badge—a silver eagle suspended from a red, white, and blue ribbon hanging from a silver bar. As my mother pinned the Eagle on my swollen chest, Bob said to the hundred or so people gathered for the ceremony.

"Last, but certainly not least, we have Pierce O'Donnell. I know for a fact that no one worked harder or wanted this pin more than Pierce. You've earned it. Congratulations!"

As the audience broke into a warm applause, I caught Phil Worrell out of the corner of my eye. He was wearing his Eagle pin and a big smile. The wink of his right eye told me that I had arrived. I belonged. I was an Eagle Scout!

That day changed my life forever.

I was now a normal, thirteen-year-old adolescent, in shape, with pimples, and my whole adult life awaiting me. After I made Eagle, people—especially most of my classmates—seemed to be nicer to me, treated me with more respect. Most importantly, I had more self-esteem and confidence. This accomplishment—which seemed unachievable—told me one thing that mattered more than anything else.

Never again would I be last pick.

EPILOGUE

If the past is prologue, my early life in Averill Park was excellent preparation for the next six decades. I graduated first in my class in high school and law school, was selected outstanding graduate in college, played small college club football (not baseball) at Georgetown, captained my high school and college football teams, served as law clerk for a US Supreme Court justice, and was blessed with a successful law practice. My wives (Connie and Dawn) and I raised five remarkable children—Meghan, Brendan, Courtney, Pierce, and Aidan—who are making their way in a troubled world far removed from the place and times of my youth. I pray for them and their generation.

My adult life has been a roller coaster ride of dizzying heights and lows. I have struggled with weight, once reaching 400 pounds before losing 160 pounds. I have two failed marriages and a Bipolar II Disorder diagnosis and (fortunately) effective treatment. From the pinnacle of the legal profession, I had a stunning, public fall from grace due solely to my spectacular lapse of judgment and hubris. In 2012, I pleaded guilty to misdemeanor federal campaign finance violations, served two months in prison, and later went bankrupt. My ten-year battle to save my coveted law license was ultimately successful, but my family and I paid a dear price.

Beginning in 2014, after I had served my time and six-month bar suspension and thanks to my beloved wife Carmen's unrelenting encouragement and loving support, I was fortunate enough to get a job as a senior trial lawyer at one of the nation's best law firms, Greenberg Glusker Fields Claman & Machtinger, in Los Angeles where I had lived since 1978. They welcomed me warmly and unconditionally, and the partnership has been mutually beneficial in so many ways. Working with the exceptionally talented associates and partners and again thanks to Carmen's continuing, unflagging assistance, I have been fortunate to attract many new clients, handling complex, high-profile lawsuits as I had before my self-inflicted wound. I must admit that a long overdue smile came to my face when one national legal publication entitled an article about my ordeal, "The Comeback Kid."

My three magnificent sisters have also done well. After majoring in drama at Mom's alma mater in Albany, Mary Eileen did graduate work at the venerable Guildhall School of Drama in London, where she was honored as the outstanding graduate. For her entire adult life, she has been an acclaimed stage, television, and movie actress in New York and Los Angeles, and she has toured the world with Tim Robbins' renowned The Actors' Gang.

Helen Kay earned her bachelor's and master's degrees at Nazareth College in Rochester, New York. After years of classroom teaching, Helen Kay became a highly respected principal at an elite public high school. Her gregarious husband, Gerry, is a successful lawyer, and my sweet niece Jessica earned undergraduate and graduate degrees with honors at my alma mater, Georgetown University.

Maureen has been similarly successful. My kindhearted sister also graduated from Nazareth College. Not surprisingly, she devoted her career to being a caring, effective benefits counselor for the elderly fortunate enough to be advised by her. Bubsy is married to Lyle, a kind retired law enforcement professional and devoted father and grandfather.

Bob Campano was my boyhood friend who not only never picked on me, he always encouraged me; I cherished his company and friendship. We forged a strong bond that lasts to this very day. Bob is retired from a rewarding forty year career with the New York State Comptroller's Office. Bob has two grown daughters and three stepchildren with his wife, Dorry. He remains an avid fisherman, delighting in stream fishing for trout and lake fishing for bass.

William Kennedy, whose smart conversation at my dad's store made me a life-long fan, is still alive at ninety-four. When still writing for the *Albany Times-Union*, Bill interviewed me in 1974 about my clerkship with Supreme Court Justice Byron R. White and the Supreme Court's landmark decision in *United States v. Nixon* rendered while I was there. It was almost an out-of-body experience to be sitting in the front parlor of my boyhood home talking with one of my genuine heroes. I congratulated him on the publication a few years earlier of his first novel, *Ink Truck*, about a newspaper strike in Albany.

"What's next, Bill?" I was eager to know.

"A novel about Legs Diamond, the Irish-American mobster," he told me.

"Title?" I followed up.

"*Legs*," he smiled.

"How original!" I winked.

Bill later became one of America's greatest novelists, winning the Pulitzer Prize for Fiction in 1984 for his novel *Ironweed*, set in Albany and later made into a movie starring Jack Nicholson and Meryl Streep. Recalling Bill's comment about the long odds against getting a novel published, *Ironweed* had been rejected by thirteen publishers. His many other critically-acclaimed novels—*Legs, Billy Phelan's Greatest Game, Quinn's Book,* and *Roscoe*—are also Albany centric. The MacArthur Foundation awarded him the coveted "Genius Grant."

Ned Pattison, whom my father repeatedly urged to run for public office, was eventually elected to Congress in 1974 after several unsuccessful bids for public office. This was a remarkable feat given the heavy Republican registration advantage. A "Watergate baby" swept into office after the scandal, Ned served with distinction for two terms. When I was considering running for Congress in Pasadena, California, in 1980, Ned encouraged me. I shouldn't have listened to him; I lost two-to-one in a heavily Republican district as Ronald Reagan was crushing President Jimmy Carter.

Miss Gehle never won the Pulitzer Prize nor served in Congress. Her accomplishments were not of this world. In 1987, she gifted her modest, gray home to a Polish refugee family with two children who had been adopted by St. Henry's Church. Miss Gehle then moved in with a lady friend from church. She died in 1989 at age seventy-four. If anyone ever earned a nonstop passage to heaven by virtue of living a life of unconditional love for her neighbors, it was my seventh grade teacher.

I later found out where my father went on that iconic Sunday trip to New York City when I met Mickey Mantle. While his army buddy Tom Romano watched me, Dad was visiting his father at the Manhattan Mental Hospital, where he had been committed for some four decades. Now I knew where Dad went every few months on Sunday for so many years.

I saw my father cry only twice while I was boy: when President Kennedy was assassinated, and when his father died shortly thereafter. My sisters and I always wondered why Dad never talked about his dad, what happened to him, and why he didn't let us meet him. Like so many other things in an Irish-Catholic family, the answer went to the grave with my father.

After my parents died, my sisters gave me the *Webster's Second*. Every now and then, I go to random pages to enjoy the origin and meaning of words. Did you know that the word "dictionary" was invented by an Englishman named John of Garland in 1220 who had written a book *Dictionarius* to help with Latin diction?

When I was nearing completion of the book, I learned that Coach Earl Retzlaff was still alive. My pal Bob Campano put me in touch with him. At age eighty-nine, he could still talk baseball, and we reminisced about That Championship Baseball Season in 1965. When I reminded him of the socks that stood by themselves, he chuckled.

"That's right, Pierce," he confirmed. "The other thing is that my wife gave me cantaloupe to eat at breakfast on the morning of the first game. After we won that afternoon, I ate cantaloupe before every game."

"Man, you were really superstitious," I remarked.

"Yeah," Coach agreed, "and I didn't even like cantaloupe!"

In 2019, Coach was inducted into the Averill Park High School Athletic Hall of Fame. Over more than fifty years, he amassed 310 victories, won several more league championships, and was league Coach of the Year numerous times. When anyone thinks about high school baseball legends in the Capital District, Earl Retzlaff is always in the conversation.

I recently did an inventory of other people and places discussed in this book. Not surprisingly, the passage of more than a half century takes its toll. We have lost my beloved parents, sweet Hunnah, Muskrat, Mr. Dibble, Skip Vigus, Aunt Louise, Uncle Jack, my cousin Jackie, Matt Graves, Jack Dempsey, all the Boys of Summer, and my Scoutmaster Bob Springer, among many others.

While I became an Eagle Scout and later made the football, basketball, and baseball teams, the bullying did not end. One guy—I'll call him Roger—kept picking on me verbally and physically. Taller and stronger than me, Roger had a chip on his shoulder the size of a redwood; he never seemed happy about anything.

When we played hockey, Roger would go out of his way to knock me down, trip me, or hit a slapshot at me in the goal when I wasn't looking. During practice on the football field, he'd clip me or hit after the play was dead. Roger roughed me up a lot and mocked my appearance, clothes, shoes, and even my gym bag. I was a much better student, causing him to insult me as a "brown noser" and the like.

One day when I was fifteen, we were in the back of the school during the lunch recess. Roger approached with his omnipresent menacing look. I'd had enough of his crap and didn't want to spend the next three years of high school in dread fear of this creep.

"Hey, Fatso," Roger greeted me as usual. "I'm hungry. What's for lunch?"

As Roger reached for my lunch bag, I grabbed his long hair, pulled him toward me, buried my knee in his groin with all the force that I could muster, slapped his face as hard as I could multiple times, and pushed him to the ground. Roger lay there motionless, moaning in pain.

"Don't you ever—you hear me—ever come near me again!" I shouted in his face as I stood over him. "If you dare, they'll carry you out of here on a stretcher."

That school yard incident landed us in the principal's office, accompanied by our fathers—who had to close their shops and rush to the high school. I was more afraid of my dad's wrath than any discipline from the principal. After I patiently detailed Roger's years of abuse, two things happened: his father made Roger apologize to me, and Roger was suspended for a week.

But the best part was what my dad told me as we drove home together.

"Pierce, why didn't you tell me about this jerk a long time ago?" he asked.

"I thought I could work it out on my own," I replied.

Dad turned to his right, paused, and said: "Well, you sure did." His look of respect is indelibly etched in my mind.

On February 18, 2020, the Boy Scouts of America filed for bankruptcy in order to deal with its mounting financial exposure from lawsuits and claims alleging decades of sexual abuse of thousands of Boy Scouts by their leaders. With assets approaching $10 billion, the national organization will not go out of business. Fortunately, local scouting continues around the country. Indeed, my Troop 26, founded in 1929, still produces Eagle Scouts.

The face of Troy has had an extreme makeover. Gone are the Troy and Proctor's movie theaters; the Fountain and Callahan's; blocks of downtown; newsstands; candy stores; fruit and vegetable stands; United Traction Company buses; F.W. Woolworth Co.; Hendrick Hudson Hotel; and Stanley's, Frear's, and Denby's department stores. On the positive side, still blessed with most of its legacy architecture, Troy is staging a strong comeback with a (finally) smart urban redevelopment plan such as repurposing the historic Hendrick Hudson Hotel into apartments and The Waterfront—a proposed half mile of mixed-use projects along the Hudson River (so unpolluted now that some fish are edible).

We lost the original Yankee Stadium and Ebbets Field; Toots Shor's is long gone, as is the New York Central Railroad and Ringling Bros. and Barnum &

Bailey Circus. The Mick died in 1995. And my beloved Brooklyn Dodgers moved to Los Angeles, the only consolations being they won five World Series. I followed them to the City of Angeles in 1978.

Averill Park was hardly immune to the inexorable march of time. The village lost its liquor store, original pharmacy, several "mom and pop" markets, A&P, appliance and gift store, news and candy store, parochial school, several bars and restaurants (Al's Burgers and Journey's End, Glass Lake, Maple Grove, and Crooked Lake Hotels), Crystal Lake Beach and Merry-Go-Round, Fireman's Field Day and Parade, and bingo on Friday evenings.

Fortunately, some things never change. St. Henry's Church, consecrated in 1870, remains a vibrant Catholic Faith Community; Averill Park High School, with its expanded physical plant, continues to be one of New York State's finest; Kay's still serves delicious pizza and pasta to hungry new generations; and the local library (founded by my mother), Larkin Funeral Home, the post office, and Volunteer Fire Department are still serving the community whose population has almost doubled since 1960. And kids can usually play ice hockey by Thanksgiving.

But not on the Old Mill Pond.

When I visited my hometown about twenty years ago, I went down to the Old Mill Pond. It was gone.[1] Literally. My boyhood fishing hole had dried up when the dam broke, and the town did not fix it. All that remained was a trickle of the stream that had once supplied the water for this man-made pond that powered Faith Knitting Mills.

When I got back to Los Angeles, this loss weighed on my mind. I wrote a poem, entitled "Old Mill Pond," expressing my feelings and reverence for this place and time in my childhood.

> OLD MILL POND
>
> There was a time
> In my youth
> When lilacs bloomed
> Late Spring, I recall
> It was across the road
> And down by the Old Mill Pond A profusion of purple
> Hanging in clusters

---

[1] I am happy to report that the pond has since been reclaimed and once again beckons young boys and girls to fish and skate.

> Cascading to water's edge
> A lovely sight, no doubt
> But it is the lilacs scent
> That triggers those vivid memories
> No flower ever smelled so sweet
> As lilacs in the mid-day heat
> Perfuming the still air
> As I sat fishing below
> Thirty-five years have passed
> Since last I smelled lilacs in bloom
> The pond is now gone
> Victim of a broken dam
> But in Springtime, I am told
> My lilacs still bloom.

Our family home has also fallen on hard times. When my parents moved to Rochester in 1992, they sold it to a couple from Albany who lovingly restored it. I'm not quite sure what happened later, but when my wife Carmen and I visited Averill Park in 2015, the house had been long abandoned, windows were broken, wood was rotting, the front and back porches had collapsed, and the building was actually leaning to one side. The yard—which Dad nursed for decades on his only day off—was overgrown with weeds, bushes, and sumac trees, and our apple and peach trees had died. This once majestic Victorian home, built before the Civil War, is now a tear down.[2]

My sadness is tempered by countless fond memories of my formative years lived so richly in this nurturing place. I have undoubtedly idealized and selectively recalled some events and people. Nonetheless, it was truly here that I was raised and developed into a young man, learning to love, laugh, cry, care, eat, play, read, write, research, pray, fish, skate, catch, throw, and hit a baseball, play and trade cards, fight, curse, ride a bike, and so many other things. The O'Donnell home was a safe house for a wide-eyed, eager-to-please, flabby boy who imagined other worlds, dreamed of conquering time, space, and even death, and fantasized about playing in the World Series for the Brooklyn Dodgers alongside Jackie, Pee Wee, and the Duke. The edifice may be fading away, but not my recollections of a youth

---

[2] Miraculously, our home was spared from the wrecking ball in 2020 when a man from New York bought it and is reportedly restoring the ruins to serve as a B&B.

joyfully lived with mom, dad, Hunnah, my three sisters, stray cats, and, of course, Nora the Ghost.

I was never much of a regular TV viewer. One series, however, fascinated me. *The Wonder Years,* a coming-of-age comedy-drama, ran for six seasons from 1988 to 1993. In the final episode, the narrator signs off with this observation that captures my feelings about my baby boomer boyhood:

> "Growing up happens in a heartbeat. One day you're in diapers, the next day you're gone. But the memories of childhood stay with us for the long haul....And the thing is, after all these years, I still look back...with wonder."

ACKNOWLEDGMENTS

A BOOK HAS MANY midwives beyond the author who brought it to life. That is particularly true for my reminiscences of a youth well lived. So many decent, loving, and patient people made my boyhood memorable and this book possible. Naturally, any mistakes are all mine.

First and foremost, I must thank my family from the bottom of my heart. Mom, Dad, Hunnah, Mary Eileen, Helen Kay, and Maureen. A son and brother could not ask for more kind, intelligent, fun loving, wiser, and caring parents and siblings. I know there is a benevolent God because I was gifted with my family.

So many people had a formative influence on my development. Too many to name, but some stand out. Mr. Dibble, Bob Springer, Coach Retzlaff, Miss Gehle, the Troy Public Library staff, all those patient bus drivers, Phil Worrell, Mrs. Dick, Muskrat, the cousins, the Brooklyn Dodgers, and my talented teachers who made learning a joy and knowledge a blessing. Hedging my bets, I better give a shout out to Nora!

One lifetime friend looms large—Bob Campano. When I was unpopular, he befriended me. When I was down, he picked me up. And when I got in trouble, he stuck by me. His comments on my manuscript were insightful and much appreciated. My favorite poet, William Butler Yeats, could have been alluding to Bob when he wrote, "Think where man's glory most begins and ends, and say my glory was I had such friends."

I am grateful to other friends who commented on my drafts: Lew Wolff, Pete Steinberg, and my sisters Mary Eileen and Helen Kay. I also want to thank all three sisters who gave me photographs of our family and Averill Park and histories of our ancestors and hometown.

The folks at Rare Bird are terrific. Thanks to publisher Tyson Cornell who saw in my manuscript something worth sharing with others. Guy Intoci is a gifted editor who made sure that the book preserved the voice of a twelve-year-old and magnificently tightened and clarified the text. Hailie Johnson designed a beautiful book. The design, production, and marketing team are in the same All-Star league with those talented folks who shepherded my earlier books.

My close and wise pals and counselors—Drew Donen, Ron Silverman, Lew Wolff, and Neal Hersh—make life fun and navigable.

My daughter Meghan and son Pierce, are pillars of loving support. Their siblings—Brendan, Courtney, and Aidan—are always in my heart.

Finally, I cannot thank enough my wife, Carmen. Her encouragement, support, and love since we married in 2013 enabled me to survive and then thrive. Carmen's two kind, very bright children—Claudia and Javier—and her four darling grandchildren have lovingly adopted me. When Carmen miraculously found my lost manuscript, I knew that I had to get it published. The book's dedication to Carmen reflects my gratitude to her in more ways than I can ever express.